THE BIRDMAN OF AUSCHWITZ

THE BIRDMAN OF AUSCHWITZ

THE LIFE OF GÜNTHER NIETHAMMER, THE ORNITHOLOGIST SEDUCED BY THE NAZIS

NICHOLAS MILTON

PEN & SWORD HISTORY

AN IMPRINT OF PEN & SWORD BOOKS LTD.
YORKSHIRE – PHILADELPHIA

First published in Great Britain in 2024 by
PEN AND SWORD HISTORY
An imprint of
Pen & Sword Books Ltd
Yorkshire – Philadelphia

ISBN 978 1 39905 981 7

A CIP catalogue record for this book is available from the British Library.

Typeset in Times New Roman 11.5/14 by
SJmagic DESIGN SERVICES, India.
Printed and bound in the UK by CPI Group (UK) Ltd.

Pen & Sword Books Limited incorporates the imprints of Atlas, Archaeology, Aviation, Discovery, Family History, Fiction, History, Maritime, Military, Military Classics, Politics, Select, Transport, True Crime, Air World, Frontline Publishing, Leo Cooper, Remember When, Seaforth Publishing, The Praetorian Press, Wharncliffe Local History, Wharncliffe Transport, Wharncliffe True Crime and White Owl.

For a complete list of Pen & Sword titles please contact
PEN & SWORD BOOKS LIMITED
George House, Units 12 & 13, Beevor Street, Off Pontefract Road,
Barnsley, South Yorkshire, S71 1HN, England
E-mail: enquiries@pen-and-sword.co.uk
Website: www.pen-and-sword.co.uk

or

PEN AND SWORD BOOKS
1950 Lawrence Rd, Havertown, PA 19083, USA
E-mail: uspen-and-sword@casematepublishers.com
Website: www.penandswordbooks.com

MIX
Paper | Supporting responsible forestry
FSC® C013604

Contents

Acknowledgements

THERE IS NO greater crime in modern history than the Holocaust. As an ornithologist and historian, I found researching the life of Günther Niethammer and his role in it a traumatic experience. It brought home to me the deeply troubling truth that the Nazis were able to seduce even the most erudite academics into helping them to cover up genocide. In writing the book I would like to thank Chris Packham, who I have known since our days together on *The Really Wild Show*, and Ed Balls for each writing a foreword and putting Niethammer's life into context. The Natural History Museum in Vienna kindly allowed me to use pictures of the bird skins he sent back from Auschwitz and the Auschwitz-Birkenau State Memorial Museum provided me with invaluable information. Telling Niethammer's story would not have been possible without the help of the wonderful team at Pen & Sword including Laura Hirst, Sarah-Beth Watkins, Lucy May, Ken Barry and especially Chris Cocks who did a painstaking job editing the text. I would also like to thank my wife Andrea and daughter Georgia for supporting me while I wrote the book, Georgia being inspired by the story to study history for her GCSE. Lest we forget it is dedicated to remembering all the victims of the Nazi regime and those who gave their lives to bring the perpetrators to justice. 'Only guard yourself and guard your soul carefully, lest you forget the things your eyes saw, and lest these things depart your heart all the days of your life, and you shall make them known to your children, and to your children's children.'

Deuteronomy 4:9

Forewords

IN 2018 I WAS honoured to be appointed the co-chair of the Holocaust Memorial Foundation Advisory Board together with the Right Honourable Sir Eric Pickles. The board is supporting the delivery of the UK's new Holocaust Memorial and Learning Centre proposed at Victoria Tower Gardens beside the Houses of Parliament.

We all share a great responsibility across society to ensure that the lessons of the Holocaust are never forgotten, and I have been inspired by the survivors I have met and deeply moved by their testimonies. With antisemitic hate crimes increasing markedly in this country as a result of the Israel-Gaza war, there could not be a more pressing need for the Holocaust Memorial and Learning Centre.

Nicholas Milton's book *The Birdman of Auschwitz* is a powerful reminder of the dreadful events of the Holocaust and of the ordinariness and complex motives of those who were a party to it.

It explores the genocide through the fascinating but hitherto little-known story of a camp guard, Doctor Günther Niethammer, who used his love of ornithology as a diversion from the terrible conditions of Auschwitz-Birkenau but also to advance his scientific career, even when it meant being complicit in Nazi crimes. His unique story is testimony to the fact that even the most erudite scientists could be seduced by the Nazis.

Niethammer served in German-occupied Poland, but we should not forget that the crimes associated with the Holocaust happened across Europe, including on British soil, which is why it is beholden on all of us to remember the Holocaust as a clear warning for the future so that it is never repeated.

Ed Balls
Co-chair of the Holocaust Memorial
Foundation Advisory Board

THIS IS AN enormously challenging story on many levels; it will undoubtedly trouble me for the rest of my life. The acts and atrocities of Nazism are beyond doubt and reproach but are they beyond forgiveness, and how might such forgiveness ever be recognised and manifest? Are one man's actions ever excusable, could they be deemed sufficiently minuscule measured against the massive scale of death and destruction? But then what are individual men but together the perpetrators of that devastation?

I came to this book motivated by the man's interest in birds, an interest I share, I came wondering if any affinity at all might build an understanding of his actions, I came asking 'how can a man with such a passion for the beauty of life have been a part of such a wicked extermination of life?' I came with no sympathy for the notion that a viable excuse might have been 'I was just following orders'. I came wondering what makes seemingly ordinary people capable of committing acts of unimaginable horror.

There are answers to these questions sewn into the terrible fabric which makes up this 'banality of evil', there is a very uncomfortable curiosity to be exercised if you have the courage to delve into the twists and turns of his life and its part in the Holocaust. For my part I found no compassion for him, I overcame any confusion around his motives and although I built a better understanding of how men behave in war, I ultimately came to despise not just him, but those who shielded and protected him from his past. Coincidentally and critically, I realised a deep respect for all those who said 'no', who refused to be a part of any killing, so many of whom were murdered because of their conscience. This book leaves me in no doubt that I would have chosen the white feather over packing my binoculars for a trip to Auschwitz.

Chris Packham CBE
Wildlife Television Presenter and Conservationist

Preface

WHEN SOVIET TROOPS were liberating Auschwitz concentration camp in January 1945, among the piles of half-burnt corpses and emaciated prisoners left behind, they were amazed to find nesting boxes for birds. They had been placed on the walls of the guard's barracks and the previous year had been used by blue tits, great tits and starlings. The Russians found the same boxes in the walled garden at the house of Rudolf Höß, the notorious camp commandant. In his safe, they also discovered a copy of a paper called '*Beobachtungen über die Vogelwelt von Auschwitz (Ost-Oberschlesien)*' or 'Observations on the birdlife of Auschwitz (Eastern Upper Silesia)' with a personal dedication from the author. The nesting boxes and research paper belonged to one of the most erudite but naive guards ever to serve at the camp, Doctor Günther Niethammer.

On his arrival in 1940 Niethammer's passion for birds soon became known throughout Auschwitz and led to him being assigned to 'special duties' by the commandant. So instead of guard duties Niethammer shot game to order for Höß and conducted the most infamous bird survey of all time. The results were written up in a research paper which was published in May 1942 in the prestigious Annals of the Natural History Museum in Vienna. In it Niethammer paid a glowing tribute to his commandant, writing, 'I owe this to the great understanding which the commandant of KL [*Konzentrationslager* or concentration camp] Auschwitz, SS-Sturmbannführer Höß, and his adjutant, SS-Obersturmführer Frommhagen, gave to the scientific development of this area and the research tasks that the German expansion in the East brings with it.'

While the admiration each man had for the other was mutual, they valued the research paper for quite different reasons. For Höß the ornithological survey helped to cover up what was really happening at Auschwitz. For Niethammer it was to be his ticket out of a camp which had become hell on earth. A religious family man with four children, he found the experience of serving as a guard there extremely traumatic. Following the survey, with Höß's blessing, he successfully applied for a transfer to carry out a study of the birds on occupied Crete. However, Niethammer could not escape the infamous camp and afterwards had to serve a second stint there before finally leaving for good at the end of 1942. He then carried out scientific studies of birds on behalf of both the Waffen-SS and the German Army in Bulgaria and Italy before in 1945 facing a marauding Red Army in the last-ditch battle for Germany.

Immediately after the war some of those responsible for the extermination of the Jews at Auschwitz were put on trial and brought to justice. The most high-profile trial was of the camp commandant, Rudolf Höß, who was hanged in 1947 in the campgrounds for crimes against humanity, *The New York Times* describing him as 'the greatest individual killer in the history of the world'. But Höß was not an individual acting on his own volition but part of a Nazi hierarchy which at its peak comprised over 4,500 people at Auschwitz alone, most of them camp guards. Niethammer was a guard who unusually Höß both knew personally and liked. Indeed, at the end of his life the commandant went out of his way to protect him, deliberately not including Niethammer in the autobiography he wrote just before he was hanged.

Niethammer was seduced by the Nazis because he desperately wanted to promote his own career, joining first the Nazi Party and then the Waffen-SS. It was a career path which led to him ending up in the most notorious extermination camp in human history. There he came face-to-face with pure evil in a place where over a million men, women and children, mostly Jews, were murdered. But before being assigned to special duties, Niethammer helped to convert the barracks at the original camp and then clear the second zone to create what would become Auschwitz II-Birkenau. Only too aware of the real purpose of Auschwitz, he turned a blind eye to the heinous treatment of the prisoners. Instead, he sought solace in counting and shooting birds, even creating a macabre museum of bird skins at the camp, working with one of the inmates.

After the war Niethammer never denied knowing what went on at Auschwitz but did not believe that he was personally responsible, like so many others, claiming to be just 'following orders'. Put on trial together with other guards who had served at the camp, he was sentenced to eight years in prison by the Polish government, but this was reduced to three years following a concerted campaign on his behalf by his fellow scientists and the British authorities. Following his release Niethammer returned to the Zoological Museum Koenig in Bonn where his career, although tainted by association with Auschwitz, still flourished until his death in 1974.

Before the war Niethammer had been an academic and scientist who had made his name as the author of a very different kind of ornithological guide. The *Handbuch der Deutschen Vogelkunde* or the *Handbook of German Ornithology* was a monumental work comprising three volumes, listing all the species then known in the country. The first two volumes were published just before the war, but the final one came out in 1942 when Niethammer was serving at Auschwitz. It was the most comprehensive set of bird books then produced and the forerunner of all our modern identification guides. If Niethammer had not joined the Nazi Party and the Waffen-SS, it is likely that today he would be celebrated as one of the greatest ornithologists of his generation.

As a fellow ornithologist and former research assistant at the Royal Society for the Protection of Birds (RSPB), I wanted to understand what motivated Niethammer. At the RSPB I worked with many similar academics who dedicated themselves to writing research papers and producing bird books including the Society's former Conservation Director, Doctor Mark Avery. What motivated them was publishing new research so that conservation policy was based on sound science. Similarly Niethammer wanted to make his mark but why he was seduced by the Nazis bewildered me. Investigating his complex life, what I uncovered was a man who decided to put his career above his conscience and as a consequence ended up at Auschwitz.

The most difficult and troubling question about Niethammer's career is whether he was complicit in the Holocaust. By piecing together his life from primary sources, people who knew him, published works and the scientific papers he produced, I hope this book helps to answer that question. When writing it I used Rudolf Höß's autobiography *Commandant of Auschwitz* as a primary reference source, well aware that it was written as a way of trying to appease his guilt and exempt his family. It is a very disturbing book to read and often I would find myself getting depressed with the darker side of human nature. This is what the writer Hannah Arendt famously referred to as 'the banality of evil' when covering Adolf Eichmann's trial. I also always had in the back of my mind another famous quote often mistakenly attributed to the philosopher Edmund Burke: 'The only thing necessary for the triumph of evil is for good men to do nothing.' I concluded that without critical thinking evil can become routine and even banal but for it to triumph all it takes is for good men to look the other way and pursue their own narrow interests.

There is a well-known saying that no birds sing at Auschwitz. In Niethammer's time birds not only sung there but also nested within the campgrounds using the bird boxes he had put up. Niethammer's paper on the birdlife of Auschwitz is testimony that the surrounding area was once rich in birds and other wildlife (now, due to the biodiversity and climate crisis, most of the species he recorded have declined or disappeared). Today on entering the gates under the infamous sign *Arbeit macht frei* or 'Works sets you free', visitors are struck by the eerie silence which hangs over the camp. It is a myth that no birds sing there, as anyone who visits at dawn or dusk in spring will testify. However, even the beauty of birdsong pales into insignificance when you are confronted by the tangible presence of evil which still pervades Auschwitz.

Chapter 1

Far Away, in the Back of Beyond, in Poland

IN EARLY JANUARY 1940 Heinrich Himmler, one of the most powerful men in Nazi Germany and the architect of the Holocaust, made a surprise visit to the Sachsenhausen concentration camp in Oranienburg, just north of Berlin. The Reichsführer-SS had become increasingly concerned about reports of 'indiscipline' among the guards so had decided to conduct a tour of the camp to find out for himself what was going on. Himmler's unannounced visits were dreaded by SS officers who lived in perpetual fear of his wrath, his displeasure often leading to rapid demotion. Despite his fearsome reputation on arrival in his official car, neither the sentry nor the prisoners recognised him and did not salute or take off their caps, putting him in a foul mood. As he toured the camp, with the commandant Walter Eisfeld[1] and an entourage of officers in tow, his anger rose at the lax regime he saw on display all around him.

Sachsenhausen concentration camp held a special place in Himmler's burgeoning empire. Constructed in the summer of 1936, it was the first new concentration camp to be established following his appointment as the Chief of the German Police in July 1936. Designed as a model camp, as well as interning prisoners it was used for the training of SS guards. In close proximity to the German capital, it enjoyed a special status and housed a wide range of prisoners, especially political ones. Its importance was underlined when in 1938 the 'Inspectorate of the Concentration Camps', the central administrative office for all concentration camps, was moved from Berlin to Oranienburg on Himmler's orders.

After visiting the site and talking to the guards, Himmler made it clear that he intended to bring the camp 'back into line' and installed a new commandant by the name of Hans Loritz.[2] A workaholic who had a history of sadism, he replaced the 'too soft' Walter Eisfeld who was sent away to another camp. Loritz was a commandant very much in

Himmler's own image who owed his position to the Reichsführer-SS and in return served him with slavish loyalty. His opinion was that everyone in the camp was treated far too leniently, SS and prisoners alike. So, he began systematically to remove the old SS guard and bring in a new, more brutal prison regime. This included selecting prisoners unable or unwilling to work and sending them to the Sonnenstein Euthanasia Centre in Saxony as an example to the rest of the inmates (euthanasia was a euphemism for extermination, the centre also being the location for the secret Aktion T4 or Action T4 programme, the mass killing of people with disabilities and mental illness by involuntary euthanasia). To bring back order he also introduced a policy of shooting undesirable or troublesome prisoners on sight, by the end of the war overseeing the killing of over 10,000 Soviet prisoners.

One of the camp commanders Loritz soon clashed with was a 39-year-old SS adjutant by the name of Rudolf Höß[3]. He was in charge of the camp's firing squad and on Himmler's orders had executed a Jehovah's Witness and conscientious objector by the name of August Dickmann on 15 September 1939, the first prisoner of conscience to be shot following the start of the war. Höß had made a name for himself by ordering all the prisoners who could not work to stand outside in freezing temperatures in January 1940, over 150 of them dying in the process. Ironically, Loritz also considered Höß too soft and worse in his eyes someone who had loyally served his failed predecessor. 'This was a bad time for me,' wrote Höß. 'Loritz was forever treading on my heels. The more so because my departure in 1938 [from Dachau where he had served as a Block Leader] to become adjutant to his most hated rival, had caused him considerable irritation ... Loritz was very resentful of this and made me only too clearly aware of his dislike.'[4]

Höß was born on 25 November 1901 in Baden-Baden in south-west Germany and was brought up in a strict Catholic home where he was the eldest of three children and the only boy. His father was a former army officer who ran a tea and coffee emporium and ensured his son led a religious and disciplined life. Originally wanting to enter the priesthood instead, when the First World War broke out, Höß served first in a military hospital and then at the age of 14 in his father's old regiment, the 21st Regiment of Dragoons. Fighting in the Mesopotamia campaign, he rose to the rank of *Feldwebel* (sergeant-in-chief) and at 17 became the youngest non-commissioned officer in the army. Wounded three times and contracting malaria, he was awarded the Iron Crescent and the Iron Cross first and second class, the highest awards for bravery in the German army.

After hearing a speech by Adolf Hitler and being won over by his nationalist fervour, Höß joined the Nazi Party in 1922 but the following year was jailed for killing a school teacher who he believed was an informer. Sentenced to ten years' hard labour, he was released in 1928 as part of an amnesty and on 1 April 1934 joined the Schutzstaffel or SS. Admiring Himmler and believing that the state needed to be rid of *untermenschen* or undesirable races, he applied to the SS-Totenkopfverbände or the Death's Head Units who administered the concentration camp system. Here he rose through the ranks and in December 1934 was sent to Dachau where he became Block Leader, four years later being made adjutant to the Sachsenhausen camp commandant Hermann Baranowski who was succeeded in September 1939 by Walter Eisfeld.

So, when in February 1940 a vacancy came across Loritz's desk to carry out a feasibility study for a new camp in southern Poland (the country had been absorbed into the Third Reich following its partition with Russia in September 1939), the commandant of Sachsenhausen put Höß's name forward. Rather than resenting the move, Höß instead seized the opportunity and conducted a comprehensive research project into the area. The resulting report so impressed Himmler that he was promoted to become the new camp commandant, Loritz being only too pleased to see him go. The new appointment was a significant promotion for Höß, who had not believed that he would be made a commandant so quickly. Recording the event in his diary he proudly wrote, 'I therefore became commandant of the quarantine camp which was to be built at Auschwitz.'[5]

The new camp was situated in southern Poland near the town of Oświęcim, the Polish name of the town, which was replaced by the German one of Auschwitz after the country's occupation. It was a small industrial town, about 75 kilometres west of the city of Kraków, in the region of Upper Silesia. The concentration camp was to be located on the outskirts of the town, centred on a former army barracks around which a so-called 'Auschwitz interest zone' (*Interessengebiet des Auschwitz*) had been identified by Höß. Approximately 40 square kilometres in size, in this zone a massive sprawling complex would grow over the next few years into the largest extermination camp in Europe.

Geographically the western and northern borders of the Auschwitz interest zone were marked by the Vistula river, the eastern by the Soła river, while the southern border ran along the roads, dykes and creeks crossing the Polish villages of Brzeszcze, Przecieszyn, Jawiszowice and Łęki-Zasole (now Zasole). The area identified for the proposed camp was composed of scattered villages and flat, waterlogged meadows, numerous streams supplying a wide variety of ponds used for breeding fish and wildfowl shooting. To the west and north of the camp were large, forested areas, woods also being located to the east towards Kraków.

The Nazis chose the site because it was in the middle of the occupied territories so it could receive prisoners from across Europe. As well as being a good strategic position for a human concentration camp, it was also home to a wide variety of wildlife, especially birds. The ponds were surrounded by extensive reedbeds which teemed with great reed and aquatic warblers. Bitterns boomed from deep inside the reeds and on the open water crested and black necked grebes nested. Wildfowl including many species of dabbling and diving ducks made the ponds their home. The Vistula was a freshwater river with numerous oxbows and gravel islands where terns, kingfishers and plovers bred. Along the margins were dense willow beds, home to marsh warblers and the enigmatic nightingale. In contrast the Soła was a very winding, cold, mountain river, the scrub along its banks supporting river warblers, willow warblers and penduline tits. The meadows, dykes and open plains surrounding the barracks contained breeding redshank, lapwing, kestrel and marsh harrier. In the forests beyond the exclusion zone jays, woodpeckers and goshawks bred while the poplar plantations were home to the exotic golden oriole.

The natural beauty of the area was, however, largely lost on Höß who instead was completely focused on his plans for developing the camp. Starting work on 30 April 1940, he threw himself into his new job but was only too aware he was being sent there to get him out of the way. 'It was far away, in the back of beyond, in Poland,' he wrote. 'There the inconvenient Höß could exercise his passion for work to his heart's content.' Despite the location, he was delighted to have the opportunity to command his own camp, 'especially as some very senior protective custody camp commanders had been waiting a long time for a commandant's post to fall vacant.' Himmler had ordered him to construct a transit camp which could house 10,000 prisoners, using the existing complex of buildings which formed the army barracks as a base. 'It is much easier to build a completely new concentration camp than to construct one quickly out of a conglomeration of buildings and barracks,' he complained, 'which require a large amount of constructional alteration.'

Höß's first job was to make the barracks secure so that they could hold prisoners by adapting the existing buildings and commissioning new ones. To lay the foundations, 300 Jewish prisoners were rounded up at gunpoint from the nearby town of Auschwitz and marched into the camp. Outside the interest zone residents in the immediate vicinity and the surrounding eight villages were then expelled by SS guards. Any homes within the exclusion zone were commandeered or demolished so that over time German colonists could move into ones east of the Soła river, part of Höß's plan to establish a new German community in the area. In the meantime, a series of permanent road closures were put in place so Polish people living nearby were kept well away from the site.

Höß had only been in Auschwitz a couple of weeks before the Inspector of the Security Police and the Security Service based in nearby Breslau began ringing him and asking when the first transports of prisoners could be sent to the camp. 'It was clear to me from the very beginning that Auschwitz could be made into a useful camp only through the hard and untiring efforts of everyone,' he wrote, 'from the commandant down to the lowest prisoner.' Despite his stated desire to prioritise constructing the camp, Höß also gave orders to complete modifications to the large villa on the site where he planned to live with his wife Hedwig Hensel and their four children.

Vowing to 'do things differently', Höß was determined from the outset to create a camp which was both better run and more efficient in 'processing' prisoners than either Dachau or Sachsenhausen where he had previously worked. For the new commandant creating Auschwitz soon became a personal crusade and to succeed he pledged to 'ignore all concentration camp tradition and customs'. As an example, to his men Höß made sure that when reveille sounded, he was the first out of bed and by the time his guards had started their day's work, he was already well into his. At night he was the last to retire, commenting, 'There were very few nights in Auschwitz when I could sleep undisturbed by urgent telephone calls.' From the beginning Höß wanted Auschwitz to be the best camp in the system, even claiming he wanted to improve the food given to the prisoners so that he would get more work out of them. 'Everything that, from my point of view, seemed wrong in the other camps, I wished to handle differently here,' he proclaimed.

Despite making plain his ideals Höß soon found that the staff sent to him did not all share his vision. 'I became bitterly aware that all the goodwill and all the best of intentions were doomed to be dashed to pieces against the human inadequacy and sheer stupidity of most of the officers and men posted to me,' he bemoaned. He was particularly critical of the 'old hands' whom he had to work with, writing that 'even the best-willed of them simply could not behave otherwise than in the way to which they had become accustomed during long service in the concentration camps. The "beginners" were quick to learn from the "old hands", but the lessons they learnt were unfortunately not the best.'

To find new personnel he could rely upon, Höß asked the Inspector of Concentration Camps, SS-Gruppenführer Richard Glücks (1889-1945), if he could spare some officers but was turned down. Eventually after much badgering, the Reichssicherheitshauptamt (the Reich Security Main Office) sent him 30 staff from his former camp at Sachsenhausen, but Höß wasn't impressed with their calibre, complaining that 'Less than ten of them were suited to my wishes and intentions.' Frustrated he wrote, 'the whole backbone about which the camp was to be built was defective from the start. From the very beginning the camp was dominated by theories which were later to produce the most evil and sinister consequences.'

So Höß had to set about his task of creating a new concentration camp with very few reliable officers who were, in his opinion, up to the job, the rest not cooperating with him due to their 'intellectual limitations, their obstinacy and malice, and above all for reasons of convenience'. When building the camp, he became increasingly convinced that his orders were not being carried out, fearing that those beneath him either didn't respect his position or worse still were seeking to undermine him. In the paranoid chain of command which existed in the camp system, no one could be relied upon to do their jobs unless through fear or intimidation. 'It was impossible for me personally to see that my orders were carried out down to the smallest detail,' he fumed, 'since this would have meant diverting my attention from my main task, the building of a serviceable camp as rapidly as possible and acting as officer in charge of the protective custody camp myself.'

Over the next few weeks Höß found himself increasingly away from the camp, having to negotiate with all the various economic offices on his own as he did not trust his executive officer to do the job, describing him as a 'complete half wit' (probably a reference to the deputy commandant Karl Fritzsche). He lamented, 'I was thus forced to take matters out of his hands and to organise the entire victualling of troops and prisoners myself.' It was not just the troops and prisoners Höß had to personally vet but also all the materials needed to build and run the camp. This involved organising all the trucks and lorries to transport the materials and the fuel for them together with visiting local farms, where he even had to collect the straw for the prison blocks. Höß recalled, 'I had to drive as far as Zakopane and Rąbka [on the Polish-Slovak border, about 60 miles from Auschwitz] to acquire cooking pots for the prisoners' kitchen, and to the Sudetenland for bed frames and palliasses.'[6]

Ironically, given the camp would in the next few years become encased in barbed wire, at first Höß couldn't find any. 'I could not lay my hands on a hundred yards of barbed wire,' he complained. 'There were mountains of it in the engineer depot at Gleiwitz. But I could not touch it without first getting authority to have it decontrolled from the senior engineer staff in Berlin. The Inspectorate of Concentration Camps refused to help in this matter.' So Höß had to steal or borrow from old field fortifications and pillboxes left behind by the Polish army. 'Thus, I acquired the steel they contained,' he wrote. 'Whenever I came across installations containing material I urgently needed, I simply had it taken away at once without worrying about the formalities. I had to help myself.'

By this time the evacuation of the first zone had largely been completed and a second exclusion zone had begun to be cleared, taking in large areas of agricultural land.

Although there were very few 'good officers' Höß could rely on, by the end of the year the SS garrison at the camp had grown to several hundred guards and by the following year would number over 700 staff (growing eventually to around 3,000 guards). The SS divided the camp into five main sections – the headquarters department (personnel, legal and other related functions), the medical unit (doctors and dentists), the political department (the Gestapo and the criminal police, the Kripo), the economic administration (including the registration and disposal of property stolen from murdered prisoners) and the camp administration (responsible for security within the camp). By far, the biggest department was the camp administration – about 75 per cent of the SS members who worked at Auschwitz performed some kind of security function. Many of these were typical Nazi recruits, most having received a rudimentary education and only a few having gone on to university (about 70 per cent of SS men in Auschwitz fell into this category; 26 per cent were non-commissioned officers above the rank of *Rottenführer* or corporal; and just 4 per cent of the total SS complement were officers or above).

Those with a university education were mainly doctors in the hospital or architects working in the SS construction offices. However, there were exceptions and a notable one was Doctor Günther Theodor Niethammer.[7] He had volunteered for the Waffen-SS in May 1940 after unsuccessfully trying to join both the army and air force [despite holding a flying licence for light aircraft he was turned down because of his age and academic background]. An ornithologist with a doctorate in avian anatomy, when the war broke out Niethammer had been based in Bonn where he was Head of Department in the Natural History Museum. After initial training he was transferred to a Waffen-SS unit in Oranienburg and then in September 1940 to a company in Auschwitz. Here he was assigned to a guard unit and stationed at the camp's infamous front gate with its *Arbeit macht frei* sign leading to the barracks.

Chapter 2

From Bird Books to the Waffen-SS

NIETHAMMER WAS BORN in Waldheim, Saxony on 28 September 1908, and came from a large Catholic family, the eighth child of Konrad Niethammer and his wife Katharina (he was the youngest boy, the couple having five sons and three daughters; they would go on to have a ninth child)[1]. His father was a paper manufacturer and local politician who had worked his way up in the business, eventually jointly owning his own paper mill called Kübler & Niethammer (situated in the Ore mountains, it was the largest private paper manufacturer in Germany). Business acumen ran in the family, Niethammer's grandfather being an entrepreneur and leading liberal politician in Saxony at the end of the nineteenth century.

At school in Dresden Niethammer excelled academically and became fascinated by natural history, particularly birds and mammals, through a love of hunting. When he was only 18 years old Niethammer went on his own to South West Africa to visit his uncle, a former colonial official living in the country. While there he crossed the Kalahari Desert using a motorcycle on a bird-watching expedition, one of the first people to make the crossing.[2] After studying zoology at Tübingen in 1927, Niethammer went on to the University of Leipzig in 1929. Here, in 1932, he completed his doctorate under Professor Johannes Meisenheimer (1873–1933) on the anatomy of the avian crop and the secretion of crop milk in pigeons (the avian crop or ingluvies is present in most omnivorous and herbivorous bird species and plays a major role in moistening and storing food;[3] it is also believed to regulate the immune system of birds – in some species ingluvies secrete 'crop milk' which is high in nutrients and energy and is fed to the young).

While studying at Leipzig he met all the leading ornithologists of the day including Hans Kummerlöwe (1903–1995), a member of the Nazi Party who soon became a close colleague and accompanied him on motorcycle expeditions to study nature, both locally and further afield. Niethammer owned a BMW motorcycle which he nicknamed 'the hen'. It was his pride and joy and on it in 1933 the pair embarked on an ornithological expedition to Turkey but nearly wrote off the motorcycle following an accident. On 1 September 1933 Niethammer married Ruth Filtzer who accompanied her new husband and Kummerlöwe on another expedition that autumn to Asia Minor but this time in car. Both expeditions resulted in a series of joint publications on the ornithology and nature of the region.

Kummerlöwe had joined the party early in 1925 and by the time Hitler came to power in 1933 had already organised a Nazi student union at Leipzig. He signed Niethammer up to the Deutsche Ornithologische Gesellschaft (German Ornithological Society) and introduced him to the man who was to become his mentor and the most important person in his career, Erwin Stresemann (1899–1972). One of the greatest ornithologists of the twentieth century, Stresemann was the curator of ornithology at the Natural History Museum in Berlin and referred to reverentially by his peers as the 'Pope of Ornithology'.[4] Secretary General, President and then Honorary President of the Society of German Ornithologists for fifty years, during the 1920s and 1930s, he had transformed ornithology from a traditional study of classification into a branch of modern biological science.

Stresemann had been looking for a long time for someone to write a book on German birds under his stewardship but hadn't found anyone suitable. Producing a guide to over 500 species (the German list is now 550) was a huge undertaking which he knew would take years to complete. The previous person to start it, Dr. le Roi, in 1913, had seen the First World War hold up the work and then he had died before making any real progress with it. Ornithologists in other countries starting similar monumental works had failed to complete them. So, Stresemann knew it was vital to get the right person if the project was to stand any chance of succeeding. It required someone with not just the knowledge and experience to research the book but also the dedication and perseverance to finish it.

Stresemann had already secured a publisher, the prestigious Akademische Verlagsgesellschaft (Academic Publishing Company) based in Leipzig. They produced a wide range of scientific tomes for the academic community and welcomed the opportunity to publish the work (the company was owned by a Jew called Leo Jolowicz who was forced out by the Nazis in 1937, the year the first book was published, he later committing suicide in 1940[5]). Stresemann had also secured the funding to produce it and had a range of contributors lined up from Niethammer's colleague Hans Kummerlöwe to other prominent ornithologists of the era including Leo von Boxberger, Holger Heinrich Dathe, Wilhelm Eichler, Hugo Hildebrandt and Helmut Sick. Impressed with the young Niethammer, Stresemann had noted how much effort he had put into his doctorate, staying up night after night to complete it and, unlike many of his other students, writing it up. Following it Niethammer had made it known that he wanted to stay within the university to carry out post-doctorate research and pursue a career in ornithology.

In 1934 Stresemann formerly asked Niethammer if he would like to produce the book working with him at the Natural History Museum in Berlin and the other contributors. As an incentive he offered Niethammer the opportunity for his name to appear first in the publication and be cited as the principal author. Being young and impressionable, Niethammer was flattered to be asked by such an eminent ornithologist and readily accepted. However, the scale of the task was considerable as there were still significant gaps in the knowledge of German birds at the time. But far from being put off by the amount of work involved, Niethammer relished it and took up the challenge with zeal. It involved researching over 500 species, reviewing journals, scientific studies and fieldwork as well as looking at skins, photographs and drawings in both public museums and private collections. After three years of painstaking research, he published the first volume in 1937 with the title *Handbuch der Deutschen Vogelkunde* (*Handbook of German Ornithology*). Produced on behalf of the German Ornithological Society, it covered the Passeres (a suborder of the largest order of birds, the Passeriformes with over 5,000 species worldwide, consisting chiefly of songbirds) and was 474 pages long with a colour plate and sixty-nine illustrations.

When it was published the *Handbuch der Deutschen Vogelkunde* was highly praised and received very good reviews in all the major ornithological journals. With its full colour plate and sixty-nine illustrations spread over twenty-four pages it broke new ground in ornithological publishing. A review in the authoritative publication *British Birds* said:

> The first volume of this excellent and compact Handbook, which we understand is to be completed this summer by

> a further volume in two sections, is now before us and reflects the greatest credit on all concerned. … The work is naturally still incomplete but has set a new standard in general European literature on this subject. A few errors and discrepancies are inevitable in a work of this kind, but the general advance is very striking. … Dr. Niethammer and his collaborators have produced a thoroughly sound and most useful work, which should afford a very valuable aid and stimulus to ornithological work in Central Europe.[6]

The success of the book paved the way for Niethammer's professional career and on the back of it in the same year he was appointed as a curator at the prestigious new Zoological Museum Koenig in Bonn by Doctor Adolf von Jordans (1892–1974) who headed up the musuem. Opened in 1934 by Alexander Koenig (1858–1940), a naturalist and philanthropist who had made his fortune in the sugar business, it was originally designed as a private institute to house his collection. In 1929 Koenig bequeathed his collection to the government and following protracted negotiations with the Reichsinnenministerium (Reich Interior Ministry), the museum opened its doors to the public on 13 May 1934. For Niethammer it was a significant promotion from his status as a post-doctorate researcher and meant that before the age of 30 he was already moving in elite ornithological circles. On taking up the position Niethammer also applied for membership of Hitler's Nationalsozialistische Deutsche Arbeiterpartei (NSDAP or Nazi Party). It was, he wrote, a decision 'which my immediate superior, Dr. A. von Jordans (now Director of the Museum in Bonn) not only approved but considered justified in consideration of the beneficial development for the work of the Museum.' Niethammer had formally applied to be a party member on 25 November 1937 but admission had been granted retrospectively to 1 May to coincide with his appointment, his party number being 5613683.[7]

Niethammer's move from being an obscure researcher to a senior curator at a state museum meant he had found himself much more beholden to the German government. While Nazi membership was not compulsory and people in the museum who were against the regime refused to join, for Niethammer it was a natural move which was designed to further his career, the ideology that it stood for being something he was much more ambivalent about. At the time Hitler had come to power in 1933, the Nazi party had over two million members but just four years later when Niethammer joined this number had doubled and by the eve of the war in 1939 over five million people were members (civil servants like Niethammer were over-represented in the party compared to the general population as, like him, many considered membership essential to their career).

A big part of the motivation for Niethammer joining the party was to take part in expeditions to discover new species, many of which were organised or sponsored by the government. Hermann Göring, the head of the Luftwaffe and the Master of the German Hunt and Forest, had a passion for falconry, hunting and conservation. To promote them he had formed the Hermann-Göring-Stiftung (Hermann Göring Foundation) which was located at the Reichsjägerhof (the Reich Hunting Lodge), near Braunschweig in northern Germany. As part of its work Göring had ordered foundation staff to collect birds of prey from across the world for his personal collection, falconry breeding programmes and party rallies. Göring already had a large collection of birds but particularly wanted to own a pure white gyrfalcon, the largest of the falcons which bred in the Arctic (the gyrfalcons plumage varies with location from dark brown to all white, the latter being particularly rare and sought after by collectors). So, in the summer of 1938 he sent an expedition to west Greenland to capture a range of gyrfalcons, especially an all-white one for his personal use.

Niethammer followed the success of the expedition with particular interest. It was headed up by the polar explorer and mining engineer Kurt Herdemerten (1900–1952) and Hans-Robert Knoespel (1915–1944), an ornithologist and falconer. They captured five gyrfalcons, four juveniles and an all-white adult bird for Göring and transported them back to the Reich. They also shot many bird specimens from phalaropes to peregrines (forty-five skins of birds collected by the expedition still reside with the Department of Zoology in the National Museum in Prague).[8]

Göring was delighted with his gyrfalcon and named it 'Polar Falke' or 'Polar Falcon'. It soon became his favourite hunting bird, the German painter Renz Waller later doing a portrait of it which hung in Carinhall, his luxurious hunting lodge and home. The other gyrfalcons from the expedition were used to set up a falconry centre at the Goldhöhe Station, which was located at an altitude of 1,400 metres in the Krkonoše Mountains in Czechoslovakia. The nearest to Arctic conditions occurring in the Reich, it was deemed the most suitable place to keep the birds (Czechoslovakia was annexed in 1938, the station becoming a research centre, later being used in the war as an Arctic training camp).

Just three weeks before Niethammer had officially applied to be a party member, in the Reich Chancellery Adolf Hitler had held a secret meeting on 5 November 1937 outlining his plans for acquiring *lebensraum* or 'living space' for the German people in Eastern Europe, a decision which would send over six million Jews to their death at Auschwitz and other concentration camps. Recorded in the Hossbach Memorandum (named after Hitler's military adjutant Colonel Fredrich Hossbach), the decision marked an infamous turning point in Nazi foreign policy, the dictator putting into practice his plans for the expansion of the German Reich and the domination of Europe.

For Niethammer, however, politics were a means to an end and the next year saw his career flourish as he developed his role as a curator at the Museum Koenig in Bonn and worked hard on the second volume of the *Handbuch der Deutschen Vogelkunde*. This was published in 1938 and this time included two colour plates and was 545 pages long. The book covered a wide variety of birds (many suborders of which are now no longer used) including the Pici (woodpeckers), Macrochires (swifts), Upupae (hoopoes), Meropes (bee-eaters), Halcyones (kingfishers), Coraciae (choughs), Caprimulgi (nightjars), Striges (owls), Cuculi (cuckoos), Accipitres (birds of prey), Gressores (waders), Phoenicopteri (flamingos), Streganopodes (water birds) and Anseres (waterfowl). Like the first, the second volume again attracted very good reviews and firmly established Niethammer as one of the most promising ornithologists of his generation. At the same time, he also found time for a second successful expedition to South West Africa with two ornithologists, Willi Issel and Walter Hoesch, who lived there (he later published a monograph about the birds of the region together with Hoesch in 1940).

Niethammer was hard at work on the third volume when in September 1939 Germany invaded Poland and the Second World War began. Like the rest of the German population, Niethammer followed events closely but was lulled into a false sense of security by the phoney war. Focused on his research, his newfound fame and work on the handbook was amply rewarded when on 1 April 1940 he was appointed curator of ornithology at the highly prestigious Natural History Museum in Vienna (following the Anschluss in 1938 Austria had been annexed into the German Reich). The person who employed him was his friend and former fellow-student Hans Kummerlöwe who was now in charge of the museum. As a leading member of the party, he had been appointed senior director of all 'scientific state museums in Vienna' in June the previous year by the Reichsministerium für Wissenschaft, Erziehung und Volksbildung (Reich Ministry of Science, Education and Culture), his appointment being confirmed by personal invitation of Adolf Hitler 'in the name of the German people'.

Kummerlöwe was very pleased with his new head of ornithology, believing in Niethammer he had attracted one of the best scientists in the Third Reich. His output was as prolific as it was varied, in 1940 alone Niethammer publishing papers on the birds at Lake Neusiedl, the breeding success of the little tern, saker falcon, red-throated pipit and yellow wagtail in Ostmark, courtship observations of South African bustards, the birds of Fukien, China (joint paper with von Jordans), the breeding success of tawny owls in the Rhineland, the cormorant in Saxony, the band-rumped storm petrel in Germany and the diet of wood pigeons (who were accused of eating the vegetables grown by German families to supplement their meagre rations).The appointment also came with a substantial renumeration and 'relocation package'. Together with his wife Ruth and children (his first son Jochen was born in 1935, a second son Gerd in 1936, a third Michael followed in 1940 and a final son Rolf would be born in 1941) Niethammer moved into a lavish residence at Blaasstraße 33 in Vienna-Döbling. The property was the former home of a Jewish woman called Rudolfine Liatscheff, née Grünspan, who had been forced to vacate it at gunpoint and sent to a concentration camp (today it is the Libyan embassy). In his new role Niethammer began work on an exciting new research project looking at breeding birds in Austria which were new for Germany.[9]

As the German Blitzkrieg swept across Western Europe, Niethammer watched in awe as the armed forces conquered first the Low Countries and then occupied France. A patriotic German citizen, despite being 32 years old, he decided to enlist, with Kummerlöwe's encouragement, his brothers having already signed up. Rather than wanting to fight for his country, Niethammer saw in the spectacular German victories new opportunities to advance his career. Despite his desire to sign up, however, the traditional German armed forces were not that keen to recruit an academic and museum curator. So, after unsuccessfully applying to both the Heer and the Luftwaffe, he then volunteered for the Waffen-SS in May 1940.

The Waffen-SS (Armed Protective Squadron) was the combat arm of the SS (Schutzstaffel) or Security Police and was an elite fighting force which had also taken on responsibility for the concentration camps. Niethammer due to his age and academic background was not selected for a frontline role but instead was designated to guard duties. However, to become a member of the Waffen-SS he still had to meet their rigid recruitment standards. This included proving his 'Aryan ancestry' and confirming his National-Socialist beliefs. Niethammer volunteered for four and a half years and after being drafted in September 1940, swore his personal oath to Adolf Hitler:

> *Ich schwöre Dir, Adolf Hitler, als Führer und Kanzler des Deutschen Reiches Treue und Tapferkeit. Wir geloben Dir und den von Dir bestimmten Vorgesetzten Gehorsam bis in den Tod. So wahr mir Gott helfe.*
>
> I swear to you, Adolf Hitler, as Führer and Chancellor of the German Reich, that I will be loyal and brave. I pledge obedience unto death to you and those you appoint to lead. So help me God.

After the oath of loyalty, Niethammer undertook basic training which covered physical fitness, small-arms proficiency and political indoctrination before being posted to Auschwitz on 16 September 1940.[10] Here they cut his hair short, vaccinated him and tattooed his blood type on the underside of his left arm near the armpit. On arriving at the camp he joined a growing garrison of guards and was assigned duties including shifts on the main gate 'G' above which was erected the infamous sign *Arbeit macht frei*. The sign had been erected by Polish prisoners with metalwork skills on the orders of Höß three months earlier (it was a cynical take on the title of an 1873 book by the lexicographer, linguist and novelist Lorenz Diefenbach in which gamblers and fraudsters discovered the path to freedom through hard work[11]). Höß believed that hard work offered to set a prisoner free but also chillingly wrote that it 'can lead to his destruction. ... Only thus can the slogan "Work Brings Freedom" be understood'.

Reflecting the infamous motto of Auschwitz, work was what drove Höß and serving the Nazi regime came above everything else in his life, including his wife and children. He believed that for prisoners 'work is a necessity and satisfies an inner need'. Those who did not or could not work he particularly despised, calling them 'idlers, loafers and other types of a-social spongers'. So, when he was setting up Auschwitz Höß was determined that any prisoners coming into the camp, regardless of their age, gender, race or physical fitness, would work (later these characteristics would be used to separate those assigned to the work detail and those sent straight to the gas chambers). For Höß work gave prisoners a purpose and a reason to exist, especially if they were Poles, Jews and other groups who were subhuman and a drain on society. 'Work helps a prisoner to get over the emptiness of imprisonment,' he wrote. 'It pushes the wretchedness of the daily round in prison into the background if it occupies his mind sufficiently; and if he does it willingly, by which I mean with an inner readiness, he will derive satisfaction from it.'

In setting up Auschwitz Höß therefore made work parties a central part of his ethos in running the camp, believing it offered prisoners a reason to stay alive. It was an ethic he shared with Niethammer who also described himself as a 'workaholic', a trait which later was to bring the two men together. 'It is true that work in the prisons and concentration camps is compulsory,' Höß wrote. 'But generally speaking, every prisoner employed on the right kind of work does it willingly. The inner satisfaction that it gives him affects his whole state of mind. On the other hand, disaffection with his work can make his life a burden.' Höß prided himself that his life had been defined by hard work and it was through dedicating himself completely to it that he has risen so far and so fast in the SS.

'All my life I have thoroughly enjoyed working,' he wrote with obvious pride:

> I have done plenty of hard, physical work, under the severest conditions, in the coal mines, in oil refineries and in brickyards. I have felled timber, cut sleepers and stacked peat. I have, with my own hands, done every sort of principal work. I can justly maintain that I know what work means, that I am fully qualified to judge another man's working efficiency.

However, Höß's work experience had been gained as a free man and he had been paid for it, not as a malnourished and beaten prisoner working for nothing at gunpoint.

In erecting the *Arbeit macht frei* sign Höß had been inspired by SS-Obergruppenführer Theodor Eicke (1892–1943), one of the key figures in the development of the concentration camp system, reflecting:

> It was Eicke's firm intention that no matter what category, those prisoners whose steady and zealous work marked them out from the others should in due course be released, regardless of what the Gestapo and the Criminal Police Office might think to the contrary. Indeed, this occasionally happened, until the war put an end to all such good intentions[12] [while most people who passed through Auschwitz were exterminated, some in the early years were released although many more died from malnutrition and over work].

On first joining the other guards at the camp Niethammer was shocked by the conditions he found there with prisoners regularly being beaten and abused but Auschwitz was not then the infamous extermination camp that it was to become over the next two years. The first mass transport of prisoners by train to the camp had taken place over three months before his arrival on 14 June 1940 when 728 Polish prisoners including a small group of Jews had arrived from a Polish prison in Tarnów. Once they had been unloaded from their carriages, the inmates were then separated into two groups: men in one and women and children in the other.

Many were political prisoners and were told by Höß that if they worked hard and abided by the rules, they could earn their freedom. However, if they didn't they were left in little doubt about their fate. Later arrivals at the camp were chillingly told by Karl Fritzsch, the deputy commandant:

> You came here not to a sanatorium, but to a German concentration camp, from which there is no other way out but through the chimney. If someone doesn't like it, they can go straight to the wires. If there are Jews in the transport, they have the right to live no longer than two weeks, priests a month, the rest three months[13] [despite Fritzsch's comments against all the odds a quarter of the first transport survived the war]

The prisoners were then registered, photographed and given a unique prisoner number which from 1941 onwards was tattooed onto their left forearm. From this point onwards, they ceased to be human beings with names and became numbers (at most other camps, their number was stitched onto their clothing rather than tattooed on their arm). A prisoner's personal possessions were confiscated and sorted in the so-called Kanada warehouses, storage facilities used to process their stolen belongings. Here the inmate's possessions were sifted through by other prisoners, valuables being separated and sent back to Germany, other useful items like shoes, glasses, hair and gold teeth also being collected. The warehouses were ironically nicknamed *Kanada*, the German spelling of Canada, because Canada was deemed a wealthy country, and the warehouses were full of people's valuables.

Prisoners who worked as part of the Kanada kommando or squad were in a privileged position. They were able to obtain extra rations and help themselves to clothing – items which could save their lives but if caught stealing they faced extreme punishment from a beating to being killed. After being parted from their possessions prisoners were then assigned to a barrack and work detail, all the first transport being given construction roles which often involved heavy physical labour. After registration the prisoners were told to undress, had their heads shaved and were forced to shower in front of other prisoners and the SS guards. The prisoner's regular clothing was then taken away and replaced by a striped uniform. This humiliating process was designed to remove any remnants of personal identity and human dignity.

The infamous Auschwitz 'uniform' resembled pyjamas with blue stripes and was made of coarse material which often irritated the skin. Men were given a cap, trousers and jacket to wear. Women wore a dress or skirt with a jacket and kerchief or scarf for their head. Some uniforms, especially those of the Kapos – prisoners who acted as guards – had pockets, other prisoners secretly sewing them into their uniforms. This was one of the privileges higher-ranking prisoners enjoyed, the pockets being extremely useful for concealing extra rations or other useful items like cutlery. On their feet, prisoners wore wooden or leather clogs. Socks were not supplied so many prisoners suffered with sores caused by rubbing, which often became infected in the poor and unhygienic camp conditions.

As well as inmates having their number tattooed on their arm, they also wore a triangle on their uniform, the colour defining the category of prisoner. Germans wore black triangles, Jews two yellow ones which formed the Star of David, political prisoners red triangles, Roma or gypsies brown ones (although they were sometimes classed as 'asocials' and given black ones), homosexuals pink triangles and Jehovah's Witnesses purple ones. Uniforms came in several sizes but people who were not a standard size were often forced to wear ones that were too large or small for them. Prisoners' clothing was often inadequate for the conditions in which they were expected to work and live, being too hot in summer and too cold in winter. As they were malnourished and lost weight the uniforms also tended to hang off them (later on, in view of the high mortality among the inmates in Auschwitz, new prisoners were often given the old uniforms and shoes of those who had just been killed).

By the time of Niethammer's arrival at Auschwitz the prisoners had already settled into a regular routine. The guards woke them up from their beds in the barracks between 4 a.m. and 4.30 a.m. (not long after his arrival this was changed to an hour later for winter). The prisoners then had between thirty and forty-five minutes to use the toilet, get dressed, make their beds, clean the barracks and have breakfast. Toilet and washing facilities usually consisted of buckets and dirty water in bowls with no soap or toilet paper and which were shared by all the prisoners. Anyone who completed these tasks too slowly faced being beaten by the guards. Prisoners were then lined up for the morning roll call on the *Appellplatz* or roll call area, a registration of all inmates in the camp including anyone who had died during the night or who was ill.

During roll call the prisoners were counted twice, any discrepancies meaning that they were recounted so the process could take hours. Throughout this time, prisoners had to stand outside – when Niethammer joined in September 1940 the temperatures were already falling and in the next few weeks came close to freezing in the early morning. Any prisoners that collapsed or helped other inmates on the Appellplatz faced beatings – anyone accused of helping a prisoner try to escape faced torture and execution. Once roll call was finished and the sun rose, prisoners were marched off to work under armed guard. Initially the work consisted of converting the existing barracks but by the time Niethammer arrived the work was also focused on clearing the second zone. The prisoners were often forced to sing marching or 'patriotic' German songs to mock, humiliate and discipline them, to the amusement of the SS officers. Keeping up with the speed of the march was essential, however exhausted or malnourished the prisoners were, those falling behind being beaten or punished by having their rations cut.

Food at the camp was always in short supply but had become much more heavily rationed since the start of the war. Before the conflict in other camps food had typically consisted of an early breakfast of bread or porridge, accompanied by tea or ersatz coffee served in tin bowls and mugs. Lunch was a vegetable soup, occasionally served with bread, and dinner would be more soup, and in some cases, bread and cheese. By the time the first mass transport of prisoners arrived at Auschwitz in June 1940 meals had become smaller and less nutritious. They consisted of soup for lunch and dinner, with just one piece of bread. These rations were further cut by some of the SS guards, who often stole or limited the amount of food that the prisoners received as a punishment. The meals only amounted to about 1,300 calories a day (the current recommendation is 2,500 calories per day for men and 2,000 calories per day for women). As food was essential for survival in the camp a black market soon developed with prisoners managing to survive by trading goods or services like sewing and reading in return for stolen rations. Anything and everything was traded, from buttons to clothing as well as clandestinely obtained goods like cutlery and cigarettes. Prisoners who worked in the Kanada warehouses or the camp kitchens were often at the centre of the black market as they had access to goods such as extra clothes and food. However, most were not so lucky, and had to barter with or steal from other prisoners.

At midday, prisoners were sometimes forced to march back for a noon roll call, and to collect their lunch (in later years lunch was brought to the prisoners to increase the time they spent working). Work typically finished at approximately 5 p.m. or 6 p.m. each day, or sundown in winter (although troublesome prisoners could be forced to work through the night). Once work had finished, prisoners were marched back to the camp to participate in evening roll call. Those that had died during the day were also brought out to the roll call to be counted. If there were inaccuracies the roll call would be repeated, and beatings were frequent. Extending roll call for long periods could also be used as a form of punishment so that the weakest prisoners would literally be dead on their feet. After the evening roll call was finally completed prisoners were sent back to their barracks, where they had 'free time'. Some prisoners used this period to barter for additional food or repair their clothing.

Most, exhausted, simply collapsed in their bunks. At 9 p.m. lights were switched off, and the prisoners were expected to sleep.

Höß's regime for running the camp was based on his belief that all prisoners had to be treated harshly and without compassion until they complied and accepted their fate. To do this he insisted that the guards treat them with severity, forcing them to work whatever their condition. 'Every prisoner tries to improve his lot and to make his conditions more tolerable,' he wrote. 'He will exploit kindness and human understanding. Unscrupulous prisoners will go to the limit and will try, by evoking sympathy, to get the better of their guards.' The interaction between prisoners and guards fascinated Höß, who believed that each was defined by the other:

> To put it crudely, guards and prisoners constitute two hostile and opposing worlds ... According to his nature he [the prisoner] either allows his enemy to vent his spite against an armour of indifference and continues to carry on more or less as before: or he becomes cunning, furtive and deceitful, and hoodwinks his opponent in order to obtain alleviations and privileges.

Despite the severity of the regime, as Höß highlighted, in the early years prisoners were released from Auschwitz and had a chance of freedom if they worked hard and agreed to conform. The camp regulations stated that periodic assessments of a prisoner's work rate and attitude had to be undertaken by the guards. Those willing to labour and who accepted Nazi ideology could in theory be released after three months. Prisoners willing to work but who proved more hostile were 're-educated' and if deemed compliant over time could be released after a year. However, prisoners who were continually antagonistic to the regime or more troublesome were detained indefinitely. This was reflected in the first transport brought to Auschwitz: out of the 728 men and women imprisoned more than 70 were released. However, with the outbreak of war the release criteria were considerably tightened. In 1940, the release of Jews was suspended and restricted for other political prisoners. In 1941 due to the number of applications to release prisoners from occupied Poland and Czechoslovakia, the procedures were tightened again, and from the autumn of 1942, almost no one was released.

CHAPTER 3

Bullies, Psychopaths and Sadists

NIETHAMMER SOON FOUND out that Höß had a low opinion of not just many of his officers like Fritzsch who served under him but also many of the guards. 'The guards who have the duty of supervising the prisoners can be divided into three district categories,' he wrote, adding, 'They can make life hell for the prisoner, but they can also make his wretched existence easier and even tolerable.' The first category Höß identified were those who were cruel, the most extreme of whom were sadists. 'Malicious, evil-minded, basically bad, brutal, inferior, common creatures regard the prisoner as an unresisting object on which they can exercise their unrestrained and often perverted desires and whims and so find relief for their inferiority complexes,' he reflected in a description which equally could have been applied to him.

> They do not know the meaning of pity or any kind, warm fellow-feeling. These seize every opportunity to terrorise the prisoners entrusted to their care, especially those against whom they have a personal grudge ... The spiritual anguish of their victims gives them particular satisfaction. No regulations, however strict, will restrain them in their evil ways.

Tellingly he also wrote, 'Woe to the prisoners under their charge when these perverted creatures have as their superiors men who acquiesce in their evil propensities, or even share in their inclinations and encourage them!'

Many of these guards were encouraged in their cruelty by the relentless Nazi propaganda about *untermenschen* (a Nazi term for non-Aryan or racially inferior people). At Auschwitz this was fuelled by the publication *Der Stürmer* (*The Stormer* or *The Attacker*), copies of which were distributed widely throughout the camp. A weekly tabloid-type newspaper, it was produced by Julius Streicher (1885–1946), the Gauleiter of Franconia and a member of the Reichstag or German Parliament. Virulently antisemitic, the magazine was renowned for its grotesque caricatures of Jews, obscene, sexually explicit material and strongly anti-communist and anti-royalist views. The first edition was produced in 1923 and after Hitler came to power in 1933 *Der Stürmer* rapidly grew into a mass-circulation tabloid. By the start of the war, it had a distribution of over 400,000 copies including all the concentration camps where it was avidly read. The explicit content in it actively encouraged guards to abuse prisoners or have sexual relations with them despite this being strictly banned. 'The Jews … did not have an easy time,' Höß wrote with gross understatement, adding they

> had to work in the gravel pit, which, for them, was very strenuous physical labour. The guards influenced by Eicke and by *Der Stürmer*, which was on show everywhere in the barracks and canteens, were particularly rough with them. They were sufficiently persecuted and tormented already as 'corrupters of the German people', even by their fellow-prisoners. When a display case containing *Der Stürmer* was put up in the protective custody camp, its effect on those prisoners who had hitherto been not at all antisemitic was immediately apparent.[1]

Despite being well read by the guards, mainly due to its pornographic content, surprisingly *Der Stürmer* was not popular with Höß who claimed to disapprove of the magazine. 'I was opposed to *Der Stürmer,* Streicher's antisemitic weekly,' he wrote,

> because of the disgusting sensationalism with which it played on people's basest instincts. Then, too, there was its perpetual and often savagely pornographic emphasis on sex. This paper caused a lot of mischief and, far from serving serious antisemitism, it did a great deal of harm. It is small wonder that after the collapse it was learnt that a Jew edited the paper and that he also wrote the worst of the inflammatory articles it contained [there is no evidence

for this assertion, Höß probably putting the blame for the content back on the Jews to deflect from the paper's virulent antisemitic editorial line].

The second category of guards were those who just did their job, which Höß thought made up the majority, he characterising them as uninterested or indifferent to the fate of the prisoners (while this may have been true when Auschwitz was being set up, over time many of these guards ended up in the first category as any sympathy gave way to antipathy). 'They carry out their tasks stolidly and discharge their duties, so far as they must, in a competent or indolent fashion.' However, even these men often treated the prisoners cruelly or with contempt due to Nazi indoctrination, Höß reflecting 'to them, too, the prisoners are mere objects that they have to supervise and guard. They scarcely regard them as human beings with lives of their own.' These guards kept strictly to the regulations, obeying them to the letter, Höß writing, 'It is too much of a strain for them to attempt to interpret those regulations sensibly. They are in general men of limited abilities.' While trying to absent them of blame, Höß also felt they caused a lot of misery in the camp. 'They have no deliberate wish to do the prisoners harm,' he wrote. 'But because of their indifference and narrow-mindedness and their desire for an easy life, they do cause a lot of harm and inflict much physical and mental anguish upon the prisoners quite unintentionally. It is primarily they, however, who enable some prisoners to obtain a domination over their fellows that is so often evil'.

The domination Höß was referring to involved the use of Kapos or Funktionshäftling (prisoner functionaries) in the camp, prisoners assigned by the SS guards to supervise other prisoners or carry out administrative tasks. They were transported to Auschwitz from Sachsenhausen concentration camp on 20 May 1940 and were assigned the numbers 1 to 30. They played a vital role in running Auschwitz as the large number of prisoners in the first transport required constant oversight. The Kapos were often recruited from violent criminals rather than from the more numerous political, religious or 'asocial' prisoners and were chosen for their cruelty toward other inmates. In Auschwitz this behaviour was actively encouraged by the SS guards as a way of keeping the other prisoners in line. The Kapos were put in charge of a prisoner work gang or *Kommando* and it was their job to brutally force prisoners to work even if they were sick or starving. In return Kapos were often spared death provided they performed their duties to the satisfaction of the SS guards. They also had privileged status within the camp system reflected in them being allowed to wear civilian clothes and have private quarters.

The third category of guard according to Höß 'consists of men who are kindly by nature, good-hearted, compassionate and able to sympathise with a fellow-human's troubles'. Niethammer fell into this category but even within it the attitude and behaviour of the guards varied considerably. 'First there are those who stick firmly and conscientiously to the regulations and will overlook no departure from them on the part of the prisoners, but who, out of kindness of heart and good nature, construe the regulations in favour of the prisoners and endeavour, so far as possible, to alleviate their situation, or at any rate not to make it necessarily hard,' reported Höß. 'There are others who are simply good-hearted, and whose naivety borders on the miraculous. They will try to gratify a prisoner's every wish, and out of sheer good nature and boundless sympathy will attempt to help him in every way. They are unable to believe that evil men exist among prisoners, too.' Niethammer fell squarely into the former category – just like following the rules of avian taxonomy he obeyed the camp regulations to the letter.

Höß believed this third category of guard was weak and easily exploited. 'Every prisoner tries to improve his lot and to make his conditions of life more tolerable,' he wrote. 'He will exploit kindness and human understanding. Unscrupulous prisoners will go to the limit and will try, by evoking sympathy, to get the better of their guards.' Reflecting his view of how prisoners should be treated, he added

> And this is the disadvantage of showing too much kindness and goodwill towards the prisoners. A single gesture of human understanding towards a strong-minded prisoner will often inaugurate a series of lapses from discipline on the part of the guard that can only end in the most severe punishment [death]. Such lapses may begin with the harmless smuggling of a letter but may lead to actual assistance in escaping.

In his first few weeks at the camp Niethammer, a highly educated man used to dealing with erudite ornithologists, researchers and scientists, soon found he had little in common with most of his fellow guards. Many of them were either bullies, psychopaths and sadists or, as Höß pointed out, men so scared of the regime that they followed the regulations religiously without questioning anything. The number of guards in the third category, 'kindly and good-hearted men' like him, were distinctly in the minority. For the 700-plus Polish prisoners many of the guards in the camp fell into the first two categories, working them to the bone to finish the hastily converted barracks. The same guards were also the ones who made them attend roll call in the courtyard several times a day where they were regularly humiliated and beaten.

As a guard Niethammer's duties included shifts manning the gate and the main tower overlooking the camp entrance where he was under orders to shoot any prisoner trying to escape. He also carried out regular checks on the inmates, supervised the work gangs and helped his fellow guards exclude people from the surrounding area of the second zone. The cruelty he witnessed by some of the more extreme guards towards the Polish prisoners, whom they treated as *untermenschen* or sub-humans, severely depressed him and left him in no doubt that he had been sent to a camp where Hitler's policies towards racially inferior races were being brutally carried out. However, Niethammer's answer to the misery he saw all around him was not to do what he could to better the lot of the prisoners or to challenge the regime but to desperately try to find a way out. In this he reflected Höß's view that most guards simply wanted 'an easy life' and so he obeyed orders and followed the regulations faithfully while being deeply shocked at what he saw going on all around him.

When not on duty many of the guards either made use of the leisure facilities at the camp which included a gym and cinema, headed to the bars and restaurants in the centre of the Auschwitz or if they had longer off would visit the city of Kraków or go home. The camp's isolated location to the west of the town of Auschwitz and its status as a concentration camp meant that guards had to apply for special passes which forbade them from talking about what was happening at the site. However, Niethammer when he had time off instead of heading into the town began to explore the fields, marshes, ditches and creeks surrounding the camp. Here he pursued his passion for ornithology and soon found out that it was an excellent location for birds. So, between shifts he would venture out in the early morning or at dusk with his binoculars and rifle to explore the area around the camp, especially taking long walks along the Vistula and Soła rivers. During these visits he began to make notes of the species he saw, recording his observations in a notebook. Any interesting species which he could not readily identify in the field or he required for his collection he shot and took back to the camp for identification and further study (it was then still common practice to shoot birds as a way of obtaining specimens or identifying difficult species, many of the natural history museums across Europe having substantial collections of bird skins donated by generations of ornithologists).

Niethammer's arrival at the camp coincided with the autumn migration when many summer visitors were heading south to be replaced by birds from Northern Europe, the Baltic and the Russian tundra. He recorded the departure of the summer warblers and the arrival of an influx of lapwings, winter thrushes like redwings and fieldfares and rarer species like the bean goose. He also discovered that Auschwitz was on the flight path for many birds migrating to Africa from the Baltic coast and Scandinavia, they using the area surrounding the camp as a feeding ground or resting place en route further south. Due to his frequent walks around the camp at dawn and dusk word soon spread among his fellow guards that Niethammer was a 'birdwatcher', much to the amusement of many who had little interest in the birdlife, just like the lives of the prisoners in their care. However, some guards took an interest, and he began to receive requests to shoot game birds including quail, partridges and snipe for the pot, to sell or send home.

Soon Niethammer's birdwatching trips went from being an eccentric pastime to an activity which was valued by his fellow SS guards. Niethammer in turn cashed in on their interest, developing a lucrative sideline in shooting birds to order. This brought him to the attention of Höß who on hearing of his birdwatching and shooting trips ordered him to report to his office. At the meeting Niethammer told a bemused but impressed Höß about the third volume of the bird book he was producing and his work at the Natural History Museums in Bonn, Berlin and Vienna. On hearing his story Höß saw an opportunity to capitalise on Niethammer's interests and ordered him to start shooting wild birds, boar and deer from the local woods for his personal consumption. So Niethammer started supplying the commandant with game who in turn gave them to his wife, visiting dignitaries and other senior SS staff whom he wanted to influence, especially at the Reichssicherheitshauptamt (Reich Security Main Office).[2]

Like many guards Niethammer had arrived at Auschwitz knowing little about the concentration camp system and still less about the day-to-day realities. However, within a few days of his arrival he can have been under no illusions about the regime in the camp and the atrocities that were taking place there, even if at this time Auschwitz had not become the notorious extermination camp it would develop into over the next couple of years. As a guard at the main gate, post G, there was a gravel pit across from the entrance where, as a keen ornithologist, Niethammer would regularly check for birds. One day some prisoners were taken there and shot. Niethammer may not have witnessed the murders in person but he would certainly have heard about them as the executions took place in public and not in a cordoned-off section of the camp (from the autumn of 1941 to the autumn of 1943, most executions were carried out in the walled-off yard of Block 11 in the main camp, in front of what infamously became known as 'Death Wall'. The condemned prisoners had to strip naked on the floor, women having separate rooms. The women were then led into the courtyard and shot first. The remaining condemned male prisoners were led to the wall in pairs. The SS executioner walked up behind each man and shot him in the back of the head with a small-calibre rifle. Kapo guards then threw the corpses onto trucks or carts and took them to the crematoria).

On 22 November 1940 the atmosphere at the camp changed irreversibly when it went from being a brutal place of incarceration with occasional shootings to a centre for mass murder. Niethammer was present when 40 Polish prisoners, considered to be among the most difficult and challenging inmates, were summarily executed by firing squad. They would be the first batch of over a million people, mainly Jews, killed at the camp. However, the loss of life went largely unnoticed by Höß, a man to whom killing had become second nature. What concerned him far more was that at the end of the month he had to give a report to Himmler on progress with converting the original barracks and creating the new camp. Despite Himmler's fearsome reputation for not wanting to hear bad news, Höß was determined to give him a detailed account of all the challenges, problems and grievances he was grappling with at the meeting. They met at Himmler's office in Berlin where he was accompanied by Heinrich Vogel, an agronomist and the head of the SS Economic and Administrative Office, responsible for managing the finances, supply systems and business projects of the SS.

Höß gave a detailed report to both men but Himmler barely spoke and showed little interest, at the end telling him bluntly that as commandant it was up to him to own the problems and get help if he needed it. Höß recalled, 'My constantly expressed fears over the danger of disease arising from inadequate sanitary arrangements, were curtly dismissed with the remark, "You only look on the dark side of things".' Sensing Himmler's displeasure Höß quickly moved on to his vision for the camp, witnessing an instant change in attitude by the Reichsführer-SS. 'He talked with animation about future plans,' he noted, 'and gave one directive after another or made notes about everything that was to be done with the land in question.'

Himmler's grand plan for the camp was to turn it into a world centre for agricultural research and development in the Third Reich. 'Auschwitz was to become *the* agricultural research station for the eastern territories,' Höß recalled, adding that as a result resources suddenly became available. Himmler, he had found out, was not interested in the depravations, brutality and squalor involved in running the camp, only as a former chicken farmer in his own warped vision for a centre which could breed super crops and cattle to feed the German people. After promising him all the necessary men and materiel he needed, Himmler addressed Vogel and ordered him to start building huge laboratories and plant nurseries on the site. 'All kinds of stock-breeding was to be pursued there,' Höß recalled. 'Vogel was to take immediate steps to gather a force of specialists; to build fisheries and to drain the lands, and to construct a dam on the Vistula that would present difficulties compared to which grievances in the camp previously described would become insignificant.' Himmler concluded the meeting by saying that he wanted to see everything in place by the time of his first visit in person.

Over the next few months progress on the camp continued apace, the Polish work gangs being pushed ever harder to complete the conversion of the barracks under the ever-watchful eye of the Kapos and armed SS guards. However, just as Höß was beginning the construction of the new buildings, he became overwhelmed with the demands placed on him and later by the continuing arrival of new prisoners. 'My efforts met with little success,' he complained, 'for I could not keep step with the rapid expansion of the camp or the constant increase in the numbers of prisoners. No sooner was a building erected that could normally accommodate over 200 people than further transport arrived consisting of a thousand or more prisoners would be drawn up at the platform.' He complained to both the Inspector of Concentration Camps and the

Reich Security Main Office but to no avail. 'The actions ordered by the Reichsführer-SS must be carried out' was the curt reply.

In the absence of any interest from Himmler, Höß drew up his own plans to enlarge the camp and to accommodate the increasing number of prisoners being sent to him: 'From the very beginning I was so absorbed, I might say obsessed, with my task that every fresh difficulty only increased my zeal. I was determined that nothing should get me down. My pride would not allow it. I lived only for my work.' That obsession left the treatment of prisoners to his officers, Höß writing 'that my many and diverse duties left me but little time for the camp and the prisoners themselves. I had to leave them entirely in the hands of individuals such as Fritzsch [Karl Fritzsch (1903–1945) deputy commandant who would first suggest using the poisonous gas Zyklon B], Meier, Siedler [Fritz Siedler (1907–1945) deputy commandant and notorious among the inmates for his brutality] and Palitzsch [Gerhard Palitzsch, 1913–1944, Report Leader, also infamous for his cruelty], distasteful persons in every respect, and I had to do this even though I was well aware that they would not run the camp as I wished and intended.'[3]

Himmler's visit to Auschwitz took place on 1 March 1941, this time accompanied by a large entourage consisting of the Gauleiter (Regional Leader) Fritz Bracht and his administrative presidents, senior police and SS from Silesia, the Inspector of Concentration Camps Richard Glücks and executives from the company IG Farben Industrie.[4] (IG or Interessengemeinschaft, meaning 'syndicate'). From its creation in Germany in 1925 IG Farben had grown into the world's largest chemical company, before the war selling its products internationally, with major business interests across Europe, the United States, and a large number of other countries around the world. Following secret negotiations with Himmler they were visiting the site at Auschwitz to establish a synthetic oil and rubber plant and to take advantage of the slave labour, the company also stating it wanted to carry out drug experiments. Himmler had assured them that he could provide an almost unlimited supply of labour and live inmates for any trials, the visit being used to draw up the contracts and finalise the deal.

Höß had been warned beforehand not to bring up difficult subjects with Himmler in front of his important guests, so the commandant decided to bide his time. Aware that Himmler wanted to impress those present, particularly the representatives from IG Farben, Höß reported back on the enlargement of the camp and progress with the exclusion from the second zone. 'With the help of plans and maps I explained to Himmler the layout of the land that was being taken over and the extensions that had been made and gave him an account of the present position,' he reported. However, when he was alone with Himmler and SS-Obergruppenführer Ernst-Heinrich Schmauser, the Police Leader in Breslau, in the car touring the zone, Höß took his chance. Outlining all his grievances, in particular the overcrowding in the camp, he waited for a response, but it again fell on deaf ears, Himmler not wanting to discuss operational issues. 'When I repeatedly begged him to stop sending any more drafts, he snubbed me abruptly,' wrote Höß. 'I could not expect any kind of help from him. On the contrary, when we were in the canteen in the SS hospital block, he started to discuss in earnest the new tasks that he had for Auschwitz.'

Himmler's new demand was to build a camp that could hold 100,000 prisoners, he indicating where in the zone this was to be built (this would become Auschwitz II-Birkenau). Both Höß and Gauleiter Bracht raised objections, pointing out the lack of utilities and drainage problems on the site which was composed of unimproved grassland and flood plain meadows. Himmler dismissed these objections with a smile, stating, 'Gentleman it will be built. My reasons for constructing it are far more important than your objections. Ten thousand prisoners are to be provided for the IG Farben Industrie according to their requirements and to increase the progress made in the constructional work.' In addition, Himmler wanted the original camp to be expanded to hold 30,000 prisoners and for the site to be used to manufacture armaments as well as being an agricultural research station.

Höß and Bracht again complained but their concerns were summarily dismissed, Himmler, telling them, 'Every means will have to be taken to accelerate the construction work. … The delivery of draft to the camp, however, cannot, on principle, be halted. The actions which I have ordered my security police to undertake, must go on. I do not appreciate the difficulties in Auschwitz.' Shortly before he departed Himmler found the time to visit Höß's family and gave the commandant detailed instructions to enlarge the house so it could be used as an 'official residence'. Höß noted that he was 'once more genial and talkative, in spite of his abruptness and irritation during our conversation a little earlier on'. The visit showed once again that Himmler became animated by discussion about agriculture, armaments or architecture but when it came to the conditions in the camp and the mass murder of prisoners, he simply wasn't interested.

CHAPTER 4

Solace in Science

AS THE CONSTRUCTION work continued apace in the second zone, Niethammer carried on with his study of birds in the immediate vicinity of the camp. By now some of the more brutal guards had established fearsome reputations. Many 'favoured' prisoners were subject to regular beatings and abuse, those emaciated by insufficient food or worn out by the hard labour often collapsing and dying. Particularly troublesome prisoners or those who did not work hard enough were shot in front of the other inmates as a warning. However, in response Niethammer literally looked the other way, spending as much time as possible outside the suffocating confines of the camp where he found solace in his scientific studies. Birds were not just Niethammer's hinterland, they were also his escape from the sadism he saw all around him.

As well as walking the fields and meadows recording birds with his binoculars, Niethammer also stalked the area for game with his rifle. Over the weeks he developed into a very good hunter, Höß greatly appreciating the game he brought back, both for his own table and to sell or giveaway to SS colleagues, depending on their rank. After he had killed the animals, Niethammer would deliver them directly to Höß's door and over time built up a rapport with the volatile commandant. For his part Höß enjoyed talking to the erudite, if eccentric, Niethammer, their conversations being a pleasant change from his other officers who continually came to him with problems. As a result, Niethammer became one of the few guards whom the commandant not only respected but liked. In turn Niethammer did everything he could to nurture the relationship, realising that to be a friend of the commandant not only guaranteed an easier life in the camp but was also the way out of it.

Soon Niethammer had filled up several notebooks with his ornithological observations and had amassed a large collection of bird skins, Höß providing him with a special area in the barracks to store them. This gave him the idea of turning his hobby into a new permanent position, one which would also be his ticket out of the camp. He decided to approach Höß directly and put in an application for alternative duties so he could concentrate on his studies full time. It was a brave move that came with considerable risk, not least because any requests for special treatment were usually declined. Niethammer knew that if his application was turned down, his standing in the camp together with his relationship with Höß and the other guards could be damaged, perhaps irrevocably.

Despite this Niethammer thought the risk worth taking as the conditions inside the camp were getting worse by the day and applying for special duties offered a way out. It was a move designed to save both his reputation and his sanity. Niethammer, a sensitive man of faith, did not want the deaths of so many prisoners on his conscience, so he sought refuge in what he knew best – bird research. What he particularly feared was becoming institutionalised by the regime and immune to the cruelty he saw dealt out daily to the inmates. Worse still, deep down he knew that if Germany lost the war, he might one day be held to account for the killings and brutality at the camp, even if in his eyes he was a witness rather than a perpetrator.

Niethammer's plan was to use the bird skins he had collected to open a natural history museum at the camp and to turn his bird notes into a scientific paper which he could submit to the natural history museums in Berlin, Bonn and Vienna. To do this he needed the blessing of Höß who after listening to his application agreed to support it, cynically seeing it as an opportunity to promote the camp and his leadership – what better way to convince visitors and the outside world that Auschwitz was not an extermination camp but a prison and centre of scientific learning than to open a museum dedicated to the study of birds and publish a research paper on it? Giving his approval, Höß agreed that Niethammer might also like to share his collection and findings with the local school. So, at the end of March 1941 Niethammer was given special permission to carry out an ornithological study of Auschwitz and its environs and was excused other duties including being on the guard rota.[1] Höß also issued an extraordinary order that no birds should be shot at Auschwitz or in the immediate vicinity except by Niethammer and one other guard. For the commandant of Auschwitz exploiting Niethammer's ornithological credentials and standing in the scientific community was an ideal way to cover up the mass murder of prisoners in the camp.

The timing of Niethammer's application also came at the right time of the war, as in the spring of 1941 the German army was still victorious on all fronts, despite having lost the Battle of Britain. The launch of its Blitzkrieg attack on the West the previous year had been devastatingly successful, Belgium, Holland and France all having fallen in a few weeks of the offensive in the summer of 1940. As well as expanding the Third Reich the changing war situation also provided more opportunities for scientific studies in the newly conquered territories. Just a week after Niethammer's application for special duties on 6 April 1941 the German army attacked Yugoslavia and Greece to secure the Balkan flank for Hitler's planned invasion of the Soviet Union and to safeguard its Romanian oil supplies. Yugoslavia capitulated within a couple of weeks and Athens fell on 27 April 1941. Just under a month later, on 20 May, German paratroopers mounted an airborne attack on the strategically important island of Crete and despite sustaining serious losses during the operation, occupied the island. Then on 22 June 1941 Hitler attacked Russia in Operation *Barbarossa*, committing most of his forces to the offensive. Due to the needs of the military, with the attack disappeared many opportunities for troops to be redeployed on other duties.

Niethammer's new role as resident ornithologist at Auschwitz had a lot of advantages apart from allowing him to pursue his passion. No longer required to do most guard duties, regularly check on inmates or supervise work gangs, he could now concentrate most of his time on his studies with the commandant's blessing. It was a move which delighted the German ornithologist, for as well as surveying birds he could now see a way out of Auschwitz. While Höß was only too happy to approve his application, there were caveats, one being that Niethammer had to be available for extra duties if required and to cover gaps in the rota when other guards were ill or away on leave. Höß also made it clear that Niethammer was to increase the amount of game he brought back for the commandant's plate (in all Niethammer supplied over forty members of the camp elite with game, listing them all in his notebook) and to carry out a detailed study of the topography and particularly the drainage of the area. This was required to fulfil Himmler's orders to build a massive new prisoner camp and grow crops at the new agricultural research station in the second zone.

Niethammer set about his new role with relish, mapping the key habitats in the zone and walking a number of set transects across it where he recorded and shot the birds he saw along the route. He also put up several nesting boxes around the camp, including around the barracks used by the guards and at Höß's house. These he monitored, recording the species that occupied each box, the number of young born and how many birds fledged. His appointment coincided with the arrival back of the summer migrants and soon the ponds in the fields surrounding the camp were alive with chiff-chaffs, wheatears, reed and sedge warblers as well as rarer species like marsh, great and river warblers. To cover all the 40 square kilometres in the Auschwitz interest zone he used a bicycle to get to his sites and a small boat to survey the ponds.

As well as his bird studies Niethammer also hunted game, on 9 June 1941 a special order being issued from the commandant's office which entitled him to shoot 'birds and predators' at the ponds surrounding Auschwitz. Wild duck were particularly in demand, on occasions when time allowed Höß accompanying him wildfowling. Niethammer also took Höß's eldest son Klaus on hunting expeditions to the forests around the zone. In recognition of his contribution to the 'life of the camp' on 2 July 1941 Niethammer was promoted from a guard SS-Schütze to a stormtrooper SS-Sturmmann on Höß's recommendation. On 25 August 1941 he sent a letter to his old mentor Erwin Stresemann. 'I am a kind of SS professional hunter, have my rifle and ride around outside the camp on a bicycle,' he wrote.[2] After recording species, shooting birds for the museum and bringing back game, Niethammer in the evenings and his spare time carried on writing the third and final volume of the *Handbuch der Deutschen Vogelkunde.*

To help with his rapidly growing collection Niethammer requested from the commandant a prisoner who had experience in taxidermy and the preservation of bird skins using arsenic soap. Remarkably following an announcement at a roll call a helper was found from among the Polish prisoners by the name of Jan Grębocki.[3] He was born in 1908 and was a forester by profession who through his work had been involved in preparing a wide variety of animals for local collectors before he was imprisoned. Like Niethammer he was also an ornithologist with experience of recording birds and was a good hunter. Following the occupation of Poland, he had been identified as someone supporting the resistance and after a Gestapo raid had been arrested and incarcerated. Grębocki was among the first prisoners to be sent to Auschwitz and bore the prison number 136. Following the roll call he was sent to see Niethammer who quizzed him on his background, what he knew about birds and his skills as a taxidermist. Impressed, Niethammer employed Grębocki to help him prepare the large number of birds he brought back to the camp, the Polish prisoner carefully gutting the birds and removing the skins which were them mounted and catalogued. Although he was still required to do hard labour, over the weeks due to the number of birds that needed preparing, Grębocki spent more and more of his time working for Niethammer. Over time due to the quality of his work, the Waffen-SS guard grew to value the Polish prisoner and the two developed a mutual respect. This also meant Grębocki was treated with less severity by the other guards although he never stopped fearing for his life.

The preservation of bird skins, especially for small or 'difficult' birds, was a notoriously long and detailed process which required intricate and painstaking work. For Nietmammer having Grębocki to help him was not only important in developing his ornithological museum, but it also saved him a lot of time which he could more usefully spend in the field doing survey work or hunting game. For Grębocki helping Niethammer was literally life changing as it kept him alive. Prisoners seen to be useful to the running of the camp generally lived longer, Niethammer's patronage giving the Polish prisoner a vital degree of protection from some of the more sadistic guards. (Grębocki survived Auschwitz but after Nietmammer left at the end of 1941 he was later imprisoned at Neuengamme concentration camp where was given the number 18434. From the end of 1944 there were no further records of him, so his fate is unknown, but he probably drowned when the ships *Cap Arcona* and *Thielebek* carrying prisoners were bombed by Allied aircraft off Lübeck on 3 May 1945. Over 5,000 people drowned in the attack on the *Cap Arcona*, mostly prisoners from concentration camps, in what was one of the largest single incidents of maritime loss of life during the war.)

Remarkably Grębocki was not the only ornithologist in Auschwitz. Wladyslaw Siwek (1907–1983), a Polish bird illustrator from Kraków, was also sent there[4] (there are no records of him meeting Niethammer although the two must have come into regular contact). On 14 January 1940 Siwek was arrested by the Gestapo on the suspicion of belonging to a resistance group and was imprisoned in the Montelupich Prison in Kraków (where later in life Niethammer would also serve a sentence). On 8 October 1940 he was transferred to the newly constructed concentration camp at Auschwitz where he was given the number 5826 and joined the other Polish prisoners. Before the war Siwek was an experienced amateur ornithologist who had produced an extensive collection of bird drawings, which he had derived both from bird skins and in the field. His first bird illustrations were detailed pen and ink drawings; later he progressed to painting beautiful and intricate colour plates. In addition to his day job as an illustrator he also studied the subject at the Academy of Art in Kraków. Like so many of his fellow countrymen, Siwek was devastated when Poland fell and was deeply depressed by Nazi brutality, so he had joined the resistance movement but had been captured.

On arriving at Auschwitz as an artist he was assigned to the painting crew in the maintenance department, which while completely beneath a man of his talents, probably saved his life. As well as compulsory hard labour and helping out with paint jobs and signs around the camp, Siwek soon put his skills to good use creating a 'business on the side'. This was drawing small pencil and watercolour portraits of his fellow prisoners who used to sit for him during periods when they were confined to barracks, the pictures often being done at night by candlelight. While the activity was dangerous – if caught by the guards both Siwek and the sitter were liable to be beaten or even shot – many inmates thought it worth the risk to have a record of their time in the camp. Siwek produced over 2,000 drawings and for many families these turned out to be the last pictures of their loved ones they saw before they were sent to their death (remarkably some of them survived and much later in 2005 were exhibited at the Centrum Judaicum in Berlin).

Despite trying to keep his art classes secret, the SS guards soon became aware of Siwek's artistic skills, and he was 'interviewed' about his work. On mentioning that he was an illustrator and had studied art at the Academy of Art in Kraków, his SS guards forced him to do a picture to see how good he was – at gunpoint. The resulting drawing of one of the guards, done under conditions of almost unimaginable stress, impressed his captors who, like his fellow prisoners, decided to make use of his talents. So, he soon started painting personal pictures to order and even decorating toys made by the prisoners for the children of the SS guards as Christmas presents.

One of the senior guards at the camp with Niethammer was SS-Sturmmann (senior private) Hans Dengler. A house painter from Munich, he had attended the School of Arts and Crafts in the city in the 1930s and continued his studies during his SS service where he soon developed a reputation for brutality. Siwek had to paint Dengler's examination pictures for him as the guard 'did not have time' to create his own artwork. However, this was his guarantee that he would live, because the 'student' needed more pictures to be painted in the same hand. In Siwek's presence he painted his own signature on one of the pictures called *The Heath*, and chillingly told him, 'Your life and your name no longer belong to you. If I wanted, I could shoot you.'

Ordinary SS guards were less demanding artistically but no less threatening. They brought passport photographs of young women and SS female guards from the neighbouring camps, whom Siwek had to paint naked in various positions. If the picture was good, he was given food from the SS canteen; if it was bad he was beaten. At the end of October 1944 Siwek was taken to the concentration camp at Sachsenhausen where he was given the number 115905. As the Russians approached the prisoners were forced to march westward, on the way seeing the fleeing motorcade of SS-Reichsführer Himmler. Siwek and the other prisoners who survived were liberated on 2 May 1945 near Lübeck. (Following Germany's surrender Siwek stayed in hospital near Hamburg where he made a remarkable recovery, after the war pursuing a very successful career as an illustrator and bird artist. He co-authored the book *Ptaki Europy* or *Birds of Europe*, drawing ninety-six colour plates and over 1,500 black and white illustrations and was affectionately known as 'the Polish Peterson' after the famous American artist and author Roger T. Peterson. He also worked first as head of education and then director at the Auschwitz Museum where he drew over fifty pictures about what life was like in the camp which were shown at international exhibitions in America, England, Japan and Germany.)

Over the spring, summer and autumn of 1941 Niethammer carried on with his ornithological studies and hunting expeditions, giving regular reports to Höß. In return the commandant showed a great deal of interest in his work, encouraging his son Klaus to go out with him whenever possible on hunting trips to the fields, ponds and woods surrounding the camp. The new bird museum at Auschwitz also began to take shape, Niethammer dedicating himself to the task and combining it with his research on the third volume of his *Handbuch der Deutschen Vogelkunde*. To populate the museum Niethammer used the large number of birds which he had either shot or trapped using nets (the latter being killed by breaking their necks or giving them a lethal injection). Afterwards Grębocki prepared the bird skins, like the inmates in the camp each being meticulously photographed and documented. The skins were then combined with pictures and information on each species to form a display. This included the bird's status and distribution based on Niethammer's painstaking work mapping their territories in and around the camp over the summer.

Preparation of the skins for display in the museum meant mounting them to be as 'real to life' as possible. Capturing the outward appearance of a bird while at the same time preserving its anatomical structures and plumage was challenging. All the skins had to be prepared in the same way, using a 'standard pose', so species could be easily compared and did not take up too much room in the confines of the camp. This was easier for some birds than others, those that had been disfigured when they were shot being much harder to mount. Large or long-billed birds due to problems with space were put into a 'compressed pose', for example by having their necks and legs folded or heads turned to the side.

The preparation of so many skins involved a lot of painstaking work, most of which was carried out by Grębocki. His first job was to record data on each bird taking measurements (length, height etc.), weighing it and recording any characteristics like moult, colour, sex or signs of breeding like a brood patch (used to incubate eggs). When this was complete, an incision was then made with a scalpel, usually in the breast of the bird, and the skin carefully cut away from the carcass. To help gut it, incisions were made at the knees, tail, forelimbs and the back of the skull so the body parts could be more easily removed. Grębocki then took any measurements of internal body organs before the skin was thoroughly cleaned of any remaining tissue, organs, blood, fat or oils (especially fatty birds required careful scraping to strip away the deposits from the skin). The skin was then washed, dried and treated with arsenic soap to preserve it, some birds also being stuffed. For this Grębocki used cotton wool and wound bandages from the camp hospital. The feathers were then smoothed, and the skin pinned in position on a board to dry. For commoner species wings were cut off, mounted and spread out to show the feather structure. The skeletons of some species were also carefully removed although this proved to be very time consuming so was only rarely done.

Niethammer the SS guard and Grębocki the prisoner may have been on opposite sides of the concentration camp divide, but they were united by their mutual love of ornithology, and both used it to forget about the horrors of the camp. By the autumn prisoners inside the camp were regularly being shot or worked to death, the birds in marked contrast at least being free before they died. While the full horrors of Auschwitz had not become apparent in the autumn of 1941, both men can have been in little doubt about where the regime was heading. For Niethammer birds were his ticket out of the camp; for Grębocki they were his best chance of survival in it. Their surgical work together in shooting and preparing the bird skins for the museum had become a macabre metaphor for the mass human suffering going on in the camp (as well as displaying the skins in the camp, Niethammer also sent a large number back to the Natural History Museum in Vienna where he worked).

Like Niethammer the camp commandant Höß lived for his work and following Himmler's visit dedicated himself to the task of clearing the second zone and building the new camp. However, except for a few favoured guards like Niethammer, he found himself becoming increasingly isolated, despairing of his fellow officers and unsupported by his master. 'Any form of friendly contact became repugnant to me,' he wrote. 'I repeatedly refused social gatherings, and was glad when I could find a plausible excuse for staying away … My family, and especially my wife, suffered on account of this, since my behaviour was often intolerable. I had eyes only for my work, my task.' To cope with the huge burden placed on him, Höß turned to alcohol and began to drink. 'Alcohol, more than anything else, was able to put me in a happy and contented frame of mind.' However, the next morning with a hangover his mood would darken, and he would again lash out at those around him.

Before the war a camp containing 10,000 prisoners had been considered exceptionally large. However, with the outbreak of hostilities both the size and the purpose of the camps had changed as had the number of prisoners being sent to them, increasing exponentially as the Third Reich had expanded throughout Europe. 'The intention of the Reichsführer-SS was that Auschwitz should become one immense prison-cum-munitions-centre,' Höß stated.

> What he said during his visit in March 1941 made this perfectly plain. The camp for 100,000 prisoners of war, the enlargement of the old camp to hold 30,000 prisoners, the earmarking of 10,000 prisoners for the synthetic rubber factory [IG Farben], all this emphasised his point. But the numbers envisaged were at this time something entirely new in the history of concentration camps.

The new camp was built on wet, undrained land near the village and agricultural community of Brzezinka or Birkenau. The construction was to be carried out in stages, with the goal of accommodating Himmler's 100,000 prisoners within a year. In the early stages, most of the labour involved in draining the area and constructing the site was carried out by thousands of Soviet prisoners of war who worked under German supervision. As time went on, they were joined by many Polish and Jewish prisoners. The labour conditions were appalling, and the death rate of the prisoners was especially high in the winter months. Polish prisoner Alfred Czeslaw Przybylski recalled:

> While digging and building the foundations, the prisoners worked in the fall, in winter and frost, standing waist-deep in water. Female prisoners at the women's prison in Birkenau worked under the same conditions. I firmly believe that the choice of building site – on wet ground, even though they could have built on ground that was dry and more suitable for construction – a choice made by professionals … was designed to exterminate the prisoners who worked on the construction and those who inhabited the buildings.[5]

While Höß concerned himself with carrying out Himmler's orders, the day-to-day running of the existing camp was mainly left to his fellow officers, in particular his deputies Fritzsch, Palitzsch and Meier who had all served at previous concentration camps and competed among themselves for ever more inhuman ways of treating the prisoners. 'For it was not I, but they, who ran the camp,' Höß protested. 'It was they who taught the Kapos, from the chief block senior down to the last block clerk, how to behave.' The Kapos were essential to the running of the camp but often treated the prisoners very badly, some becoming as sadistic as the guards. 'They trained the block leaders and told them how to treat the prisoners,' Höß wrote. 'It was a factor of decisive importance in Auschwitz-Birkenau where the masses of prisoners could not be supervised. One would have thought a common fate and the miseries shared would have led to a steadfast and unshakeable feeling of comradeship and cooperation, but this was far from being the case.'

Yet the Kapos were merely a reflection of the brutal and sadistic regime at the camp created by Höß which saw them treat their fellow prisoners ever more harshly in a desperate bid to keep themselves alive. In such an environment well-meaning men could be turned from being benign to cruelly manipulating the most vulnerable prisoners in a matter of weeks which is why Niethammer knew he had to leave. ‘Even people, who in ordinary life outside the camp were at all times considerate and good-natured, became capable, in the hard conditions of imprisonment, of bullying their fellow-prisoners mercilessly, if by so doing they could make their own lives a little bit easier.’ Höß wrote callously. ‘More merciless yet was the behaviour of those who were naturally egotistical, cold and even criminally inclined, and who rode rough-shod and without pity over the misery of their fellow-prisoners when they could thereby gain even the pettiest advantage for themselves.’ Höß sadistically noted that the physical and psychological effects of such treatment was far worse coming from the Kapos than the guards. ‘The treatment they received from the guards, however brutal, arbitrary and cruel, never affected them psychologically to the same extent as did this attitude on the part of their fellow-inmates.’

CHAPTER 5

Auschwitz II-Birkenau: A New Camp

THE CONSTRUCTION OF the new camp began in earnest in October 1941 while Niethammer carried on with his scientific studies and populated his bird museum. The building work was supervised by the 'Central Building Authority of the Waffen-SS and Police, Auschwitz, Upper Silesia', which was headed by Sturmbannführer (Major) Karl Bischoff (1897–1950) who oversaw the construction of Auschwitz II-Birkenau. Under him the Architects or Blueprint Office was headed by Hauptscharführer (First Sergeant-Major) Otto Wichmann. He was responsible for preparing the construction plans, which were drawn up by SS officers who had studied architecture or engineering at university, together with several prisoners who had relevant technical training. Herta Soswinski, a prisoner who worked as a clerk at the Building Authority, recalled:

> The task of the Bauleitung [Building Authority] was the overall planning of all the construction works within Auschwitz, including living quarters, medical facilities, crematoria, gas chambers ... The Bauleitung was not only responsible for the planning, but also for the labour itself, the allocation of materials and supervision. The SS men who worked on the plans, were also active at the building sites, when necessary.

The Kapos were managed by Niethammer's fellow guards and while he was surveying the birds at the site, they were supervising the Polish prisoners who were now being put to work building the new camp. By early October 10,000 prisoners were working on the new site following the Polish village of Brzezinka or Birkenau being cleared of people in the spring. Encouraged by Höß, his guards pushed many of the prisoners to the limit as the construction work continued apace – felling trees, levelling the ground, mining gravel, building roads and laying foundations for the new huts and barracks. They also demolished the empty village buildings, over sixty prisoners dying a day due to exhaustion, punishment beatings, starvation and disease, the guards treating their fate with callous indifference. 'It is the guards and the supervisors who create the opportunity for such behaviour,' Höß noted. 'They do either out of indifference, since they are too lazy to stop such activities, or else, being themselves base and cruel by nature, they permit it because they enjoy the spectacle provided, and indeed even encourage the bullying, since they derive a satanic pleasure from watching the prisoners torment one another.' In the deviant and immoral atmosphere which characterised the camp, the Kapos often became as hated as the guards, many after a while needing no encouragement to beat their fellow prisoners. 'Their mean, brutal and cowardly natures and their criminal tendencies led them to torment their fellow-prisoners both physically and mentally,' Höß observed, adding, 'and even to harass them to death out of pure sadism.'

In contrast to the main camp where most of the buildings were brick, in Birkenau they were mainly uniform wooden huts, more suitable for animal rather than human habitation. They had no efficient drainage system and little insulation against the bitter cold. Originally intended to house some 550 prisoners each, due to the number of transports arriving at the camp over three times that number ended up being crammed inside. The extreme overcrowding and lack of sanitary facilities led to raw sewage covering the floor and a very high death rate due to dysentery and disease. A former prisoner recalled the conditions inside the huts at Birkenau:

> On rainy days, the packed-earth floor of the huts turned into a swamp because of the lack of drainage. These huts were originally intended to house 500 people. Building manager Dejaco's [Walter, 1909–1978, Austrian architect, Dejaco was a member of the SS construction office at Auschwitz. From November 1941 he headed the planning department] order to build a third lower layer of bunks increased the huts' capacity to 800–1,000, and often, not 4 but 10–12 prisoners would lie on each bunk.

In the summer and autumn of 1941, the war continued to go well for Germany. Following the launch of Operation *Barbarossa*, the attack on the Soviet Union on 22 June 1941, German forces in three huge army groups had made major inroads across a 1,000-mile front in what was the biggest land invasion in history. Three million German troops, together with half a million Romanian and other Axis soldiers, had poured across the border in an attack spearheaded by 3,600 tanks backed up by more than half a million support vehicles and 750,000 horses (one horse for every four men, they proved a lot more reliable than many of the German vehicles).

In the sky overhead a thousand aircraft had bombarded Soviet military positions and airfields. Within a few weeks, the Red Army had been driven back hundreds of miles and hundreds of thousands of prisoners had been captured, the Germans making rapid progress towards Moscow. However, in August Hitler had diverted his armies south to occupy the Ukraine and the Caucasus to secure the oilfields. When they were redeployed towards Moscow, heavy autumnal rains turned the land into a quagmire and the Wehrmacht got bogged down. The subsequent attack on the Soviet capital, Operation *Typhoon*, saw German forces stall at the gates of Moscow, the result of a stream of Soviet counterattacks combined with the atrocious winter weather.

The first Soviet prisoners of war had been transported to Auschwitz in July and August 1941 following Germany's invasion and were not registered but were placed in the isolated Block 11 in the barracks where they were treated with severe brutality. Forced to work in the pits extracting sand and gravel using picks, shovels and their hands, many of them died in the process. Over the next few months over 9,000 Soviet prisoners were transported to the camp and were allocated to nine blocks to the left of the *Arbeit macht frei* sign. Two of the blocks, numbers 3 and 24, were double-storeyed and the remaining seven, numbered 1–2, 12–14 and 22–23, were single-storeyed, all the blocks being separated from the other buildings by an electrified barbed-wire fence.

In late August 1941 an infamous precedent was set in the notorious history of the camp when the first prisoners were murdered with Zyklon B gas. Zyklon B was the trade name of a cyanide-based gas which had been invented in Germany in the early 1920s as a pesticide and fumigant. Supplied to the camp by the firm Tesch & Stabenow, it was in constant use to kill vermin and a large supply of tins were kept in the storerooms. Originally its use was restricted to employees of Tesch & Stabenow but later medical staff at the camp were permitted to use it. It was composed of hydrogen cyanide or prussic acid which was found to be highly poisonous to humans when the pellets were exposed to air, death typically occurring in an average person within a few minutes of inhaling it.

Fritzsch, the deputy commandant, after learning about its effects decided to experiment with its use on twenty to thirty Soviet prisoners to see how effective it would be in killing them. Choosing a windowless room in the basement of Block 11, he rounded up the prisoners at gunpoint and locked them in the building. The gas was then released into the room via a special vent, to his satisfaction most of the prisoners dying. Pleased with the results, Fitzsch reported to Höß that the gas had the potential to kill large numbers of people and would be much more efficient than shooting them. The first case of mass murder using Zyklon B gas at Auschwitz had taken place.

Höß on hearing of the trial asked to see for himself, so a larger experiment with about a hundred Soviet prisoners was arranged for a couple of days later. The prisoners were packed into six rooms in the block and Zyklon B gas was again released into them, Höß watching as the prisoners died and then afterwards inspecting the corpses:

> The gassing was carried out in the detention cells of block 11. Protected by a gasmask, I watched the killing myself. In the crowded cells death came instantaneously the moment the Zyklon B was thrown in. A short, almost smothered cry, and it was all over. During this first experience of gassing people, I did not fully realize what was happening perhaps because I was too impressed by the whole procedure.[1]

Höß was so impressed with the results that he ordered its use on a larger scale so on 3 September immediately after evening roll call, 700 Soviet POWs, 250 Polish patients from the camp hospital and ten criminal prisoners were rounded up. They were placed in twenty-eight rooms in the basement of the block used as a mortuary, the windows being sealed with soil. 'The Russians were ordered to undress in an anteroom; they then quietly entered the mortuary, for they had been told they were to be deloused,' he wrote:

> The whole transport exactly filled the mortuary to capacity. The doors were then sealed, and the gas shaken down through the holes in the roof. I do not know how long this killing took. For a little while a humming sound could be heard. When the powder was thrown in, there were cries of 'Gas!' then a great bellowing, and the trapped prisoners hurled themselves against both the doors. But the doors held.

Höß continued:

> They were opened several hours later, so that the place might be aired. It was then that I saw, for the first time, gassed bodies in the mass. It made me feel uncomfortable and I shuddered, although I had imagined that death by gassing would be worse than it was. I had always thought that the victims would experience a terrible choking sensation. But the bodies, without exception, showed no signs of convulsion. The doctors explained to me that the prussic acid had a paralyzing effect on the lungs, but its action was so quick and strong that death came before the convulsions could set in, and in this its effects differed from those produced by carbon monoxide or by a general oxygen deficiency.

However, when Palitzsch, the SS guard, checked the bodies he found that a few of the prisoners were still alive, due to some windows not being properly sealed. So, after the windows were made airtight, more gas was introduced and by that night all the prisoners were dead.

While many prisoners died quickly, another SS guard Perry Broad recalled the nightmare that some of the victims endured when they suddenly realised their fate:

> A number of victims noticed that the covers had been removed from the six holes in the ceiling [of the gas chamber]. They screamed in terror when a head, covered in

> a gasmask, appeared at one of the holes. The 'disinfectors' went to work. … Using a hammer and chisel, they opened some innocuous-looking tins which bore the inscription 'Zyklon, to be used against vermin. Attention, poison! To be opened by trained personnel only.' As soon as the tins were opened, their contents were thrown through the holes, and the covers were replaced immediately … about two minutes later, the screams died down, and only muffled groans could be heard. Most of the victims had already lost consciousness. Two more minutes passed, and Grabner [Maximillian Grabner, 1905–1948, Gestapo chief at Auschwitz in command of Block 11] stopped looking at his watch. Absolute silence prevailed.

Despite the effectiveness of the gas in killing the prisoners, Block 11 was deemed unsuitable as the basement was difficult to seal completely and to aerate after the prisoners had been killed. So Höß ordered Fritzsch to find an alternative site. He chose the crematorium at the camp, where after modifications were made to the morgue to turn it into a gas chamber, more than 700 victims were able to be murdered there at once using Zyklon B.

The experiments using the gas were a closely guarded secret, as was any news from outside the camp. Although they were kept in the dark by the guards about the infamous gassing, a group of prisoners did know what was going on outside the camp, courtesy of an illegal wireless set which they had smuggled in. Although anyone caught possessing a radio or listening to it clandestinely was liable to be executed instantly, the prisoners had managed to keep it hidden from the guards. For desperate inmates it was their one contact with the outside world and as the war turned against Germany it gave them a glimmer of hope that one day they may be free. Höß knew that a radio was present in the camp, but his SS guards had no sooner found one then another was smuggled in with the help of the local population. 'They were kept fully informed about Germany's "true position" by the enemy news broadcasts,' Höß stated. 'It was not difficult to listen to these enemy broadcasts, since there were plenty of wireless sets in Auschwitz.' Surprisingly, he added, 'They were listened to even in my own house.'

News from the outside world also filtered in courtesy of illegal letters which were smuggled in by local people and even by SS guards, usually in exchange for goods. New arrivals to the camp also brought in news from the war and when it was confirmed that the Wehrmacht had stalled at the gates of Moscow, there was elation among the prisoners. However, many still despaired of their fate, believing that the end of the war was a long way off and German forces were still far from beaten. After a few months most prisoners in the camp lived one day at a time, their only goal being to survive until the next day. 'It was this uncertainty and fear which, psychologically speaking, made imprisonment so hard for the Pole,' reflected Höß. 'He lived in a perpetual state of anxiety as to what may befall him each day. He might at any time be swept away by an epidemic against which his weakened physical condition could offer no resistance.'

It was not just physical violence that was a constant threat in Auschwitz but also disease, prisoners being very susceptible to a variety of conditions, a result of being malnourished and having weak immune systems. The camp's sewer system was often overwhelmed or broken and with few toilets or washing facilities in the barracks, excrement was everywhere, and prisoners weren't able to clean themselves or readily change their clothes. With few doctors or medicines available, dysentery and scabies were common, killing many of the weakest inmates. Dysentery, a painful and often fatal illness, was endemic in the camp, caused by the water and food supply often being contaminated with the prisoners' faeces. Many prisoners also suffered from scabies, an itchy, highly contagious skin condition which resulted in a painful rash on their bodies composed of small red bumps and blisters.

Serious epidemics of typhoid fever, tuberculosis and typhus also broke out in Auschwitz. Following an outbreak of typhoid fever, many prisoners died due to the infected water supply in the camp and from tuberculosis, the airborne bacteria rapidly spreading from prisoner to prisoner due to the severe overcrowding. As the camp expanded, more and more prisoners were crammed into the blocks, 1,200 to 1,300 men typically being accommodated in a single one-storey block. There they slept on three-tier bunk beds, up to six in each, while some were forced to sleep on the floor. Bouts of typhus also broke out, spread by lice or fleas, killing over half of the people in the camp who contracted it (including several years later Anne Frank who died of typhus in the camp at the age of 15). Prisoners believed to have contracted a contagious disease were isolated in a room called a *Durchgangszimmer* (walk-through room); if the doctor confirmed the diagnosis and declared the patient terminal, they were killed quickly by the SS guards together with anybody thought to have been in contact with them. As an extra prevention against typhus each prisoner's head was shaved when they arrived at the camp.

The incidence of disease and the dreadful conditions in the camp led many prisoners to become severely depressed, some deciding the only way out was to commit suicide. Out of fear for their lives most prisoners acquiesced to the brutal regime, but a minority rebelled and some even tried to escape. In the early days escape was still possible, but all the prisoners knew that if they failed or were caught, they would be put to death. The best opportunity for escape was during the construction work of the new camp when the Kapos and the guards were not looking. To stand any chance of success someone trying to escape had to have the help of their fellow prisoners and local people in the surrounding villages. Höß wrote in July 1940 to the commander of SS and police in Wrocław that 'the local population is fanatically Polish and … ready to do anything against the hated camp SS garrison. Every prisoner who manages to escape can count on all possible help as soon as he reaches the first Polish homestead.'

The first successful escape had happened on 6 July 1940, when a Polish prisoner, Tadeusz Wiejowski, walked out of the camp with the aid of Polish civilian workers who were employed by the SS to help with the construction work (local civilians from the surrounding villages and the town of Auschwitz with specialist skills like electricians and plumbers were hired by the SS to help with the construction of the camp).[2] When the escape came to the attention of Höß, he ordered that the five Polish workers who helped the prisoner were themselves to be imprisoned in the camp (only one survived the war but he died shortly afterwards). 'Many were tempted into flight in order to escape,' Höß wrote:

> Flight was not very difficult from Auschwitz, where opportunities for escape were innumerable. The necessary preparations are easily made, and it was a simple matter to avoid or outwit the guards. A little courage and a bit of luck were all that was needed. When a man stakes everything on one throw, he must also of course reckon that if it goes wrong the result may be his death.

Despite Höß claiming the contrary, escapes from the camp were not easy but they did happen. In the autumn of 1941, seven Soviet prisoners escaped, the local Polish resistance group recruiting two of them into their Sosienki partisan unit while the five others were smuggled to other resistance groups operating in the mountains. In response the SS carried out savage reprisals, Höß reporting, 'But these projects of escape always involved the prospect of reprisals, the arrest of family and relations, and the liquidation of ten or more fellow sufferers,' cynically adding, 'Many of those who tried to escape cared little about reprisals and were prepared to try their luck. Once beyond the ring of sentry posts, the local civilian population would help them on their way. The rest was no problem. One way or another, it was the solution of their problems.'

Höß took a particularly hard line against prisoners who tried to abscond, on one occasion ordering the parents of a man who had escaped to be arrested at their home in Poland. They were then brought to the camp and around their necks were hung signs saying that they would remain in the camp until their son surrendered himself. Other officers were even crueler. Fritzsch, his deputy, regularly made indiscriminate arrests while touring the camp as a warning to anyone thinking of trying to escape. He locked them into punishment cells, leaving them there with no food and water until they died.

The main fate, however, of those who tried unsuccessfully to escape was that they were shot. As an example to the other prisoners, the dead person would be brought back to the camp and the other prisoners would be forced to parade past the corpse. 'Many were frightened by this spectacle,' Höß noted, 'and abandoned their plans as result. But there were others who did not hesitate to make the attempt despite everything, hoping that they would be among the lucky ninety per cent who succeeded.' This figure even in the first year of the camp was an exaggeration, conjured up by Höß to make Auschwitz seem less secure than it was and to give the impression that prisoners had a chance of escape when most did not. More accurately he added, 'What can have passed through the minds of the prisoners as they marched past the corpse of a dead comrade? If I read their expression rightly, I saw horror at his fate, sympathy for the unlucky man and a determination to exact revenge when the time came.' If they were unlucky enough to be caught alive, they were hanged, Höß remarking, 'I saw the same expression on the faces of the prisoners when they were paraded to watch the hangings.

Only terror, and a fear least a similar fate overtake themselves, were here more in evidence.'

It was not just prisoners who were killed at the camp but also 'hostages'. These were Polish prisoners who were kept alive so they could be killed on demand to keep the local population in check or in retaliation for partisan attacks, usually on the orders of the Reich Security Main Office. 'Most of the hostages had been in the camp for a considerable time' wrote Höß, 'and the fact that they were hostages was unknown both to them and the camp authorities. Then one day a teleprinter message would arrive from the security police or from the Reich Security Main Office, stating that the prisoners named therein were to be shot or hanged as hostages.'

After the prisoners had been shot, usually by firing squad, or hanged a report would then be sent back to the police, usually within hours of the original request (after 1941 they were either hanged or shot in the back of the neck with a revolver, those in hospital being killed by lethal injection). Despite not knowing that they were hostages, Höß stated that those who had been in the camp a while 'usually knew what this meant or had at least a very shrewd idea'. A kangaroo court was also set up in the camp called the Kattowitz military court, which tried camp prisoners for a range of 'crimes' from stealing food to helping the resistance. With the help of an interpreter, they were interrogated over their actions and then tried although the final sentence was never in any doubt, most being put straight to death.

Prisoners went to their deaths with very different emotions. Political prisoners, noted Höß, often admitted their 'crimes' and met their fate bravely, especially the women. 'Some of the women answered bravely for what they had done,' he said. 'In most cases the death sentence was pronounced and carried out forthwith. Like the hostages, they'll met their death with calm and resignation, convinced that they are sacrificing themselves for their country. I often saw in their eyes a fanaticism that reminded me of Jehovah's Witnesses when they went to their death.' However, criminals condemned by the court went to their death without the same conviction. 'Men who had taken part in robberies with violence, gang crimes and so on, died in a very different way,' Höß reported. 'They were either callous and sullen to the last, or else they whined and cried out for mercy.'

While Niethammer was now assigned to 'special duties', he still resided at the camp and although not involved in the day-to-day running of Auschwitz, he would have heard from other guards about what was going on in the guardrooms, canteens and barracks. Increasingly concerned about the brutal regime and how prisoners were treated, he became even more focused on finding a way out. The only way out of Auschwitz was to get a transfer to another part of the Waffen-SS or to a scientific establishment, both of which required Höß's consent. So Niethammer decided his best chance was to make a case for extending his ornithological studies to other parts of the conquered territories. To gain wider support he therefore decided to approach his ornithological colleagues to see if anybody was prepared to back his transfer request.

As part of carrying out his bird survey work and completing the third volume of the *Handbuch der Deutschen Vogelkunde*, Niethammer was in regular contact with a wide range of fellow ornithologists at the state museums in Bonn, Berlin and Vienna and at the prestigious Kaiser Wilhelm Institute for Biology in Berlin. Founded in 1911 to promote the natural sciences, the institution enjoyed a very high reputation among both the scientific community and the Nazi hierarchy. An umbrella body for a wide range of different organisations including testing and research stations, it was one of the foremost institutes in the Third Reich (following the rise to power of the Nazis the Kaiser Wilhelm Institute became increasingly involved in developing weapons research and production, later giving scientific credence to the medical and eugenics experiments carried out at Auschwitz and other concentration camps). There his key contact was a Professor Fritz von Wettstein (1895–1945) an Austrian-born zoologist who specialised in botany.[3] A staunch national socialist and one of the leading scientists of his generation, he had enjoyed a rapid rise within the academic establishment.

Wettstein had trained in natural history in Vienna and just after the First World War in 1919 left Austria to become an assistant at the Kaiser Wilhelm Institute for Biology in Berlin. He was later appointed professor of botany at the University of Gottingen where from 1925–1931 he made collecting trips to South West Africa (Namibia), South Africa and East Africa (Tanzania). In these expeditions he was accompanied by his father, Richard Wettstein, a world authority on botany. His taxonomic system, the Wettstein system, was one of the earliest classifications to be based on evolutionary biology and had revolutionised botany.

Wettstein's illustrious father died in 1931 and he was left with the monumental task of editing the 5th edition of his totemic work, the *Handbuch der Systematischen Botanik* (*Handbook of Systematic Botany*) which had first appeared in 1901. From 1931–1934 Wettstein was professor of botany at the University of Munich before becoming the director of the Kaiser Wilhelm Institute for Biology where he specialised in plant classification, physiology and cytogenetics. Wettstein's background and editing the *Handbuch der Systematischen Botanik* meant that he had much in common with Niethammer who was busy finalising the third volume of his own *Handbuch der Deutschen Vogelkunde.*

When Wettstein received a letter from Niethammer about his ornithological research at Auschwitz and his desire to extend his studies to other parts of the Third Reich, the director of the Kaiser Wilhelm Institute saw a golden opportunity to recruit a leading zoologist to his staff and put his institute firmly on the map. By the end of 1941 the Third Reich was geographically at its zenith encompassing the greater part of the European continent. German rule in the east extended to most of the Baltic states, Belorussia (now Belarus), Ukraine, Russia up to Moscow, Poland, the protectorate of Bohemia-Moravia (the former Czechoslovakia), Serbia and Greece (where the occupation was shared with the Italians) and the nominally independent satellite states of Slovakia, Croatia, Hungary, Romania and Bulgaria. In the west from the summer of 1940 Norway, Denmark, the Netherlands and Belgium were all under German occupation, as was a large part of France (and the whole country from November 1942).

These areas were ruthlessly exploited economically by the Germans to provide men and material for their war effort. However, the Nazis were also keen to exploit them for their scientific value, putting in place programmes to record and monitor their natural resources with the aim of utilizing them for the Third Reich. Hermann Göring took a particular interest in the natural history of the conquered territories in his role as the Master of the German Hunt and Forest. Reichsführer-SS Heinrich Himmler also actively supported scientific studies, financing an expedition to Tibet before the war which looked at the zoology, botany, ethnology and geophysics of the region. Wettstein saw in Niethammer's letter the potential to extend this pioneering work to the newly conquered territories in the Mediterranean and the East and to win favour with both Göring and Himmler. He had already planned and got permission for an expedition to compare the biodiversity of the newly occupied peninsula of the Peloponnese, the southernmost tip of Greece, with the island of Crete. This was to take place in the spring of 1942 when he had assembled a team of biologists to carry out an ecological survey of the island. So, Wettstein wrote to Höß requesting that Niethammer join the expedition because of his scientific training and ornithological skills.

The study was coordinated by the Department of Science at the Reich Research Council, part of the Oberkommando der Wehrmacht (OKW) or the High Command of the Defence Forces, who also sponsored Niethammer's paper on the birds of Auschwitz. Founded in 1938, the OKW coordinated the German armed forces and wielded huge influence, setting the strategic direction for the war. It had oversight over the individual high commands of the country's armed forces: the Army (Heer), Navy (Kriegsmarine) and Air Force (Luftwaffe). Located in the Maybach complex of underground buildings, 20 kilometres south of Berlin in Wünsdorf near Zossen, the OKW was responsible for planning all the activities of the armed forces and was managed by Generalfeldmarschall (field marshal) Wilhelm Keitel who reported directly to Hitler. The Reich Research Council's role had been redefined by a Führer decree for wartime, he stating, 'The necessity to develop all available resources most efficiently in the interest of the State dictates that a concerted effort be made not only in peace but primarily also in wartime to engage scientific research and to orient it towards the desired targets.'

On receiving the request from the OKW, Höß had little choice but to agree to Niethammer's transfer although he was disappointed to lose a good guard and in particular the regular supply of game which he brought to his home. However, Höß made it a stipulation of the transfer that Niethammer's ornithological studies at Auschwitz be written up and got agreement that his name was to be kept on the reserve list of guards available for duty at Auschwitz. At the time Niethammer, who was delighted at finally being able to leave the camp, readily agreed to the stipulations. Finally, after a year at Auschwitz in which he had witnessed the horrors of the camp but also carried out a unique bird survey, he was moving on. In his role as a guard, he had been part of an operation to convert the original barracks into a prison camp and construct a new extermination centre at Auschwitz II-Birkenau. This work experience would have major consequences for him later in life. However, at the time Niethammer was just relieved to be leaving behind the infamous camp, receiving his transfer at the end of 1941. He went home that Christmas to his family in their palatial villa in Vienna a very happy man.

CHAPTER 6

Fortress Crete: Birds and the Resistance

THE YEAR 1942, which was to be a pivotal one for both Niethammer and the German army, started with him receiving a letter from the OKW confirming his employment as a zoologist with the Department of Science and assigning him to the Crete expedition which was being led by Wettstein. The previous year, on 6 April 1941, the Wehrmacht, supported by Hungarian and Bulgarian forces, had attacked Yugoslavia and Greece in support of the stalling Italian invasion of the country. This has helped to secure Germany's Balkan flank prior to the invasion of the Soviet Union a month later and had safeguarded its Romanian oil supplies from possible Allied attack.

Control of the southern Balkans, commanding the Eastern Mediterranean, had also allowed Germany to attack British lines of communications with Egypt. Following the attack both Yugoslavia and Greece had fallen quickly after which the Germans had invaded Crete on 20 May 1941 in a massive airborne assault. However, German paratroopers had been met by stiff resistance from Allied soldiers and the Cretan population. Although the Germans had eventually overwhelmed the defenders, the loss of so many paratroopers had forced them to abandon further airborne operations. Generaloberst Kurt Student (1890–1978), commander of the invasion force, had dubbed Crete 'the graveyard of the German paratroopers' and a 'disastrous victory'.[1]

Situated about 160 kilometres from the mainland of Greece, Crete has over 1,000 kilometres of coastline and was strategically important because it controlled access to the Eastern Mediterranean and was the main transit base for the Luftwaffe to supply Rommel's forces in North Africa. The largest Greek island, it measures 260 x 60 kilometres and contains major limestone mountain ranges separated by high, rocky terrain and gorges. The three highest mountains are the Lefka Ori or White Mountains at 2,453 metres in the west, Mount Ida in the centre which at 2,456 metres is the highest point on the island, and the Dikti mountains at 2,148 metres in the eastern part of the island. As well as birds, the terrain provided ideal hiding places for resistance groups, who used the inaccessibility of the island's interior to hide from the Germans. By the time of Niethammer's arrival on the island in the early spring of 1942, resistance to the German occupation was rapidly growing and the army found itself under regular attack from the partisan groups hiding in the mountains. Organised with the aid of British Secret Services, the raids had already begun to take their toll on the occupying forces.

In response German forces had taken severe reprisals against Cretans across the island thought to be harbouring saboteurs and introduced curfews and other draconian measures to keep the local population in check. This had started with the infamous Massacre of Kondomari (Greek: Σφαγή στο Κοντομαρί), the mass shooting of male villagers by a squad of German paratroopers on 2 June 1941, two days after the island had fallen. Ordered by Generaloberst Kurt Student, the shootings were in retaliation for Cretans helping the British in the battle for the island.

When Niethammer reported to the main German army base many of the surrounding mountain areas were inaccessible due to partisans, the access roads being dangerous and difficult to pass. To secure their position the Germans had heavily fortified key strategic parts of the island, creating what Student boasted was 'Festung Kreta' (Fortress Crete). The Germans occupied the island's three western settlements (Khania, Heraklion and Rethymno) and had their headquarters in Khania, whilst the Italians occupied the eastern part of the island. However, most of the remoter parts which supported the greatest variety of birds were completely unprotected. The island was therefore a far from safe or accessible place to carry out an ornithological survey.

Despite the perils, Wettstein was determined to carry out the expedition, the last ornithological surveys of the island having been carried out over fifteen years earlier by the British soldier, intelligence officer and ornithologist Richard Meinertzhagen (1878–1967) in 1920 and the ornithologist Dr. Gindo Schiebel in 1926. Wettstein was particularly keen to assess the birdlife of the island in comparison to the mainland where surveys had already been carried out of the Peloponnese, the peninsula which formed the southernmost tip of Greece. The Crete survey team was led by Dr. Wettstein and consisted of Niethammer and three other members – Dr. Hans Stubbe (1902–1980), a professor of genetics, zoology and ornithology at the Kaiser Wilhelm Institute for Biology in Berlin, and two soldiers with an interest in ornithology – Leutnant Behnke and Obergefreiter B. Mihan (*Obergefreiter* is approximately equivalent to a senior lance-corporal, the rank normally given to a soldier who commands a squad).[2]

Given the security situation on the island and the extensive area they had to cover, the team decided that they would work out a series of transects which covered all the main habitats present including the outer lying islands. The range of habitats was extremely varied – apart from the mountains and their foothills it included gorges, scrubland, the sea, the coastal strip and cliffs, estuaries, freshwater lakes (both natural and artificial), streams and seasonal rivers. The survey was made even more challenging by the island having a long history of birds being shot by the local population which meant that many species were very wary and difficult to approach.

The birdlife of Crete was particularly important because as well as resident species, the island was also a very important stopping-off point for birds migrating from Europe to Africa and vice versa. It therefore functioned as a flyway for species wintering in East Africa but breeding in Eastern and Northern Europe. Wettstein and Niethammer knew that more than 300 species were thought to use the island but there was not an up-to-date species list of either resident or migratory species. They were keen to assess the populations of rare species like the Eleonora's falcon and the Ruppell's warbler, which were thought to have their main European breeding populations on Crete. However, they also wanted to survey the populations of colourful resident birds such as the red-backed shrike or butcher bird which impaled its victims on thorns, the dramatic pink, black and white hoopoe with its magnificent crest and the exotic yellow and black golden oriole whose whistled call rang out from the scrub and olive groves.

Other habitats on the island held an array of interesting species. In the skies overhead cliff swallows replaced the house martins Niethammer knew so well from Auschwitz and in the mountains the large alpine swift with its white belly screamed around the crags. From the scrub-covered slopes the velvet-crowned warbler – the male with a shiny black cap and a striking red eye – called while below it the chukar, a partridge species like the red grouse, occurred on the steep, rocky hillsides. Spending most of their time on the ground, chukars took flight for short distances only when they felt threatened (their sentinel ability to detect approaching people on several occasions saving the team by giving away partisans hiding in the rocks). Although wetlands were in short supply on the island, the few present still held a variety of herons, as well as smaller wading birds such as the rare avocet, marsh sandpiper and black-winged stilt, with its characteristic black and white plumage and long pink legs.

Marsh harriers could also be seen quartering over the marshes, but it was the birds associated with the mountains that particularly excited Wettstein and Niethammer. Here smaller birds such as the imperial thrush, lemon finch and alpine chough found a home together with an impressive range of birds of prey including buzzards, golden eagles, Bonelli's eagles and vultures, including griffon vultures. However, the species they particularly wanted to survey were the lammergeier or bearded vulture (now on the list of endangered species, in 1942 it was still common on Crete) and the Eurasian black vulture (now extinct on the island, it was also known as the cinereous vulture *Aegypius monachus*). Back at their base in between air raids Wettstein and Niethammer went to bed at night lulled to sleep by the calls of scops owls. The smallest owl in Europe, they could be heard calling near the Germans' military headquarters in the capital, where their monotonously repeated '*poo*' call competed with the drone of Luftwaffe transport planes which took off day and night.

To assess the birds of Crete the team's series of transects, which dissected the island, had as their focal point the capital Heraklion in the centre of the island. The transects ran eastward to the village Zakros, westward to the coastal town of Kissamos and southward to Messara Bay. The transects also included paths up the three main mountains on the island and expeditions by boat to the surrounding small islands. It was decided to start the fieldwork at the beginning of April 1942 and carry on throughout the bird breeding season until the end of July. Niethammer agreed with Wettstein that the focus of the research should be on the breeding birds although any visitor or migrants found during the survey period would also be recorded.

Due to the distances involved and the constant threat from the resistance much of the survey work was done from the back of a Kübelwagen (a bucket car), a light and versatile vehicle designed by Ferdinand Porsche (1875–1951) and based on the Volkswagen Beetle.[3] Although only a two-wheel drive, the Kübelwagen proved ideal for the survey due to its light weight, flat and smooth underbody and good ground clearance, meaning the car could cope with the rugged terrain. So, in early April the survey started in earnest, three Kübelwagen's being deployed, two for the expedition team and the third for the German guards. At areas along the transect which supported good habitat the team would stop and do a more systematic survey, while the soldiers kept guard. Any bird that could not be readily identified using binoculars and Niethammer's guide was shot. Most nights due to security considerations the team would head back to the military base at Khania.

While Niethammer was busy starting his survey of the birds on Crete, back in Auschwitz concentration camp his former boss Höß was beginning the mass extermination of the Jews. While he mostly left the job of herding the prisoners into the gas chambers to his officers and guards, Höß did when time allowed supervise the process, making sure he was present after any 'incident' had taken place. 'They were taken from the detraining platform to the "cottage" – to bunker I – across the meadows where later building site II was located,' he wrote. 'The transport was conducted by Aumeier [Hans, 1906–1948, deputy commandant] and Palitzsch and some of the other block leaders.' Their job was to reassure the prisoners, which they often did by asking them about their skills and experience. As they were led away from the *Judenrampe*, this misled them into thinking they were going to be put to work. On arrival at the 'cottage', they were told to undress, most going calmly into the rooms to be 'disinfected', believing they would be assigned to a trade afterwards.

Despite the elaborate measures the guards and Sonderkommados put in place to deceive the victims about their fate, during the early transports some of the prisoners on arriving at the cottage panicked. Believing they were about to be suffocated or gassed, their shouting soon caused others in the group to become hysterical. In response to the unrest the guards moved in quickly and forced the prisoners into the chambers at gunpoint before slamming the doors shut and bolting them. Following this incident being reported to Höß, he ordered that any difficult, rebellious, or hysterical prisoners should be singled out straight away by the guards. After being taken to the back of the building they were then shot using a pistol with a silencer. 'The presence and calm behaviour of the Special Detachment [the Sonderkommando consisted of prisoners, mainly Jews, forced to work for the SS herding other prisoners into the gas chambers and disposing of the corpses] served to reassure those who were worried or who suspected what was about to happen,' Höß wrote. 'A further calming effect was obtained by members of the Special Detachment accompanying them into the rooms and remaining with them until the last moment, while an SS man also stood in the doorway until the end.'

For the efficient running of the camp, it was very important to Höß that the arrival, selection and gassing of 'non able' prisoners should take place in a calm and orderly way without any hysteria. To do this he relied on the Sonderkommando who under severe duress played a key role in processing the prisoners. On arrival at the 'undressing cottages' many people were reluctant to take off their clothes, the Special Detachment convincing them it was for their own benefit and encouraging them to do it quickly 'so it would soon be over'. The less time the victims had to think about what was happening to them, the easier they were to manipulate and control. Höß bragged:

> The eager help given by the Special Detachment in encouraging them to undress and in conducting them into the gas chambers was most remarkable. I have never known, nor heard, of any of its members giving these people who were about to be gassed the slightest hint of what lay ahead of them ... On the contrary, they did everything in their power to deceive them and particularly to pacify the suspicious ones. Though they might refuse to believe the SS men, they had complete faith in these members of their own race and to reassure them and keep them calm the Special Detachments therefore always consisted of Jews who themselves came from the same districts as did the people on whom a particular action was to be carried out.

To pacify the prisoners the Special Detachment would answer questions about life in the camp, many prisoners asking after the fate of family and friends who had previously been to Auschwitz. In response they would lie, often with conviction, believing it was better for the victims not to know the fate that awaited them and as importantly fearing for their own lives. Some of the women, sensing what was going to happen and wanting to save their babies, would hide them among the piles of clothes. However, the Special Detachment under supervision from the SS would meticulously search through the piles and return the children to their mothers, persuading them that everything was going to be alright. Many of the younger children unsettled by all the commotion would cry, particularly when they were undressed, the Sonderkommandos encouraging their mothers to comfort them. 'They became calm and entered the gas chambers, playing or joking with one another and carrying their toys,' wrote Höß with supreme callousness. 'I noticed that women who either guessed or knew what awaited them nevertheless found the courage to joke with the children to encourage them, despite the mortal terror visible in their own eyes.'

Despite Höß standing stony faced and not talking to the prisoners, some of the braver ones on seeing his uniform or noticing that he was in charge approached him directly as they filed past. One woman came up to him and pointing to her four children who were helping each other over the rough ground, whispered in his ear, 'How can you bring yourself to kill such beautiful, darling children? Have you no heart at all?' before she was pulled away by a guard. Another prescient old man, his eyes glowering with hatred, hissed to him, 'Germany will pay a heavy penance for this mass murder of the Jews' and then walked defiantly into the chamber.[4]

Another prisoner who caught Höß's attention was a young woman who was busily helping the children and the older women undress. 'During the selection she had had two small children with her, and her agitated behaviour and appearance had brought her to my notice at once. She did not look in the least like a Jewess,' he cynically observed.

> Now her children were no longer with her. She waited until the end, helping the women who were not undressed and who had several children with them, encouraging them and calming the children. She went with the very last ones into the gas chamber. Standing in the doorway, she said: 'I knew all the time that we were being brought to Auschwitz to be gassed. When the selection took place, I avoided being put with the able-bodied ones, as I wished to look after the children. I wanted to go through it all, fully conscious of what was happening. I hope that it will be quick. Goodbye.'

While many prisoners who were ignorant of their fate or even suspicious went to their deaths in a quiet and dignified way, occasionally women would suddenly start screaming or shrieking hysterically, crying out to God and tearing at their hair. Like the men who showed signs of being rebellious or difficult, they were quickly removed by the guards and taken away behind the building where out of sight they were shot in the back of the neck. Others who only suddenly realised their fate in the cottage started cursing and damning the guards, the Special Detachment quickly leaving the room fearing they would be lynched. 'I remember, too, a woman who tried to throw her children out of the gas chamber, just as the door was closing,' wrote Höß. 'Weeping she called out: "At least let my precious children live."'

During the spring of 1942 while Niethammer basked in the sun on Crete counting birds, thousands of men, women and children walked unsuspecting to their deaths in the gas chambers he had guarded, under the blossom-laden fruit trees of the 'cottage' orchard ('this picture of death in the midst of life remains with me to this day,' wrote Höß after the war while on trial). One of the most traumatic parts of the process was the splitting up of families on the Judenrampe, the selection being overseen by 'SS doctors'. This part of the process was, Höß knew, the most likely to lead to rebellion as families were separated so he took a particular interest in ensuring that it was done as efficiently as possible. Despite all the reassurance given to the families by the guards and the Sonderkommandos that they were soon to be reunited with their loved ones, many refused to be split up so the guards had to resort to using force.

For many of the highly traumatised people being unloaded from the cattle trucks this was a clear sign that Auschwitz was not a work camp but a place where prisoners were treated brutally and with little compassion. For those people who already knew in their hearts that they were going to be killed, it simply reinforced their worst fears. The topic had been openly discussed among some Jews living in the ghettos across the occupied countries but most people either didn't want to hear or believe it. 'The process of selection, which took place on the unloading platforms, was in itself rich in incident,' recalled Höß:

> The breaking up of families, and the separation of the men from the women and children, caused much agitation and spread anxiety throughout the whole transport. This was

> increased by the further separation from the others of those capable of work. Families wished at all costs to remain together. Those who had been selected ran back to rejoin their relations. Mothers with children tried to join their husbands, or old people attempted to find those of their children who had been selected for work, and who had been led away.

On the Judenrampe the SS officers often struggled to maintain control despite the presence of guards, guns and dogs. Höß had given strict instructions that guns were not to be fired and force kept to a minimum to avoid spreading further panic and fear at a critical stage in the process. Despite this there were often chaotic scenes as families struggled to stay together and frequently the selection procedure had to be repeated a second time. The platforms were also quite narrow meaning people who had already spent days crammed into cattle cars were again forced to rub against each other, causing further distress. As a result, agitation and anger rapidly spread through the crowd, causing the guards to use force to restore order, often with their rifle butts. Under pressure to process the transport as quickly as possible, they had to ensure there was enough time to clear the platforms of people and their possessions before the next train arrived.

The prisoners' desire to stick together as families was often the cause of most 'incidents' during the day, any delays in processing the transports having to be reported to Höß. 'As I have already frequently said, the Jews have strongly developed family feelings,' he noted:

> They stick together like limpets. Nevertheless, according to my observations, they lack solidarity. One would have thought that in a situation such as this they would inevitably help and protect one another. But no, quite the contrary. I have often known and heard of Jews, particularly those from Western Europe, who revealed the addresses of those members of their race still in hiding [while this did happen, Höß's assertion that it happened often was not true, the close-knit Jewish community doing everything it could to protect those in hiding]. One woman, already in the gas chamber, shouted out to a non-commissioned officer the address of

> a Jewish family. A man who, to judge by his clothes and deportment, appeared to be of very good standing, gave me, while actually undressing, a piece of paper on which was a list of the addresses of Dutch families who were hiding Jews [there is no way of verifying these assertions but they are likely to be Höß trying to portray the Jews as duplicitous and treacherous, even towards their own people, a Nazi stereotype]. I do not know what induced the Jews to give such information. Was it for reasons of personal revenge or were they jealous that these others should survive?

It was not just the Jewish prisoners who Höß regarded as more than capable of betrayal but also the Sonnderkommandos or Special Detachment squads who supervised their last journey to the gas chamber and disposed of the corpses. All of them were only too aware that the fate they saw daily befalling their fellow Jews was at some point waiting in store for them. So, the way they stayed alive for as long as possible was to become useful to the guards and to establish a relationship with some of the 'softer ones' like Niethammer. A few, however, in their attempts to impress the guards became sadistic like so many of the Germans they served, this cruelly serving to reinforce Nazi stereotypes.

'The attitude of the men of the Special Detachment was also strange. They were all well aware that once the actions were completed, they, too, would meet exactly the same fate as that suffered by these thousands of their own race, to whose destruction they had contributed so greatly,' noted Höß. Many of the Sonderkommandos used at Auschwitz from 1942 onwards were Jews who on arrival at the camp had been specially selected for the task and by the next year over 400 were employed at Birkenau. Under threat of death, they were given no choice, the other alternatives being to join those being gassed or commit suicide which many did. Usually strong, able-bodied men were chosen whom the Nazis could coerce or blackmail into working for them. They were either trusted members of the community like doctors whose job it was to lead people to the undressing rooms or conversely prisoners with a criminal record whom the Nazis tasked with taking away and disposing of the corpses.

Due to their usefulness to the guards, the Sonderkommandos were given separate accommodation and extra food in comparison to the other prisoners. They were also treated better, not being subjected to the arbitrary beatings and killings that other inmates regularly endured. Some were even able to keep goods and possessions like cigarettes and pictures and trade these with other prisoners. This gave them a special status in the camp but as *Geheimnisträger* or bearers of secrets, SS policy dictated that they should be killed every three months. The first job of the new set of Sonderkommados was therefore to bury their predecessors. However, as the number of transports arriving at the camp multiplied, some Sonderkommandos with special skills deemed particularly useful to keeping the camp running were allowed to live longer although few survived the war.

Höß deluded himself that rather than serving under severe duress some of them actually excelled at the work: 'Yet the eagerness with which they carried out their duties never ceased to amaze me,' he wrote:

> Not only did they never divulge to the victims their impending fate, and were considerately helpful to them while they undressed, but they were also quite prepared to use violence on those who resisted. Then again, when it was a question of removing the troublemakers and holding them while they were shot, they would lead them out in such a way that the victims never saw the noncommissioned officer standing there with his gun ready, and he was able to place its muzzle against the back of their necks without their noticing it. It was the same story when they dealt with the sick and the invalids, who could not be taken into the gas chambers. And it was all done in such a matter-of-course manner that they might themselves have been the exterminators.

Although most Sonderkommandos took their secrets to the grave, a few became determined to document the gruesome process and record the Nazis crimes against humanity for posterity. So, on scraps of stolen paper, they recorded their daily work – the bodies being taken from the gas chambers, the extraction of the gold teeth and the hair being cut off, the corpses being dragged to the pits or to the crematoria. Then stoking the fires in the pits, the surplus fat being drained off, and the mountain of burning corpses being constantly turned over so that the draught could fan the flames. Afterwards the bits of paper were buried in the ground with the hope that one day they could be used to tell the world of the atrocities and help indite those responsible. (The manuscripts are now kept primarily in the archive of the Auschwitz-Birkenau State Memorial Museum. They are recognised as some of the most important testimony to be produced about the Holocaust because they were contemporaneous eyewitness accounts written about the operation of the gas chambers in Birkenau.)

Höß often watched the Sonderkommandos and what struck him most was the 'callous indifference' to their work rather than their almost superhuman endurance to carry on under the most appalling conditions imaginable. 'They carried out all these tasks with a callous indifference as though it were all part of an ordinary day's work,' he wrote. 'While they dragged the corpses about, they ate or they smoked. They did not stop eating even when engaged on the grisly job of burning corpses which had been lying for some time in mass graves.' Some Sonderkommandos even had the truly horrendous job of burning their own friends and family. 'It happened repeatedly that Jews of the Special Detachment would come upon the bodies of close relatives among the corpses, and even among the living as they entered the gas chambers. They were obviously affected by this, but it never led to any incident,' observed Höß with cold-blooded indifference:

> I myself saw a case of this sort. Once when bodies were being carried from a gas chamber to the fire pit, a man of the Special Detachment suddenly stopped and stood for a moment as though rooted to the spot. Then he continued to drag out a body with his comrades. I asked the Capo what was up. He explained that the corpse was that of the Jew's wife. I watched him for a while but noticed nothing peculiar in his behaviour. He continued to drag corpses along, just as he had done before. When I visited the Detachment a little later, he was sitting with the others and eating, as though nothing had happened.

The incident left Höß wondering at the prisoner's ability to detach himself from everything that was most precious in his life, writing, 'Was he really able to hide his emotions so completely, or had he become too brutalized to care even about this?' The whole experience of Auschwitz left Höß bewildered, asking himself where the Jews in the Sonderkommandos found the will to keep on working in what had become hell on earth. 'Where did the Jews of the Special Detachment derive the strength to carry on night and day with their grisly work?' he asked.

> Did they hope that some whim of fortune might at the last moment snatch them from the jaws of death? Or had they become so dulled by the accumulation of horror that they were no longer capable even of ending their own lives and thus escaping from this 'existence'? I have certainly watched them closely enough, but I have never really been able to get to the bottom of their behaviour.

What he singularly failed to recognise in the face of so much suffering was the enduring strength of the human spirit – and even in the most awful conditions imaginable the steely determination of some Jews to survive so that humanity would one day learn the truth.

Chapter 7

Observations on the Birdlife of Auschwitz

IN MAY 1942, not long after Niethammer had started his studies on Crete, his paper on the birdlife of Auschwitz was published in the prestigious Annals of the Natural History Museum in Vienna. The paper was included in volume 52 of the museum's periodical on pages 164–199 and included four plates. Its publication was another feather in his cap and helped to establish Niethammer as one of the foremost ornithologists in the Third Reich. The article was edited and approved for publication by Nietmammer's boss Hans Kummerlöwe, a staunch party member who was extremely well thought of in the Nazi party. Niethammer had met him first early in his career while studying at Leipzig; Kummerlöwe had also been a contributor to his book the *Handbuch der Deutschen Vogelkunde.*

Niethammer's paper was called '*Beobachtungen über die Vogelwelt von Auschwitz (Ost-Oberschlesien)*' or 'Observations on the birdlife of Auschwitz (Eastern Upper Silesia)' and after his name he was credited with currently serving in the Waffen-SS.[1] The paper was written in a very personal, almost conversational style and although the survey wasn't comprehensive or scientifically rigorous, Kummerlöwe was probably only too aware of the conditions under which it had been produced. It started off with a detailed description of the study area and then contained a list of birds seen at the camp ordered according to the classification Niethammer had used in his *Handbuch der Deutschen Vogelkunde.* The most striking aspect of the paper was the moving dedication at the beginning to the commandant Rudolf Höß and his adjutant SS-Obersturmführer Frommhagen (Erich Frommhagen, 1912–1945, he served as Höß's personal assistant from 1 November 1940 until 1 November 1941). The introduction read:

> In the period from October 1940 to August 1941 I had the opportunity to get to know the surroundings of Auschwitz

> and at the same time carry out special duties to survey the birdlife. In the fall and winter months and the early spring too my service in the Waffen-SS left me little time for ornithological observations. So, I devoted myself to the task in the last week of May, in June and July, enabling me to get a fairly complete picture of the birdlife of this interesting and still completely unknown new German eastern territory, especially the breeding birds occurring there. I owe this to the great understanding which the commandant of KL [*Konzentrationslager* or concentration camp] Auschwitz, SS-Sturmbannführer Höß, and his adjutant, SS-Obersturmführer Frommhagen, gave to the scientific development of this area and the research tasks that the German expansion in the East brings with it.

The timing of his survey work was significant as it showed that Niethammer would have helped to convert the barracks at Auschwitz I and clear the second zone before he started his special duties. His glowing tribute to Höß was entirely sincere, when Soviet troops liberated Auschwitz in 1945, they were amazed to find in Höß's safe a copy of the paper with a handwritten dedication from Niethammer.

In the introduction Niethammer also carefully defined the boundaries of his research, writing:

> The city of Auschwitz lies on the Soła river just above the confluence of the Soła and the Upper Vistula [the Vistula is a tributary of the Soła]. Belonging to Austria (Galicia) until the First World War, Auschwitz was then on the border of the German Reich which ran along the Vistula. The area referred to here finishes directly to the east of the old German territory; in the west it is bordered by the Vistula and to the east by the Soła. My activity was located in this 'intermediate catchment' area. It stretches from the mouth of the Soła into the Vistula, southwards up to the Soła beyond the village of Raisko and beyond the villages of Babitz, Birkenau, Plawy and Harmense to a forest north of Brzeszcze. This 5,500-ha area, whose highest elevation is 245m and lowest is 230m above sea level, sits to the south and stretches to the steep foothills of the West Beskydy,

> which I did not take into account. Also, to the north and east of the city of Auschwitz I have, generally, not included all terrain lying outside the Vistula–Soła angle, since I wanted to carry out intensive research in a small area in preference to a more superficial one of a much larger area.

The area of Niethammer's research was important as it showed that he had been surveying the site when the second camp was being constructed by the Polish and Russian prisoners, which would become Auschwitz II-Birkenau. As the work gangs were deployed across the second zone to prepare the ground, many dying in the process, it seems inconceivable that Niethammer did not witness their treatment. Each of the villages in Niethammer's survey had been cleared of its Polish population and during his survey stood lifeless and deserted but would soon become sub-camps of Auschwitz. As Auschwitz grew each of these former villages would be turned into satellite camps where men and women, mostly favoured Polish women prisoners, would be used for farming, including growing crops, rearing cattle and poultry, breeding rabbits and tending the fishponds.

The paper then set out to describe the ecology of the area, Niethammer describing it rather grandly as the 'Biotope Design'. The most important component of the biotope was the very high water table which fed the large number of ponds in the area, Niethammer stating:

> The country surrounded by the Soła and Vistula is for the most part a loess soil [very fertile soil with an abundance of silt particles] used for arable farming and an alluvial soil [soil deposited by surface water] used for river gravel. Since the groundwater level is very high everywhere (often only 30–40cm from the surface), a stagnant wetness can be observed in many places. Moreover, the amount of rainfall is significant; it is about 800mm per year. Numerous small ponds rich in fish and crabs are scattered over the whole area. In addition, many fishponds have been created, which alone for the village of Harmense make up around 250ha [hectares].

The areas rich soil fertility was the reason that Himmler wanted to create an agricultural research station on the site, using the deserted villages cleared by the Germans as laboratories. The reference to the river gravel was significant as it was this resource that the Russian prisoners had to mine to build the second camp, often by hand under appalling conditions. The village of Harmense which was deserted when Niethammer wrote the paper would soon be turned into two sub-camps. In December 1941 at about the time Niethammer left the camp, fifty Polish prisoners were billeted on the second floor of a manor house there, about 2 kilometres from Birkenau. They occupied rooms separated from the rest of the house by a barred, padlocked door and were employed farming poultry, rabbits and fish.

In the opening passages of the paper Niethammer painted a picture of an area rich in wildlife, paying particular attention to the fish, plants and mammals as well as the birds. Fish were particularly important to the area, the former Polish population using the extensive range of ponds to raise carp, the ditches and dykes also teeming with rudd, tench, loach and dwarf catfish. The Vistula river was also extensively fished, it containing perch, ruffe, tench, carp, roach, eel, pike and barbel together with rarer species like burbot and gudgeon. On Höß's orders all the ponds were used to farm fish both for his family's consumption and to feed his officers, all soldiers being prohibited from fishing them. (Höß's order of 9 June 1941 prohibited all shooting at the ponds except for Niethammer and another SS guard Ernst Merzinger and any bathing or fishing in the ponds. Any soldiers wishing to fish were told to do so in the Soła or Vistula, Höß adding that he would punish violators of these prohibitions severely.[2])

In addition to the fish, Niethammer described the area as being rich in plants typical of river floodplains including dense areas of willow, poplar and alder scrub and extensive reed and sedge beds, while the dams were planted with poplars and oaks. The reedbeds like the fishponds were extensively farmed by the Polish inhabitants before they were expelled, Niethammer noting that as they were cut in rotation annually 'only a small stock of last year's reeds [are] available, which is why local inhabitants of birds such as great reed warblers, bitterns etc. only occasionally occur in large numbers'. The reedbeds were also home to lots of small birds like the aquatic warbler while the ponds supported great crested and black-necked grebes.

Flowers typical of flood plains were common, Niethammer recording marsh lousewort, cotton grass, horsetail, purple loosestrife, arrowhead and water chestnut. To survey the ponds Niethammer had to take off his boots and walk through many of them barefoot with a survey net, he complaining, 'The prickly fruits [of water chestnut] make it all the more unpleasant and noticeable for those who have to wade barefoot in the ponds.' Sweeping his net from side to side, Niethammer noted that the pond water supported a diverse range of insects and molluscs especially mussels and the ditches teemed with amphibians, he commenting, 'Extremely richly blessed are the ponds with water frogs and also green toads, common toads and tree frogs are not uncommon.'

During his survey Niethammer was surprised to come across a raised bog on two small islands between the village of Harmense and the Vistula. The bog was used to grow blackberries, cranberries and blueberries which thrived among the heather and low poplars. Like the reeds the berries were cultivated by the local Polish population before they were ejected, Niethammer noting that although now overgrown, it supported 'the meadow pipit, which I have not found anywhere else in the area as a breeding bird as well as the rare black-tailed godwit'.

Niethammer also dedicated a section to comparing the Soła and Vistula rivers. The Soła was a mountain river which he described as 'mostly clear, greenish water and a wide riverbed of medium coarse gravel and coarse-grained sand' (the Soła originates in the Western Beskids mountain range near the border with Slovakia). The river was constantly prone to flooding, especially in the summer months, he noting that it carried 'most of its floods in March, June and July, so right in the breeding season'. This left the nests of the terns and common plovers on the islands in the middle of the river in constant danger of being washed away, as were those of the sand matin and kingfisher who made their nests in the sandy banks at the edge of the Soła. Along some sections dense willow stands formed a belt along the edge, which he photographed for one of the plates, recording that they supported nightingales and marsh warblers, while the water was rich in fish including eel, pike, roach, chub and burbot.

In contrast to the Soła, the Vistula was a freshwater river whose murky water, graduated slopes and narrow riverbed provided a more specialised habitat, the banks being composed of dense willow scrub combined with poplar, oak, hazelnut, alder and buckthorn. Here Niethammer expected to find the rare penduline tit but to his frustration he could not prove it was breeding, instead finding the area rich in river and willow warblers.

Along the banks he also found otter spraints, saw weasels and counted many muskrats which he described as a 'nuisance everywhere'. Native to North America, the muskrat was introduced to Poland and other European countries early in the twentieth century. Found in wetlands all along the Vistula, it provided the local Polish population with fur and meat but caused widespread ecological damage. The mammals' burrows led to serious bank erosion along the river and at night they would enter the local villages to eat the crops. In response Niethammer shot as many as he could, presenting them to Höß with other game.

Under a section called 'Field, village, forest', Niethammer reported on the birds he had found around the former settlements in the second zone after the Germans had expelled the Polish residents. He wrote, 'The villages [Raisko, Babitz, Birkenau, Plawy and Harmense] ... are more or less dissolved settlements, whose houses are mostly built in the wooden style and covered with straw or reeds. Tall trees (oak, poplar, linden, elm, alders, etc.) provide shade in the hot summer months.' At the time he wrote the paper all of them would have been deserted, the houses, shops, schools and other village buildings eerily empty but Niethammer provided no comment on this other than to describe them as 'dissolved'. Most were surrounded by farms, the larger ones of Raisko and Harmense also having estates with parkland. (Höß's order of 9 June 1941 also prohibited anyone entering the area around the Raisko park, which had originally been cordoned off and used as a cemetery for German soldiers. However, Höß stated they had long since been transferred to the 'Heroes' Cemetery in Bielitz'.[3]) In the parkland and the scattered forests around the villages he found jays, wood pigeons and greater spotted woodpeckers. Along the field margins and rows of poplar trees he recorded cuckoos, whitethroats, yellowhammers, chaffinches and the exotic golden oriole. In the deserted villages magpies had taken up residence after the Polish population had left, he admiring their audacity but finding them wary and difficult to hunt. In the nearby water meadows used for hay he found a large number of nesting redshanks and lapwings, their haunting alarm calls giving away their presence.

In the paper Niethammer made a particular point of comparing his study area with similar biotopes in Germany and found some striking differences. Absent were many of the species he would have expected to see, including corn bunting, red-breasted merganser, wren, pied flycatcher, dipper, long-tailed tit, buzzard and the chiffchaff.

What puzzled him was the rarity of the blackbird and song thrush, both of which did not occur in the local villages. The normally ubiquitous grey wagtail was a rarity on the Soła river, the kingfisher and the crested lark also being seldom seen. He was also struck by the lack of birds of prey in the area, only marsh harriers and kestrels being common. (Niethammer did not give reasons for the differences, the most likely explanation for the absence of many of species being he simply failed to record them. However, pollution, hunting and the previous severe winters would also have played a part.)

The remainder of the paper was given over to a systematic list of the birds Niethammer had seen, heard or shot across the study area during his survey. The list amounted to 124 species of both breeding and wintering birds, a good but not spectacular tally. In the list Niethammer often cross-referenced his findings with those of Dr Otto Natrop (1876–1956), a German ornithologist who took Polish citizenship so he could focus on the status and distribution of birds in the country. (During his lifetime he also accumulated a huge collection of Silesian bird skins which he preserved himself but had to abandon when Breslau fell at the end of the war – miraculously his collection survived and much of it was saved.[4]) Niethammer's species list often referred to birds that Natrop had recorded in the local area but which he had not been able to find. (A comparison with species lists compiled by Natrop shows that from an ornithological perspective Niethammer recorded most of species to be found in the area but there were some species which he either could not confirm, like penduline tits, or could not find, like the woodchat shrike. However, Natrop had more time to compile his list and greater local knowledge of the different habitats).

A typical entry in Niethammer's list gave the status of the bird (common, rare, breeding, winter visitor etc.), the date(s) he had first seen, heard or shot it, the location (e.g. on the Soła river), if he could find it any information on the nest and the number of young raised together with any personal anecdotes, Niethammer liking to write about the 'jizz' of the bird. While most of the entries gave basic ornithological data, some contained more interesting pieces of information such as unusual bird behaviour or observations on what was happening in the local area, both at the barracks and in the surrounding villages. A few entries also referred to some of his fellow officers who supplied him with information. A typical entry for the golden oriole, an exotic and secretive bright yellow bird with black wings and a distinctive fluting whistle call, read:

> Oriolus oriolus (L.) – Oriole
> A very common breeding bird both in the pond area and in the riparian zones of the Vistula and Soła and on the tree-lined field margins. The first appeared on May 7th at the Soła. On May 12th, an adult yellow male flew in the morning hours across the open fields near Dwory, where there was not a group of trees far and wide. On May 29th I found a nest with an egg in it on an oak tree that had only a very small amount of leaves. The nest, about 5m high, was therefore clearly visible from all directions. On June 5th I watched another nest building couple at the Soła. Females and males always flew together with nesting material to the building site. In the last days of July I still heard various males whistle but on 5th August they only made themselves noticeable by frequently uttered 'chrä' calls.

Some entries, however, indicated his clear frustration at not being able to find a particular species, such as the entry for the blackbird:

> Turdus merula L. – Blackbird.
> On 13th April, at dusk, in the willow scrub on the Soła I turned up a blackbird. I didn't see any more until 14th June and would not have believed that the blackbird even occurs here. That day I found a nest with 5 fresh eggs in an elder tree shrub about 1.5 m high in the scrub zone of the Soła. Of the adults I only saw the female fly from the nest and heard the male later start to sing. But I wasn't able to see both the adults. If one considers how familiar the blackbird is in the cities of western and central Germany, one is downright astounded by such a shy bird. It may be said that the blackbird is by far the shyest songbird there is. In the city of Auschwitz, as in Myslowitz, the blackbird is missing and from all the smaller towns. She continues to breed in the woods near Brzeszcze, where I also observed young on 10th August.

Another species inexplicably missing from the immediate area around the Auschwitz I barracks was a bird immortalised in plays, poems and songs by William Shakespeare and John Keats. 'Strangely enough, the nightingale is missing here,' he wrote, although it was common in the surrounding zone. With only the sounds of the camp to keep him awake at night, Niethammer missed the bird's extraordinary melodic song with its fast succession of high, low and rich notes which few other species could match. Other birds, however, flourished such as the sand martin which bred in the many banks created by the camp's construction, Niethammer recording that it 'brings up its brood happily'. And just like the camp records for the inmates, Niethammer meticulously recorded every detail, noting for a shot falcon that it weighed 200g and its testicles measured 5 x 3mm (birds' testicles are found within the abdominal cavity, situated on either side of the backbone adjacent to the left and right kidney).

Niethammer's list started with the crows, jackdaws and rooks which were frequent visitors to the Auschwitz I barracks, they occasionally sitting on the *Arbeit macht frei* sign. 'Among the huge flocks of crows that roamed in late autumn or stayed at Auschwitz throughout the winter, hooded crows were always represented as individuals or in small groups,' he wrote. 'I never saw more than 100 together. Often quarrels broke out between crows and rooks over a piece of food, the rooks always losing out.' In the village of Harmense he recorded them working together to drive ruffe (a small freshwater fish) into ditches where they could be picked off at will, much like the prisoners at the camp. In the winter thousands of rooks and jackdaws roamed the site, one being caught with a Polish ring. He commented 'A rook caught here in January wore a Polish ring, whose origin could not be determined more precisely, like numerous retrievals of birds with Polish rings that are being processed, it is waiting in Rossitten.'

The Rossitten Bird Observatory or Vogelwarte Rossitten was the world's oldest ornithological observatory. Established by the German ornithologist Johannes Thienemann in 1901, it was located on the Curonian Spit at Rossitten, East Prussia on the south-eastern coast of the Baltic Sea (today a UNESCO World Heritage Site shared between Russia and Lithuania, all the Germans being expelled from the spit in 1945). Located on the East Atlantic Flyway, between ten and twenty million birds would fly over the spit during the spring and autumn migrations, so it was of vital importance for ringing research. From 1936 the observatory had been headed up by Ernst Schüz, the curator of the bird museum in Stuttgart who like Niethammer had studied under the esteemed German ornithologist Erwin Stresemann. The Rossitten Observatory had then been taken over by the Kaiser Wilhelm Institute, with Schüz specialising in ringing studies on white storks.

The white stork, one of Europe's biggest and most recognisable birds, nested in close proximity to human habitation throughout the area, often on rooftops. A long-distant migrant, they were known to winter in South Africa with over a quarter of the European breeding population occurring in Poland. This included Auschwitz where Niethammer recorded seven nests in many of the villages in his survey area such as Plawy, Harmense and Birkenau. When in 1941 Niethammer had sent off his Polish bird rings to the observatory, Schüz was heavily involved in his research on white storks and his staff had been conscripted, so many of the rings had not been processed. Schüz's predecessor, Thienemann, had discovered that white storks that bred in eastern Prussia migrated to south-east Africa while those to the west migrated to the south-west of the continent. So, for his research Schüz had taken young storks from the eastern part of the migratory divide and moved them to the western side, finding that they had taken a south-westerly route following the adults. In contrast, when the young were released only after all the adults had gone, he found that they reverted to migrating to south-eastern Africa.

Schüz's pioneering research on white storks had brought him to the attention of Reichsführer-SS Heinrich Himmler. He had long wanted to get the Boers in South Africa to rebel against the ruling British and in white storks thought that he had found the avian answer. In 1940 a dead stork was found on a farm in the northern Transvaal with a message sent by the resistance in Nazi-occupied Holland on a piece of tape sewn around its leg. It read: 'To our South African brothers: we, the people of Bergen op Zoom, tell you that living under German occupation is just hell.' When Himmler learnt of the message it gave him the idea of using the birds to send propaganda of his own to the Boers in a bid to get them to overthrow their British oppressors and undermine the South African war effort. So, he asked Schüz to investigate attaching propaganda leaflets in Afrikaans to the legs of the storks, the birds already being famous in European folklore for carrying babies in cloth bundles. Schüz was extremely sceptical about the idea but in 1942, on Himmler's direct orders, began test flights for the wonderfully codenamed project *Storchbein-Propaganda* or 'stork-leg propaganda'.[5] These trials continued until it was found that a thousand birds would be required for every ten leaflets that reached their target and the bird-brained plan was then quietly dropped.

In Poland storks were protected because having one on your roof was considered lucky, their excitable bill rattling during courtship also being seen as applause for the coming summer. However, for Niethammer they were a trophy species which, like so many other birds at Auschwitz, he shot to display in his bird museum at the camp. For many of the commoner species he shot multiple specimens so that he could dissect and compare them, he noting that the stomach contents of five jackdaws contained 'remnants of eggshells, otherwise grains and, beetles, insect pupae and some pebbles'.

The magpie was another species he shot in large numbers so he could study the feather changes associated with the moult. 'The magpie is a very common breeding bird near Auschwitz, especially in gardens, along streets and in isolated groups of trees,' he wrote. 'During the winter, many magpies stayed in gardens and sheltered in houses, where they often sat on the roofs.' In the village of Harmense after the Polish population had been expelled, he noted some remarkable behaviour. In the absence of humans, the magpies worked together in a large flock to kill the domesticated ducks that had been left behind by the villagers. Niethammer recorded, 'In August [1941] things happened at Harmense, several families of magpies formed a mob of 40–50 birds together. This strong troop attacked very young domestic ducks several times, killed and ate them.'

Jays were a species that Niethammer particularly wanted for his collection because of their colourful plumage, but they were rare outside the larger local forests. So, when on 20 July 1941 he came across a jay family where the adults were feeding the begging young out of the nest, he shot both an adult and a juvenile with his Mauser or Karabiner 98k rifle. 'Shot the adult and a young just as the feeding was in progress,' he wrote. 'The parent bird had just fed it a large green caterpillar and had an insect pupa in its beak which it was just about to hand over. In the stomach next to caterpillars and insects were lots of blueberries.' In contrast, the starling was a common bird at Auschwitz and was one of the few birds to nest in the barracks, Niethammer commenting, 'The surroundings of Auschwitz are filled with starlings, they are literally saturated, and nest in all possible and impossible places. The hanging nesting boxes [that Niethammer had put up around the camp] will have contributed to their success. Moreover, most of the tree cavities were also occupied by starlings.'

As well as starlings, the black redstart made its home in the barracks. A small bird about the size of a robin, it had successfully adapted to living in industrial and urban areas which mimicked the scree slopes of its Alpine home. The bird's name came from the plumage of the male, which was grey-black in colour with a red tail which it flicked open when startled. Niethammer described it as 'one of the most common birds in the area. In all villages and in Auschwitz it breeds in large numbers.' He had first observed it on 29 March at a 'large complex building' at Auschwitz, probably a reference to the Kanada storage buildings and workshops associated with the camp. Here among the buildings, he had seen a couple of male birds singing. In the following two weeks the black redstart turned up all over the camp, Niethammer stating, 'the species appeared everywhere, on April 13th I noted large numbers arriving on the Soła with one in almost every willow bush.' On 25 June he found a nest in a brickyard at the camp, where amongst the bricks piled up by the prisoners the female had built 'a loose cup of grass lined with hair, wool and feathers', the hair and wool once belonging to the prisoners.

Another bird to make its home in the barracks and a far more visible one was the barn swallow which Niethammer again described as 'a very common breeding bird everywhere'. He recorded the first bird arriving in the camp on 1 April but very cold and wet weather in that month and early May had seen many of the birds die, like the inmates starving to death due to lack of food (swallows feed on insects caught on the wing) and the inclement conditions. 'At the beginning of May the weather was again very cold and rainy, and many barn swallows perished,' he wrote. 'In one case I witnessed this process: a swallow flew quite feebly over a pond near Harmense and finally settled down exhausted on the shore. From here, after a few minutes, she rose again into the air, flew in a big arc but suddenly crashed and fell on the water where she lay helpless but still alive [it seems to have been lost on Niethammer that many prisoners shared the same fate].' A pair of birds had created their mud nest in the barracks where he was staying and managed to raise two broods. 'A couple who raised the first brood in our barracks started the second brood in July and on 14th July had a clutch of 3 eggs,' he reported. The young were fed on insects, particularly flies which were very common, swarms of them feeding on both the living and the dead.

Niethammer clearly enjoyed the survey work, the job of studying and shooting birds being much safer than studying and shooting prisoners or the enemy during a time of war. Many of the bird entries hint at his pleasure in finding a particular species, even if his scientific training prevented him from expressing it. On 14 June he came across a large group of yellow wagtails in a field, a summer migrant characterised by its bright lemon plumage and almost comical habits of picking up insects while wagging its tail and bobbing its head. 'The yellow wagtail is with the lapwing a character bird of the wet meadows, especially those that lie between the ponds or on their limits. Here it is a very common breeding bird that lives in a small area and reaches a high population density,' he wrote, adding:

> I noticed the first male feeding on 14th June. At the end of June there were riots in places as many yellow wagtails formed large flocks consisting primarily of adult birds who worked together on freshly ploughed fields in search of food. In a bird's stomach I found large caterpillars and on 4th July I observed a pair on an oak tree eagerly picking off the caterpillars of the oak moth.

Niethammer was also pleased to find the hoopoe, an exotic-looking bird with a pinkish-brown body, striking black and white wings, a long black downcurved bill, and a long pinkish-brown crest which it raises when excited.

> I was amazed to see the hoopoe as a breeding bird in early June and had to consult [presumably Natrop] as I had never heard him before. In Auschwitz the bird is extremely secretive and during the narrow breeding season rarely seen. On 23rd June I surprised an adult bird with food in its beak. The nest was apparently somewhere in a pollarded willow although I at first questioned whether the location was appropriate enough. This breeding pair lived on a street lined with pollarded willows at the exit of Harmense village, a second pair stuck to the high trees which existed

> along the supply ditch for the ponds at Raisko. On 15th July I again saw a hoopoe with food in its beak; in the following days I observed the young fledging daily in the breeding area of this bird.

While Niethammer did most of the survey on his own, his enthusiasm for birds was shared by at least some of his fellow guards. On 15 August he reported that 'Untersturmführer Thomsen saw a goshawk on 15th August near Birkenau [while guarding the Soviet prisoners building the Auschwitz II-Birkenau camp], while another guard and fellow birder, Merzinger, had seen a male black grouse displaying in the spring near the village of Raisko.' It was at this time that the local inhabitants of the village were being forcibly expelled at gunpoint by the guards, so it is likely that Merzinger came across a lek of displaying birds at dawn when clearing the area.

Many of the vacated buildings in the village were commandeered and the fields taken over and turned into a camp farm. Over the summer the work preparing the fields was done by work groups of Polish male prisoners who walked there each day under armed guard from the main barracks at Auschwitz. From 1942 onwards they were increasingly replaced by women and with the opening of Auschwitz II-Birkenau, the women were quartered there permanently. Here they were assigned to two Kommandos – horticulture and plant research. The first Kommando grew vegetables in greenhouses for the SS, cultivated flowerbeds, and worked in the nearby fields. They also ran a shop where SS men, their families, and civilian workers could purchase vegetables, fruit and flowers. The second Kommando worked in an experimental station where they cultivated the plant *Taraxacum kok-saghyzot*, often abbreviated to TKS, a native dandelion to Central Asia. Also known as the Kazakh or Russian dandelion, it was used to produce high-quality rubber for the German war effort. Many of the women had degrees in biology, chemistry or agronomy with civilian scientists, mostly from Russia, also being employed there.

Despite being an expert ornithologist Niethammer relied a lot on shooting as a way of identifying difficult species, over the ten-month period of the survey from October 1940 to August 1941 killing hundreds of birds. However, on one occasion he used his Mauser rifle to try to save one. On the evening of 25 June, he had been watching a little grebe at a pond when he saw it disappear into the reeds quickly followed by a muskrat. Soon afterwards he witnessed a violent shaking of the reeds and suspected that the muskrat had attacked the bird, so he shot at the reeds from six to eight metres in an attempt to save it.

> At the relevant point there was now a muskrat in the water and a little grebe male without a head. The shotgun had perforated the muskrat's head and body of the little grebe like a sieve. The head of the little grebe was nowhere to be found, the stump of the bird's neck was already cold but the body still warm. All indications therefore point to the assumption that the muskrat dragged the little grebe in its mouth. That she was able to subdue an adult little grebe seems not yet clearly proven to me. The bird may also have become a victim of a stoat, which in turn was again disturbed during its meal by the muskrat [while mostly vegetarian, muskrats will eat fish, small mammals and young birds].

While most of the species accounts were innocuous, the timing of some brought into sharp focus the moral ambiguity of carrying out a bird survey while just a short distance away people were being murdered in the most appalling circumstances. While ten Polish prisoners were being deliberately left to starve to death in their cells by Fritzsch, the deputy commandant, Niethammer heard a nightingale singing outside. And in late August 1941 when the first Russian prisoners were being gassed using Zyklon B, he recorded eight curlews flying over a pond within sight of the windowless room in the basement of Block 11. Niethammer was not just surveying birds, he was using them to turn a blind eye to the horrors going on in the camp.

The paper finished with four plates which illustrated the range of habitats and birds in the survey area, Niethammer taking the photographs himself. He owned a Leica camera with a telephoto lens and was clearly proud of the results (although by today's standards they seem crude). The first picture taken in June 1941 showed one of the large ponds between the village of Harmense and the Vistula river. Niethammer commented that crested, black-necked and little grebes bred here together with mallard, garganey, moorhen and pochard. It also showed small islands on which meadow pipits and godwits bred. The second picture was taken on 16 August 1941 and showed two snipe at the bottom of a drained pond at Harmense and is the only photograph of birds (despite a reed rather obtrusively being in front of the snipe, Niethammer was clearly pleased with the picture as snipe are extremely shy and difficult birds to photograph).

The third picture taken in early June 1941 showed the riverbed of the Soła, about 5 kilometres from Auschwitz viewed upstream, in the background the Beskids Mountains where the river originated (the photograph is particularly haunting for as well as birds, the river was also used to dump raw effluent, ground bones and human ashes from the crematoria at Auschwitz). Niethammer stated, 'The character bird of the shore scrub in the foreground is the marsh warbler, on the opposite bank the nightingale. On the shingle beach and on shingle islands it is not uncommon to find the ringed plover.' The final photograph taken in early June 1941 showed the scrub on the east bank of the Soła river, about 2 kilometres from the town of Auschwitz. A few tall trees stand out above the shrubbery, which consisted mainly of willows, poplars and oaks. Niethammer recorded that the characteristic breeding birds of this habitat were willow warbler, nightingale, the golden oriole and pheasant.

When Niethammer's paper was published it was widely praised in ornithological circles, Kummerlöwe promoting it among Austrian ornithologists and Stresemann doing the same among German ones. Based on the survey Niethammer produced two short supplementary articles which were published in the *Reports of the Association of Silesian Ornithologists* in 1942 and a year later a two-page follow-up in the Annals of the Natural History Museum in Vienna. Still a serving member of the Waffen-SS, Niethammer also sent a copy to Höß at Auschwitz to thank him for his support, adding in ink at the top a personal dedication.

Birds apart, chillingly the paper helped to deflect from what was really happening at the camp. Since the invasion of the Soviet Union the year before, reports had begun to reach the Allies of mass murder, especially of Jews in the occupied territories in the east and in the concentration camp system, reports which the Germans denied (most historians believe that the Allies didn't learn that the Holocaust was happening until August 1942). While at the time the paper provoked little comment outside of the Austrian, German and Polish ornithological community, it helped reinforce Nazi propaganda that Auschwitz was a prison camp involved in scientific research rather an extermination camp involved in genocide.

CHAPTER 8

The Pope of Ornithology

IN CONTRAST TO the survey work at Auschwitz which was done in a secluded and heavily guarded area where the local population had been forcefully expelled, in Crete Niethammer found that his ornithological studies were soon being impacted by the war. After the German invasion of the island in 1941, the following spring had seen the army bring up large military reinforcements to support Rommel's forces in North Africa. The airfields of Crete were of great strategic importance as the main transit base for the Luftwaffe to supply the Afrika Korps. From here the Luftwaffe also undertook photo-reconnaissance operations, bombed enemy positions, and attacked British convoys across the south-eastern Mediterranean. In response, the British high command in Egypt became determined to disrupt the supply route and started covert communications with the local resistance on the island about sabotage missions.

For Niethammer and the other ornithologists carrying out their bird studies around the island in their Kübelwagens this meant they had to put in place extra security. Often finding themselves in remote parts of the island and carrying out survey work away from their vehicles or off track, this made them particularly vulnerable to a surprise attack from a local resistance group in the mountains. As a result, the two soldiers in the team, Leutnant Behnke and Obergefreiter Mihan, asked for more troops to protect the party but this was refused. However, in early June the war came to them when the team found their base at Heraklion under attack after the British sent three groups from the Special Boat Squadron and one from the Special Air Service to Crete to disrupt their war effort.

The aim of Operation *Albumen* was to sabotage aircraft and installations on the airfields at the capital and three other settlements.[1] The Heraklion raid was led by Major George Jellicoe (1918–2007) who commanded the Special Boat Squadron and included four members of the Free French forces and a lieutenant from the Greek army. The group was transferred to Crete on board the Free Greek submarine *Triton*, and after considerable delays rowed ashore in three inflatable boats. The party had intended to land at Karteros beach, but instead after getting their bearings wrong came ashore in the Gulf of Malia at dawn on 10 June, two days behind schedule. Following their late arrival at the wrong landing site, the men had to march overland to reach the airfield. Hiding by day from German patrols and marching by night, they finally arrived at the airfield on the night of 12/13 June. There they found the Luftwaffe were flying night operations, so the raiding party had to postpone their attack until the following evening. Breaking into the airfield during an air raid while it was being attacked by RAF bombers, they destroyed about 20 Ju 88 transport aircraft with Lewes bombs. All six of the sabotage party escaped but the group was betrayed by some of the local inhabitants who took them in, one of the Free French commandos being killed and three captured. However, after evading the trap, Jellicoe managed to reach Egypt with the only other surviving member of the team.

The outcome of all the covert raids by the Special Boat Squadron and Special Air Service was 12 German soldiers killed, 25 aircraft destroyed, with many more planes damaged. In a savage reprisal, the Germans executed 50 local people in Heraklion the next day. For Niethammer the consequence of the raids was that the danger associated with his bird survey had increased considerably, any help from the local population now being completely out of the question. So, at the peak of the bird breeding season, Niethammer's party had to stay together rather than split up due to the worsening security situation. This meant that to his frustration he had to scale back some of his plans for surveying the more remote parts of the island.

As well as the publication of Niethammer's paper on the birdlife of Auschwitz, the year 1942 also saw the publication of the third and final volume of the *Handbuch der Deutschen Vogelkunde*. The handbook was 568 pages long and it came with 32 illustrations and a single colour plate (the use of colour at this stage in the war being highly unusual and showing the importance attached to the handbook). Again, produced on behalf of the German Ornithological Society by the academic publishing company in Leipzig, it retailed at a price of 18 reichsmarks. The book featured contributions from a range of German ornithologists including Kummerlöwe and Stresemann, Niethammer stating in the introduction that the book covered most of the new 'Greater Germany' and he was currently employed with the Waffen-SS. Like the previous two volumes it received very good reviews, Stresemann stating in a leading German ornithological journal:

> The 3rd volume of the 'Handbook' has been much awaited by all ornithologists and is published in the same good format as Volumes 1 and 2 despite the war. It contains the petrels, grebes, loons, pigeons, sandgrouse, auks, waders, gulls, bustards, cranes, rails and gallinaceous birds. The format of the 3rd volume is the same as that of the earlier volumes. An addendum to Volume 1 and 2 takes into account new developments, likewise one in Volume 3 has the misprint and corrections noted for Volumes 1 and 2. The quality of the new book is as good as the others: Volume 3 is in every way worthy of his two predecessors, so that there is now a work totaling three volumes which is excellent value to anyone who is interested in birds and an indispensable tool for the more serious ornithologist. No ornithological reference library should be without a copy, it is a reliable and quick way for anyone who wants to find the best way to promote German cooperation on ornithology and provides information on all the important questions, so far as this is possible within the framework of a 'Handbook'.

As Niethammer was carrying out his survey he received a telegram with the welcome news that the author of the review and his great mentor Erwin Stresemann, the esteemed curator of the Ornithological Department in the Museum of Natural History in Berlin, was going to join him in Crete. Following the German occupation of the island he had successfully lobbied for a project to produce a film on the natural heritage of Crete with Dr. Horst Siewert (1902–1943) as the project leader. Siewert was well known for his outstanding wildlife photography, filmmaking and his scientific publications which included papers on several birds of prey, the great bustard and the rare black stork. He was also the founder and manager of a game reserve close to Joachimsthal in the Schorfheide municipality near Berlin where Hermann Göring had his palatial country residence, Carinhall (today a UNESCO biosphere reserve).

Stresemann, as well as being known by his contemporaries as the 'Pope of Ornithology', was also the best-connected ornithologist in Nazi Germany. He had given Niethammer his big break when he had commissioned him to write the *Handbuch der Deutschen Vogelkunde,* numerous other students also benefitting from his patronage and contacts. Like Niethammer his own relationship with the Nazi government had vacillated over time. Although at 49 he was too old for military service when war broke out in 1939, two years later he was called up and the scientific work of the museum ground to a halt. As a reserve lieutenant in the Luftwaffe, he was employed as an adjutant or military support officer and a staff writer at the Luftwaffe's headquarters, the Reichsluftfahrtministerium in Berlin. This position had brought him into contact again with Göring and other high-ranking Nazis. So, when he heard about Wettstein's expedition to Crete, he had submitted the project proposal to make a natural history film about the island which had been rubber-stamped. Stresemann, however, had not always enjoyed such a close relationship with the regime. When Hitler had been elected, he had opposed the Nazis and in 1934 wrote to a close friend in New York:

> The state no longer serves the wellbeing of the individual, but the individual is there to safeguard the structure of the state and has to act in a manner that the leadership thinks fit. For people who have always striven for the development of personal individuality and see the decline of higher culture in the oppression of the tolerance of the educated classes, the change signifies a catastrophe; and like me the vast majority of scientists, artists and industrialists condemn it ... There is actually no point in inwardly opposing this development, which can no longer be halted and affects everyone, but I cannot help standing grief stricken by the ruins of an incomparably happier past for those of our education. ... Through this exaggerated antisemitism we have raised the world's opinion against us; ... It could be that this enables us to form alliances – but the thought that war could be again on the agenda is a horror for all those who experienced 1914–1918. You can hardly imagine how they 'moan' about it in our circles, but one has to be very

> careful, for the secret surveillance (in particular by low-level officials) is as well organised as today's Soviet State.[2]

Just like his protégé Niethammer, Stresemann also had a monumental work on avian biology published regularly from 1914 until 1934, simply called *Aves* or *Birds*, part of the prestigious *Handbuch der Zoologie*. In 1934 it ran to over 900 pages and had glowing reviews. At the university where he taught a diverse range of pupils, as the Nazis' grip on academia took hold, he became increasingly shocked by the changing political mood, in particular the rise of antisemitism on the campus and the number of his post-graduate and doctoral students who turned up in military uniforms. On one field trip north-west of Berlin Stresemann and his students came across a preventive detention camp (a forerunner of the concentration camps) run by the Sturmabteilung or SA. Unsure what it was, Stresemann confronted the armed guards and asked if he could see around. At gunpoint he found himself taken inside and interrogated, only returning to the university two days later.

Despite his views of Nazism, Stresemann still represented the German government at a very successful 8th International Ornithological Congress held in Oxford, England, that year, where as president he organised the event with the English secretary, the Reverend Francis Jourdain (1865–1940), a notable ornithologist and zoologist. One participant, Rolf Nohrig, who observed Stresemann in action with ornithologists of both genders, wrote that the event

> moved Stresemann to the forefront of the scientific attention of a large international circle and displayed his special social skills even to strangers. Extremely well dressed, even for the England of those days, a monocle in his right eye, brilliant and cheerful, witty and ironic, a wonderful dancer, surrounded by the attention of beautiful women, to which he responded gladly, he was an extraordinary President of the International Ornithological Congress and it would be hard to emulate in his perfection.[3]

Stresemann also went on much longer field trips, completing a five-month sojourn to the United States where he was offered a senior position at Yale University but turned it down. The Nazi regime now sought to seduce him, Hermann Göring himself offering Stresemann a role as the official Expert Advisor to the Reich Forestry Office (a position which much to Stresemann's delight included nature conservation). He was also given the title of 'Reich Hunting Councillor' and tasked with helping to organise an international exhibition of game hunting in Berlin. Seduced, when the Sudeten crisis brought the world to the brink of war in 1938, he welcomed the annexation believing it would pave the way for peace and new birdwatching expeditions.

At the end of August 1939 Stresemann was delighted to receive a large number of bird skins from the ornithologist Dr Ernst Schäfer (1910–1992) who had just returned from a very high-level expedition to Tibet or 'The Roof of the World'.[4] Soon afterwards the bird skins were deposited with the Berlin Natural History Museum who had enthusiastically supported the trip, he declaring them a very important contribution to the collection. Stresemann like the rest of the population could now see that war was all but inevitable, he commenting in a letter to a friend, 'the situation appears to be very uneasy and to quote the words of Wilhelm Busch "some are creeping around and looking depressed".' Concerned that he would be drafted into the armed forces despite his age, he was also worried about what that would mean for the museum in his absence. However, after war broke out the following month the success of the German Blitzkrieg and the easy victories soon convinced him that Germany was going to win the war and with it, exciting scientific expeditions would be required to catalogue the newly conquered territories.

After the signing of the German–Soviet pact which carved up Poland, Stresemann contacted leading ornithologists in Russia with a view to publishing another even more ambitious book, the *Atlas der Verbrietung Palaakitsher Vogel* or *Atlas of the Distribution of Palaearctic Birds*. In another letter to a friend, he heaped praise on German military might, writing, 'It is an exemplary triumph of our military traditions and our superior leadership.' Following the swift victories in the West, Stresemann watched awestruck as the Blitzkrieg was turned against the Soviet Union, writing on 15 November 1941 at the height of German success, 'And then I look again spellbound at this little spot of Germany, which has set this huge world in motion and dared to reshape it, and feel my share of the responsibility for the success of this gigantic objective.' Despite his support for the war, he still tried to assist a Russian ornithologist who was captured by the advancing Germans and wrote to him asking for help.

So, when the opportunity arose to follow in the footsteps of Wettstein and Niethammer in visiting Crete, Stresemann jumped at the chance and made sure that his project got given the go-ahead by the German high command. He made his first recce of the island in 1941 just after it fell to the Germans and returned there in July 1942, just ahead of Siewert who began filming in August, starting with the extremely rare wild bezoar goats in the Lefka Ori Mountains. Stresemann had received permission and the funding for a two-month shoot from the commander of Crete, Alexander Andrae (1888–1979), and discussed the project with both Wettstein and Niethammer whose breeding bird survey had just finished. He also made sure that he got on the good side of the commander by taking him and his senior officers on a duck shoot.

Siewert then spent six weeks from mid-October to the end of November in a tent camp with hides high up in the mountains where he stayed, a few hours' steep climb from the nearest village of Samaria. This 'high camp' stood on a broad rocky outcrop at the foot of a very steep rock face, 1,100 metres high, that golden eagles regularly passed by in search of prey. The camp was surrounded by sparse mountain forest composed of old Kermes oak bushes and Cretan cypresses. While filming Siewert was able to add extra species to Niethammer's bird list for the island, recording the first long-eared owl on 2 November 1942. He also found other notable animals including the first record of the edible dormouse, a total of twelve specimens being collected and the second only record of a wild cat.

The most important species that Stresemann and Siewert wanted to film was the globally threatened Eurasian black vulture, the species widely believed to be extinct on the island by the ornithological community. The earliest record from Crete of a black vulture dated back to 1843–1845 when the Hungarian zoologist Frivaldszky and his collectors saw the species near a snow-covered peak. The Austrian ornithologist Guido Schiebel (1881–1956) recorded thirty-five griffon vultures near a donkey carcass on 30 May 1925, just east of Heraklion, and among them was one large individual which he believed was a black vulture. However, there had been no sightings since, and it was widely believed that the species had disappeared from the island. Despite this Siewert was determined to find it and started his search of the most likely mountain locations based on historical records and the advice of Niethammer and the other Crete survey team. After weeks of searching, to Stresemann's delight he wrote that he had filmed six griffon vultures and two black vultures at carrion on 11 November 1942. Sadly on his return the film was not of a high-enough quality to identify the species. But for Stresemann, it was proof enough that the black vulture occurred on the island, he publishing another observation of two individuals together near Panagia on the island of Thasos on 4 April 1944. (After the war the records were questioned, the lack of evidence and the wartime conditions under which the film was made meaning that the black vulture wasn't included in any bird guides to Crete. However, in 1999 a small exhibition of Horst Siewert's work was opened in the East Prussian State Museum in Lüneburg, featuring pre-war wildlife photos, drawings and publications, salvaged from his parents' home after the war. Among the photographs in the collection was a slightly out of focus picture with five griffon vultures and one black vulture, this being the only verifiable record of the species on Crete.)

The German high command were so pleased with the initial rushes from the film that the shoot was extended until the end of the year and then into 1943. However, the next year tragedy struck on 20 June 1943 when Siewert had a heart attack when filming the bezoar goats and died at the scene (he had kept a detailed diary of the expedition which together with his notes on filming was published by Stresemann in the project report and formed part of the exhibition on his life in 1999). After Siewert's death, Stresemann arranged for Heinz Sielmann (1917–2006), the renowned German wildlife filmmaker, to complete the film. As part of his research, he visited the reserve at Joachimsthal near Berlin where Siewert's records were kept at his parents' house. When finally finished, the film was widely shown in German cinemas and army camps across Crete where it was highly praised.

Following the film being completed the bird skins from both Niethammer's survey and the film together with other animal specimens were sent to the museum in Berlin for Stresemann to study on his return. Stresemann also published his own paper focusing on the migratory and wintering birds of the island, listing twelve new species out of a total of 200 and citing Niethammer (who had mainly surveyed breeding birds). He dedicated it to the late memory of Dr. Horst Siewert, bemoaning the fact he was only 40 when he died and generously made him the principal author. Called 'Ueberblick über die Vögel Kretas und den Vogelzug in der Aegaeisor' or 'Overview of the birds of Crete and the bird migration in the Aegean', it ran to 16 pages and was published in the prestigious *Journal für Ornithologie* in October 1943.[5]

Chapter 9

Prisoners of War

WHAT WAS TRULY remarkably about Stresemann's Crete paper was not just the birds it listed but the contributors. Listed among the German troops serving on the island and Stresemann's fellow ornithologists was a soldier called George Waterston (1911–1980), a second lieutenant in the Royal Artillery. He had fought against the Germans in the Battle of Crete and after being captured was then imprisoned securely behind barbed wire. His inclusion as a serving prisoner of war was therefore nothing short of extraordinary. In the paper before the list of birds Stresemann had recorded on the island, he had surreptitiously incorporated him into the acknowledgements, writing:

> I welcome some notes from Colonel Seer, who had been deployed in Crete since the summer of 1941. Lt. G Waterston kindly let me include the ornithological observations he made in the spring of 1941 on Crete (on the south side of Suda Bay).

Waterston was incarcerated in the camp Oflag or *Offizierslager* (officer camp) VII-B, located in Eichstätt, Bavaria, in southern Germany where his prison number was 3695. There he had befriended three other prisoners who shared his passion for birds and had also found themselves in captivity, each being interned in a succession of POW camps across Germany before ending up at Oflag VII-B. Edward Buxton (1912–1989) was a second lieutenant and an intelligence officer with 1st Independent Company (later to become the 1st Commandos) who had been captured in Norway in 1940. Peter Conder (1919–1993) was also a second lieutenant with the Royal Corps of Signals who had been captured following the fall of France in the same year. The last of the trio, John Barrett (1913–1999), was a pilot and squadron leader with Bomber Command who had been shot down on a raid over Germany and captured. The four prisoners together had formed a truly remarkable bird club behind barbed wire which they used to while away the time and survive the squalor, brutality and stupefying boredom of the camp.

Waterston was born in Edinburgh on 10 April 1911, the eldest of seven children, his father being director of George Waterston & Sons, a long-established family firm of printers and stationers in the city. The firm dated back to 1752 when it made sealing wax and over the intervening years had become so well thought of that it was given the prestigious honour of printing the Scottish pound note. Waterston was fascinated by birds from an early age and soon began making lists of the species he had seen. As a teenager he collected eggs and kept them in immaculate moss-lined drawers in a cabinet in his bedroom. He also set up his own birdwatching club with some friends which would eventually become the Midlothian Ornithological Club. Had it not been for the war, Waterston's hobby may well have stayed confined to birding sites near his Scottish home.

Waterston's destiny was always to enter the family firm and after attending Edinburgh Academy he joined them as a junior partner. This gave him both the financial security and more importantly the freedom he craved to pursue his favourite hobby, ornithology. However, despite his obvious wealth and privilege, Waterston suffered his whole life from a kidney condition and was frequently very ill but he never let it limit his birdwatching or his collecting. He took many of his specimens to the Royal Scottish Museum where he was befriended by an elderly retired surgeon and Rear Admiral called John H. Stenhouse, the keeper of the natural history section.

Stenhouse was impressed with the knowledge and enthusiasm of the young ornithologist and took him under his wing. In his spare time Stenhouse was a regular visitor to Fair Isle, the remote island between Shetland and Orkney where he studied birds which used the island as a staging post – by shooting them. Stenhouse showed Waterston many of the bird skins he had collected there, the younger man making a mental note of the island's potential to become a centre for ornithology. Closer to home he also became involved in helping set up and run a bird observatory on the Isle of May. Anchored in the Firth of Forth, the island was a magical but noisy mix of seabirds, seals and smuggling, the cliffs literally heaving with nesting seabirds in early summer. In 1934 the Isle of May became Scotland's first bird observatory, funded by Waterston and other generous benefactors.

A couple of years later Waterston helped to set up the Scottish Ornithologists' Club and became one of the driving forces behind Scottish ornithology. He also undertook expeditions abroad, in 1937 visiting Finnish Lapland where after unwittingly straying across the Russian border he found himself arrested. Incarcerated and then interrogated by a Soviet intelligence officer, his explanation that he was on a birdwatching expedition was treated with scepticism. During his days in captivity, he whiled away the time observing a pair of red-throated pipits just outside the jail until he was eventually released. In the years leading up to the war much of his time and effort was spent visiting Fair Isle, a place that would become a second home to him and eventually dominate his life. Inspired by tales from his time with Stenhouse, he visited the remote island every summer with the aim of setting up an observatory on the island, like the one on the Isle of May. On these trips he would carefully record all the species he saw, like Niethammer doing his survey work with a gun in one hand and a pair of binoculars in the other.

When war broke out Waterston volunteered for the Territorial Army and was assigned to the Royal Artillery. To his great joy in 1940 he found himself stationed on an island in the Firth of Forth, manning the gun emplacements in case of invasion. For Waterston it was an ideal posting as he could record the bird species he saw flying past, unlike most of his fellow recruits who were bored silly by the long hours spent keeping watch. In January he was delighted to find an exhausted little auk washed up on the shore and in July he shot a whimbrel which he had great pleasure in eating. The next year his luck changed, although he didn't know it at the time, when he found himself on a troopship bound for Crete.

To Waterston the island held out the opportunity of discovering lots of new Mediterranean species, a prospect he relished. After landing there in the spring he was assigned to a coastal battery east of the city of Chania and again to his delight found he had ample time to sea watch, keeping an eye out for both enemy vessels and birds. He recorded all the species he saw in a notebook, sarcastically writing SECRET on the cover in case it fell into enemy hands. The first species he saw was a Sardinian warbler in the scrub by the gun emplacement on 20 April and the last entry in the notebook was made on 10 May when he saw a woodchat shrike. Days later hundreds of elite German *Fallschirmjäger* parachuted from the sky and Waterston soon found his battery isolated and then overrun. Out of ammunition they abandoned the gun and headed further along the coast where they came across other British soldiers who after bloody fighting were waiting to be being evacuated. However, there was no room for Waterston or many of the other troops in the few boats available and he was left behind to take his chances. After days on the run without adequate water, marching under the baking hot Cretan sun took its toll and he contracted cholera and suffered from acute dysentery. By the time he was captured on 1 June Waterston was a very ill man incapable of putting up any resistance.

After time spent recovering in hospital Waterston then found himself in a series of prisoner of war camps before ending up with Buxton, Conder and Barrett in Oflag. VII-B. For the four soldiers birdwatching soon became more than a way of whiling away the days, it became a lifeline for surviving the ordeal. In a previous camp Buxton had been sent a copy of Niethammer's *Handbook of German Ornithology* by a fellow Swiss ornithologist and this became their bible, each of the soldiers consulting it whenever they found a bird. Seeing Stresemann's name as the joint author of the book, Buxton remembered they had met at the 8th International Ornithological Congress at Skokholm in 1934. Although it was a very long shot Buxton decided to write to him, courtesy of the *Deutsche Ornithologische Gesellschaft* in Berlin. Well aware that the congress had happened eight years earlier and been attended by hundreds of ornithologists, Buxton knew it was a tenuous link but felt he had nothing to lose. Getting permission from the camp commandant to write, Buxton sent off his letter to Stresemann reminding him of the happy time they had spent together before the war and asking for books, journals and bird rings. After passing through the camp censor the audacious letter was delivered to a surprised Stresemann who although he could not recall Buxton, decided to start a correspondence with him and Waterston (he later said he remembered several Buxtons but could not place John). After all war or no war, they were all fellow birdwatchers.

Soon the three men were regularly exchanging bird notes and news, in one letter Stresemann telling them about the invasion of the collared dove across Europe bringing with it new and exciting ornithological opportunities (a barely disguised metaphor for the German Blitzkrieg and the conquered territories). In another letter not long after the invasion of Russia he wrote, 'We had a most successful meeting of the Deutsche Ornithologische Gesellschaft a month ago, attended by about 140 members and many guests. It lasted three successive days (including an excursion to see birds of prey).' In turn the prisoners told him about the birds they had seen around the camp and that they were all members of the British Ornithologists' Union (founded in 1858, the BOU is one of the world's oldest ornithological organisations with an international membership stretching across the globe. It also maintains the British list, the official list of all the birds seen in Britain). The exchanges, although purely about ornithological matters, were not without considerable risk, both to the prisoners and to Stresemann, as the correspondence had to pass through the camp censor and any suspect letters were immediately sent to the Gestapo. Despite this they continued to write to each other, Stresemann also sending them bird rings and back copies of the *Journal für Ornithologie* which he edited.

In late 1942 Stresemann wrote a letter about his time on Crete and some of the birds he had seen on the island. In his reply Waterston told the German ornithologist that he had also been on the island during the invasion and included with the letter the bird sightings he had written down in his 'secret' notebook. On 2 August 1943 Stresemann wrote back on Deutsche Ornithologische Gesellschaft headed paper, addressing it to 'Lieut. George Waterston, British Prisoner of War, Nr. 3695, Oflag. VII B, Eichstätt:

> Dear Sir
> I have been greatly surprised by getting your Notes on the birds of Crete together with your interesting letter. Until now I had no idea that in present times our ornithological journals, the *Journal für Ornithologie, Ornithologische Monatsberichte and Vogelug*, would be of some use to Members of the B.O.U.
>
> Your list looks rather complete considering the districts in which your observations have been made, and some of your records are certainly worth publishing. Emberisa hortulana [Ortolan bunting] on 25.3 looks extremly [sic] early. In 1942 and 1943 the birds of Crete had been studied by several German ornithologists, who also did some collecting, and a first report by Dr. Niethammer will soon be out in print. One of our best-known bird photographers, Horst Siewert, has made a marvellous film on Birdlife in the White Mountains, including Lammergeier and Griffon Vultur [sic], which I hope you and your comrades will be able to see one day.

> I have not seen the *Journal of Animal Ecology* since 1939, and therefore did miss your paper on the Fulmar. Neither had I any opportunity of reading Mr. John Buxton's paper on the Oystercatcher publ. late in 1939. Ornithologists will have a hard time after the war if they want to read all the important stuff published in the meantime, across the water. Have you seen my review of Herr Ruiter's paper on the breeding biology of the Redstart? I wish you could add to this [one of Waterston's fellow POWs John Buxton studied the redstart while imprisoned and after the war used the observations in his New Naturalist monograph *The Redstart* published in 1950].
>
> I shall try to send you a copy of the *Ibis* [journal of the BOU] for Jan. 1939 hoping that you may be able to return ist [sic] before long to the library of the Deutsche Ornithologische Gesellschaft. It's our only copy, you know. The *Ibis* for 1940 ist [sic] not represented in any of our libraries; I saw it at the Paris Museum.
>
> It would be very nice if we could remain in touch with [one] another. With my best wishes
>
> Yours sincerely
> Erwin Stresemann[1]

As a result of their correspondence and exchange of bird records, Waterston was able to make the unique boast that he was the only serving British soldier to contribute to a German scientific paper in wartime (it was a boast that he would continue to dine out on for years after the war). His fame even spread to featuring in *The Prisoner of War*, the official journal of the prisoner of war department of the Red Cross and St. John War Organisation based in St. James's Palace in London. Delivered free to the next of kin of all prisoners, the December 1943 issue featured an article called 'Their Country Life – and Interests Carry on in Spite of Captivity in a Foreign Land'. It started:

> Surprising as it may be to many of us, the pleasures of a nature lover are not necessarily denied him when he enters a German prison camp. Birdwatching, bee-keeping, the study of wildlife in general – these, we might suppose, are

> solitary country pursuits for the leisure hours of a free man, for which no place or privacy could be found in the life of a prisoner of war. And yet, somehow, in spite of everything, he does manage to fit them in – and in a way, too, that gives pleasure at the same time to more of his neighbours than might ever be possible at home.

Although it did not name him or any of the other prisoners, the article went on to give details of the birdwatching group at Oflag. VII-B. It stated:

> Here, for instance, is an account from an enthusiast of a systematic birdwatching group at Oflag VIIB, where 'we have at least two really good ornithologists and many keen amateurs'. Bird boxes have been placed in most trees and every week a detailed list is posted up, telling of all new birds seen in the camp, whether residents or casual visitors, etc., and on a large map is shown where they spend their winter months. From dawn to dusk every day all nests in the camp are under observation and detailed daily reports are kept. For instance, the time the female arrived at the nest; length of time there; number of times mate fed her whilst she was sitting, etc.; time first egg was hatched: number of times young were fed, and all that sort of thing. Mirrors on the end of sticks are used to enable us to look into nests. All birds in this camp seem to be far more tame than any wild birds in England – especially swallows. One nest of swallows on a beam in the hospital collapsed when the two parent birds tried to feed their young together. Despite their fall to the ground, the half-grown young were not hurt. Later a nest was made for them in a round milk tin which was wired to the beam. The parents watched all this with great interest and then carried on as usual. [The article also inspired 'The Forger' character in the 1963 film *The Great Escape* called Colin Blythe played by Donald Pleasance (1919–1995). In it, Blythe gives an ornithology lecture to some of the men, whistling the song of a warbler and showing them how to draw the masked shrike, as cover for their escape activities.]

Not long after the newsletter came out Stresemann received a visit from the Gestapo, unhappy with his correspondence in English with British prisoners of war following a tip-off. Due to the changing wartime situation, the German ornithologist sensibly deciding that it was not a good idea to continue it.

After his bird survey on Crete was over, Niethammer and the other members of the team had to return to operational duty. For Niethammer as a member of the Waffen-SS that meant returning to being a camp guard at the notorious Auschwitz concentration camp. Following spending over three months employed on the island of Crete, it must have been very difficult to go back to a place that had haunted him and from which he had spent so long trying to leave. However, the camp commandant Höß was keen to have him back as during his absence the camp had expanded massively, and he was short of good guards. In the intervening eight months Niethammer had been away, Auschwitz had been transformed from being a concentration camp holding hundreds of prisoners to an extermination camp 'processing' thousands of people, including for the first time large numbers of Jews.

Chapter 10

The Final Solution

NIETHAMMER ARRIVED BACK at the camp in September 1942 as the autumn leaves were turning bronze, red and gold in the 'cottage' orchard and the trees surrounding the camp. During his time away both the political and the camp landscape had changed beyond recognition. In January 1942 at the Wannsee Conference in Berlin the SS and representatives of the German government ministries had agreed on the 'Final Solution', the infamous Nazi plan to kill the 11 million Jews in Europe by deporting them using trains to the extermination camps in occupied Poland and other conquered territories. The plan was coordinated by SS General Reinhard Heydrich, the chief of the Reich Security Main Office and the representative of Reichsführer-SS chief Heinrich Himmler. He said:

> during the course of the Final Solution, the Jews will be deployed under appropriate supervision at a suitable form of labor deployment in the East. In large labor columns, separated by gender, able-bodied Jews will be brought to those regions to build roads, whereby a large number will doubtlessly be lost through natural reduction. Any final remnant that survives will doubtless consist of the elements most capable of resistance. They must be dealt with appropriately, since, representing the fruit of natural selection, they are to be regarded as the core of a new Jewish revival.[1]

The beginning of the mass extermination of Jews at Auschwitz had started in earnest in January 1942, just weeks after Niethammer had left the camp. On 1 March the Inspectorate of Concentration Camps had officially opened the second camp at Auschwitz, known as Auschwitz II-Birkenau or Auschwitz II, to 'process' the Jews. That month 69,000 Jews from France and 27,000 Jews from Slovakia had arrived at the camp, the first mass transports. They were followed on 26 March by the first 2,000 women prisoners (out of 130,000 who 'lived in' the camp during its existence). May saw the start of the deportation to Auschwitz of over 300,000 Jews from Poland and 23,000 Jews from Germany and Austria. In response that spring the infamous so-called *Judenrampe*, located between Auschwitz I and Auschwitz II-Birkenau, was built. It was here that the transports by rail to the camp arrived containing Jews, as well as Poles, Russians, Romanies (gypsies), homosexuals and other prisoners for 'processing'.

At the new camp Auschwitz II-Birkenau temporary gas chambers had been put into operation and on 4 May the SS had carried out the first selection of prisoners to be murdered there. The original gas chambers were housed in a specially adapted farmhouse whose owner had been expelled at gun point. The house stood outside the fence of the Birkenau camp, Höß and Adolf Eichmann, the Reich Security Main Office representative in charge of deportation, selecting the location together during a visit. Eichmann was head of the Jewish section IV B4 in the Reich Security Main Office and had been tasked by Himmler with carrying out the Final Solution.'I myself first got to know him after I had received from the Reichsführer-SS the orders for the destruction of the Jews,' recalled Höß, 'when he visited me at Auschwitz to discuss the exact details of the extermination process.' The adaptation work involved partially walling up the windows, sealing the house and knocking down the interior walls. Two barracks for undressing were also erected nearby. According to Höß, about 800 people at a time could be killed in the house, the commandant being impressed with Eichmann's knowledge, commenting he was 'a vivacious, active man in his thirties, and always full of energy. He was constantly hatching new ideas and perpetually on the lookout for innovations and improvements. He could never rest. He was obsessed with the Jewish question and the order which had been given for its final solution.'

Both Höß and Eichmann agreed that the converted farmhouse was not large enough to exterminate the number of Jews arriving at the camp so to increase the number who could be processed together they 'hatched a new idea' to construct four much larger gas chambers and crematoria at Birkenau.

Where Höß and Eichmann differed was on whether 'able-bodied' Jews should be selected for work or exterminated in the gas chambers, Höß commenting:

> Eichmann was also a determined opponent of the idea of selecting from the transports Jews who were fit for work. He regarded it as a constant danger to his scheme for a 'final solution', because of the possibility of mass escapes or some other event occurring which would enable the Jews to survive. In his view action should be taken against every Jew that could be got hold of, and such actions ought to be pursued to their conclusion as quickly as possible, since it was impossible to anticipate the final result of the war [of the estimated 1.3 million people sent to Auschwitz, more than 1.1 million died at the camp, mostly Jews].[2]

Of the 10,000 Russian prisoners who Niethammer had watched build the camp at Auschwitz II-Birkenau the previous year, by the summer of 1942 only a few hundred were still left alive. Höß commented, 'They arrived from the military prisoner-of-war camp at Lamsdorf in Upper Silesia and were in very poor condition. They reached the camp after many weeks marching. They had been given hardly any food on the march, during halts on the way being simply turned out into the nearest fields and there told to "graze" like cattle on anything edible they could find.' However, on arrival at the camp they were treated even more brutally as communist enemies of the state. Most of them died from typhus, undernourishment and overwork. Höß wrote:

> They were willing to work but were incapable of doing so because of their weakened condition. I remember very clearly how we were continually giving them food when first they arrived at the base camp but in vain. Their weakened bodies could no longer function. Their whole constitution was finished and done for. They died like flies from general physical exhaustion, or from the most trifling maladies which their debilitated constitutions could no longer resist.

Such was their hunger that cases of cannibalism were not uncommon, Höß coming across a Russian prisoner lying dead between piles of bricks at Birkenau whose body had been ripped open and the liver removed. Another prisoner saw someone scavenging in the bottom of an empty food bucket and pushed him on to the electrified fence before running off with the food. 'They had become animals,' reflected Höß, 'who sought only food.'

As a result of their treatment, in June, there was a mutiny among the remaining prisoners and a mass breakout from the camp at Birkenau. Some of the Russian prisoners had learnt that their fellow prisoners had been gassed and fearing they were all going to die, they had fled. The guards panicked and opened fire, killing over 300 prisoners. 'A great many of them were shot,' wrote Höß, 'but many managed to get clear away [in fact only seven escaped]. ... Those who were recaptured gave as a reason for this mass escape their fear that they were to be gassed, for they had been told that they were to be transferred to a newly built sector of the camp.' In response the Nazis took elaborate measures to make sure that in future prisoners were not aware of their fate.

In July 1942 while Niethammer was busy surveying birds on Crete, Himmler had made his second and last visit to Auschwitz. The inspection had lasted two days and he was again accompanied by Gauleiter (Regional Leader) Fritz Bracht, SS-Obergruppenführer Ernst-Heinrich Schmauser, the Police Leader in Breslau, and Dr Hans Kammler (1901–1945?), an *SS-Obergruppenführer* responsible for Nazi civil engineering projects who was in charge of the construction of the concentration camps (he was later put in charge of the V-2 rocket and jet programmes). Following Himmler's arrival, the party went to the SS officers' mess where Höß with the aid of maps showed how much of the new camp had been constructed. Afterwards they visited the architect's office where Kammler showed the Reichsführer-SS what the final camp would look like with the aid of construction drawings and models. Both men also outlined the huge logistical challenges involved in delivering such an ambitious construction project within the timescale specified by Himmler who, like on his previous visit, remained unmoved by their protestations.

'Himmler listened with interest, enquired about some technical details and expressed agreement with the scheme as a whole,' Höß recalled, 'but he showed no concern over the difficulties which Kammler had repeatedly brought to his notice.' After the meeting Himmler toured the site, firstly inspecting progress with the agricultural research station at the village of Raisko, then he toured the construction site at Birkenau, visiting the Russian, Romani and Jewish quarters. He then climbed the gate tower, where Niethammer kept watch, to get a bird's-eye view of the camp, to see the land drainage works which had taken place so the buildings could be constructed. Himmler then watched the prisoners at work building the new camp and toured the inmates' accommodation, kitchen and hospital. Recalled Höß:

> He saw the emaciated victims of disease (the causes of which were bluntly explained by the doctor), he saw the crowded hospital block, he learnt of the mortality among the children in the gypsy camp, and he saw children there suffering from the terrible disease called Noma [gangrene of the face and mouth, Noma occurred in malnourished children debilitated by other diseases. The mortality rate was very high, survivors being left with severe facial deformities]. ... He also saw the overcrowded huts and the primitive and insufficient latrines and wash houses. The doctors told him about the high rate of sickness and death and, above all, the reasons for it.

Throughout it all Himmler remained completely dispassionate and silent. However, back at the camp he furiously told Höß and Kammler that they were in charge and needed to take responsibility for the conditions. 'I want to hear no more difficulties,' he yelled. 'An SS officer does not recognise difficulties; when they arise, his task is to remove them at once by his own efforts! How this is to be done is your worry, not mine!'

Following the inspection of the camp at Birkenau Himmler met one of the transports of Jews which had just arrived at the Judenrampe and watched as the able-bodied prisoners were separated from those who were destined to go directly to the gas chambers. He then watched as about 400 Jews were led at gunpoint to the adapted farmhouse at the new camp, forced to undress and then gassed with Zyklon B after being told they were going for a shower. Himmler again looked on in silence, paying particular attention not to the suffering of the prisoners but to how the officers and guards managed the process. Afterwards he toured the IG Farben rubber factory which contained the pick of the prisoners and where conditions and rations were generally more favourable than in the main camp. Turning to Höß and Kammler he said, 'You complain about difficulties but look at what IG Farben Industrie have done in one year, and under similar difficulties!' Asking the head of the company how efficient the camp workers were, many of whom had been specially chosen because of their skills, he received an evasive reply. So, a seething Himmler told Höß to make sure they worked harder, even though rations had been cut on his orders due to the huge number of prisoners arriving daily at the camp.

From the synthetic rubber factory Himmler then went to the camp sewage treatment works which due to a lack of materials had not been completed. As a result, raw effluent was being discharged directly into the Soła river . 'It was one of the worst spots in Auschwitz,' noted Höß, 'and it affected everyone. The drainage water from the base camp was discharged, without any purification worth mentioning, directly into the Soła. The population was constantly exposed to the danger of infection, because of the diseases which were always rampant in the camp.' The effluent had also killed much of the wildlife for over a quarter of a mile down the river, dead fish floating to the surface due to lack of oxygen and a thick, toxic scum forming at the margins and oxbows in the river. Bracht pointed out the impact that the pollution was having both on the prisoners and the population downstream and asked for urgent assistance but Himmler was again uninterested, stating matter of factly that 'Kammler will apply all his energies to the problem.'

After the sewage works, Himmler visited the horticulture and rubber plantation at the village of Raisko. Here he inspected the vegetables and flowers grown in greenhouses for the SS, visited the shop selling the produce and toured the agricultural experimental station where they cultivated the plant Taraxacum kok-saghyzot to produce the rubber. Impressed with the station, his mood lightened, Höß noting that he 'always found it more interesting and more pleasant to hear positives rather than negatives. The SS officer counted himself lucky and enviable, who had only positives to report, or who was skilful enough to represent negatives as positives!' That evening a special dinner was laid on for the Reichsführer-SS, Höß inviting all the officers at the camp under his command. They were all introduced individually to Himmler and if they interested him, he enquired in a perfunctory way about their work and family. Over the dinner, which included wild game shot at the camp and vegetables grown in the greenhouses (Himmler was vegetarian so a special meal was prepared for him), he quizzed Höß about his officers and which ones showed potential. 'I seized the opportunity to tell him about the troubles I had with my staff and how many of the officers were completely unfit to serve in a concentration camp or to command troops,' stated Höß. 'I begged him to give me some replacements and to increase the strength of the guards.' Himmler was again dismissive:

> You will be amazed at the impossible officer material with which we will have to be satisfied in the end! I need every officer, junior officer and man, who is capable of serving in the front line. For the same reasons it is impossible to increase the strength of the guard. You will have to think up some technical ways of economising in guards.

Himmler's suggestion to make up the shortfall in guards was to use dogs, telling Höß that he would get one of his experts in dog handling to show him how the animals could be used to control prisoners. The guards already used German shepherd dogs to patrol the grounds and to control the prisoners at the Judenrampe but following Himmler's order their use expanded, the dogs being taught to terrify the prisoners and to attack on command. (Many of the guards had their own dogs including the infamous female camp guard Irma Grese [1923–1945] who came to Auschwitz in March 1943 and used two huge German shepherds as part of her brutal reign in the Birkenau women's camp. Survivors recall her riding around the camp on a bicycle with a dog on either side, accompanying the female inmates on their 16-kilometre march to work. If they couldn't keep up with the column, she ordered her dogs to attack them without mercy.) Following the breakout of Soviet prisoners the previous month, Himmler also made it plain that the number of escapes from the camp was unacceptably high. 'I approve of every means,' he berated Höß, 'I repeat every means, being used to prevent these escapes. This escape disease, which has become rampant in Auschwitz, must be eradicated!'

After the dinner party was over Himmler departed for Bracht's house in the nearby town of Kattowitz where he was staying that evening, Kammler and Höß accompanying him, Himmler also requesting that

Hedwig, Höß's wife, join them. There, away from the camp to Höß's surprise Himmler relaxed and became genial and talkative. 'Although during the day Himmler was occasionally very ill-humoured and angry and even downright unfriendly, yet this evening, and among this small company, he was a changed person,' recalled Höß. 'He was in the best of spirits, took a leading part in the conversation and was extremely amiable, especially toward the ladies, the Gauleiter's wife and my own wife.' Although he hardly ever drank or smoked, Himmler had a couple of glasses of red wine and a cigarette, the other guests emulating him. During the evening, he discussed the education of their children, the new buildings that would be built in Germania after the war, his favourite books and paintings, the development of the SS and his visits to the front with Hitler. However, Höß noted he avoided saying anything about the camp and ignored all attempts to cajole him into doing so. 'Everyone was under the spell of his good humour and lively conversation,' Höß said. 'I had never known him like that before.'

The next day Himmler's tour of the camp continued. He inspected the barracks at the original base and the kitchens, the workshops, the stables, the Kanada sorting warehouse, the equipment works or Deutsche Ausrüstungswerke, the butcher's shop, bakery, the timber yard and the troops supply depot. At each he made detailed enquiries as to their operation and how many prisoners were involved in running each operation. Among the buildings that Himmler toured was Niethammer's bird museum where he was given a personal tour by Höß. Here he looked at the exhibits with interest, noting the preserved skins of over a hundred species which had been shot in and around the camp. Höß explained about the project with pride and that the guard responsible had been given 'special duties' to carry it out and was now finishing off a bird tour on Crete. He also informed the Reichsführer-SS that Niethammer had written up the survey and it had been published as a scientific paper in the prestigious journal of the Natural History Museum in Vienna. Himmler nodded his approval, indicating that other camps should undertake similar surveys (the fact that many of the birds were now rare, because like the prisoners they had been shot, was lost on both men and Höß failed to point that Auschwitz, through its drainage of the land surrounding the new camp and its discharge of raw effluent into the Soła river, was slowly but surely destroying and poisoning their habitat).

Following his tour of the bird museum and other support functions Himmler asked to do an inspection of the women's camp. Here according to Höß he saw 'the cramped quarters, the insufficient latrine accommodation, and the deficient water supply, and he got the administrative officer to show him the stocks of clothing. Everywhere he saw the deficiencies. He had every detail of the rationing system and the extra allowances for the heavy workers explained to him.' Several women had been lined up for the Reichsführer-SS to inspect who had been charged with various crimes, mostly stealing or because of their religious views. To set an example to all the female prisoners, a woman accused of prostitution was brought before him for whipping. She was according to Höß, 'a prostitute who was continually breaking in and stealing whatever she could lay her hands on [in fact many of the women accused of prostitution were political or religious prisoners who were trying to survive, many driven to bartering for food or other comforts in return for sexual favours]'.

Permission had to be gained from Himmler to whip the woman, who after hearing about what she had been accused of, readily gave his consent. So, in front of the Reichsführer-SS, Höß, the other officers, guards and the assembled prisoners she was hauled in, turned around, had her prison top dragged up before she was handcuffed to the wall. The woman was then repeatedly stuck with a horse whip until she bled. Once the punishment was over, she was dragged from the room by the guards screaming in pain, her cries echoing around the women's camp. Himmler then turned his attention to the line-up of other women in the room, most being Polish. Each was forced by the guards to stand in front of him where he quizzed them on what they had done, the conditions in the camp and what work they had been employed doing. Any who refused to answer were whipped. On hearing their testimonies, a lucky few who were deemed 'hard workers' were released, Höß impressing on them how fortunate they were that the Reichsführer-SS was a compassionate man. This, like the whipping of the prostitute, was meant to send a clear signal to the other women in the camp.

Himmler was particularly taken by the female Jehovah's Witnesses in the line-up who displayed purple triangles on their prison clothes. Unlike Jews or the Sinti and Roma gypsies, Jehovah's Witnesses had the opportunity to escape persecution and being sent to a camp if they renounced their religious beliefs. Despite facing beatings, maltreatment and torture, many refused to give up their religion, Himmler perversely admiring them because of their fanatical faith despite having none himself. (Jehovah's Witnesses were subjected to intense persecution under the regime because they were unwilling to accept the authority of the state, refused to give the Nazi salute and were strongly opposed to the war as a matter of conscience. An estimated 1,400 Jehovah's Witnesses from Germany and other occupied countries died or were murdered in concentration camps, many hundreds also being killed for refusing to serve in the army.)

After the inspection of the women's camp, Himmler returned to Höß's office where he addressed his assembled entourage. 'I have now made a thorough inspection of Auschwitz. I have seen everything, and I have seen enough of the deficiencies and difficulties,' he told them uncompromisingly, adding:

> and I have heard enough of them from you. You will have to manage as best you can. We are now in the middle of a war, and we must learn to think in terms of war. The actions, which I have ordered the security police to carry out, will not be stopped under any circumstances, least of all because of the lack of accommodation and so on, which I have been shown. Eichmann's programme will continue to be carried out and will be intensified month on month. You must see to it that swift progress is made with the building of Birkenau.

He then gave explicit instructions that the gypsies in the camp were to be exterminated as were Jews who were unable to work. He also gave orders that a new armaments factory was to be built on the site and that the agricultural research was to be expanded as rapidly as possible in support of the German war effort.

When it came to the different categories of prisoner, Himmler chillingly told Höß:

> The gypsies are to be destroyed. The Jews who are unfit for work are to be destroyed with the same ruthlessness. Soon the labour camps at the armaments factories will absorb the first large contingents of able-bodied Jews, and that will give you some breathing space again. Armaments factories will also be built in Auschwitz camp, so prepare yourselves

> for that. Kammler will give you far-reaching support in matters connected with their construction. The agricultural experiments will be intensively pursued, for the results are urgently required.

With that Himmler brought the conversation to a close after having told Höß he was satisfied with the progress to date and thanking him for his service. To show his faith in his commandant he then promoted Höß to *Obersturmbannführer* or senior assault-unit leader, seven ranks below Himmler in the SS hierarchy, and equivalent to the military rank of *Oberstleutnant* or lieutenant colonel in the army (Eichmann had been promoted to *Obersturmbannführer* in 1940 prior to him being charged by Himmler with coordinating the Final Solution at the Wannsee Conference in January 1942).

After the meeting was over, Höß took Himmler to his house where he admired the furniture (much of it made of wood from local forests by prisoners in the workshops and some from the bones of the prisoners themselves) and then spent the remainder of the afternoon talking to Höß's wife Hedwig and playing with his four children. (Höß had a 12-year-old son Klaus who accompanied Niethammer on his game-shooting expeditions, 10- and 9-year-old daughters by the name of Heidetraud and Brigette and a young son, 5-year-old Hans-Jürgen. He was to have another daughter Annegret who would be born in Auschwitz on 7 November 1943.) Himmler also met one of the Jehovah's Witnesses from the camp whom Höß employed as a maid to keep his house clean and look after the children. Höß employed two women to do this who worked on a rota around the clock and were employed for more than three years. At first, he was afraid that they would try to indoctrinate the children but the women never spoke to his family about religion, Höß commenting that this was really remarkable, given their 'fanatical attitude'.

In contrast to the other prisoners female Jehovah's Witnesses were much in demand by all the SS officers and were nicknamed 'bible-bees' or 'bible-worms'. One of them worked for an SS officer and did everything he asked without needing to be told, but refused to touch his uniform, cap or boots or have anything to do with his military life. Most of them, however, worked the land including at the agricultural research station at Harmense and the other sub-camps where they worked with

Poles, Czechs, Ukranians and some Russians. 'Unfortunately, there were too few of them,' complained Höß:

> I have always regarded Jehovah's Witnesses as poor, misguided creatures, who were nevertheless happy in their own way. Despite their more or less fanatical attitude they were much in demand. They were employed as servants in the homes of SS-men with large families, the Waffen-SS clubhouse, and even in the SS officers' mess … They needed no supervision or guards. They were diligent and willing workers, for such was the will of Jehovah. Most of them were middle-aged German women but there were also a number of younger Dutch girls. My wife often said that she herself could not have seen to everything better than did these two women. The care that they bestowed on the children, both big and small, was particularly touching. The children loved them as though they were members of the family.

After spending time with his family and Jehovah's Witness maid, at the end of the afternoon Höß drove Himmler to the airport where he caught his flight to Berlin. 'So ended Himmler's great inspection of Auschwitz,' wrote Höß. 'He saw everything, knew what the ultimate results would be. Was his remark "Even I cannot help" intentional?'[3]

Himmler's visit was to have one important but unexpected consequence – it was to alert the Allies to what was really going on in the camp. The Polish resistance, which operated both outside and inside the camp, had been given a tip-off about his visit and following it their spies in the camp reported that he was present when about 400 Jews were murdered with Zyklon B gas in the converted farmstead or so-called Bunker no. 2 (two huts near Bunker I and three near Bunker 2 were erected so the victims could undress, the hut supporting Bunker 2 was the largest and could hold about 1,200 people). The information was conveyed to the Polish government-in-exile in London by Edward Schulte (1891-1966), a German industrialist and secret anti-Nazi, who wrote a detailed report of the visit based on the intelligence. This was one of the first pieces of eyewitness evidence from an authoritative German source about the extermination of Jews in the gas chambers of Auschwitz.

Chapter 11

Death Duties

FROM THE AUTUMN of 1940 the Allies had been regularly informed about the development of the camp and the building works that were happening there but had not got a detailed account of the extermination of the Jews in the gas chambers. They had received uncorroborated information that the killing of the Jews had begun the next year when a few hundred had been gassed in the sealed room at the barracks. However, Polish resistance reports stated that the extermination had started in earnest in January 1942 when transports had first arrived from across the country. 'The Jews from Upper Silesia [the region containing Auschwitz] were the first to be dealt with. These Jews were arrested by the Kattowitz Police Unit and taken in drafts by train to a siding on the west side of the Auschwitz–Dziedzice railway line where they were unloaded,' recalled Höß. 'So far as I can remember, these drafts never consisted of more than 1,000 prisoners.'

On the Judenrampe those destined to be exterminated were led away by the guards, those too ill to be taken to the gas chambers were separated and out of sight shot in the back of the head with a pistol. The long line of people were then led to the outbuildings near Bunker 2 and told to undress before being led to the 'rooms', as they were called by the guards, so they could be deloused. In the new camp at Birkenau there were five rooms in total, each being filled with prisoners at the same time, the gasproof doors then being securely sealed, and the contents of the gas canisters pumped into the rooms through special vents. After half an hour the doors were re-opened (there were two at either end of the room) and the bodies were taken out. Any gold teeth were removed from the corpses and the hair cut from the women. The bodies were then brought to the pits in small trolleys which ran on rails while the victim's clothes, gold teeth and hair were taken by lorry to the Kanada sorting office. Höß outlined the process:

> The whole operation, including assistance given during the undressing, the filling of the bunker, the emptying of the bunker, the removal of the corpses, as well as the preparation and filling up of the mass graves, was carried out by a special detachment of Jews, who were separately accommodated and who, in accordance with Eichmann's orders, were themselves liquidated after every big action.

One of the guards who arrived at Auschwitz in September 1942 along with Niethammer was Oskar Gröning (1921–2018). Although thirteen years younger than the German ornithologist, like Niethammer the 21-year-old soon found the camp to be an oppressive and brutal place hiding a very dark secret. Like all the new guards on reporting for duty he immediately witnessed the arrival of a transport at the Judenrampe. 'I was standing at the ramp,' he stated 'and my task was to be part of the group supervising the luggage from an incoming transport.'[1] He watched on in silence as the men were separated from the women and children, and the SS doctors then selected who was fit to work and who should be gassed immediately. 'Sick people were lifted on to lorries,' he recalled. 'Red Cross lorries – they always tried to create the impression that people had nothing to fear.' Gröning estimated that on the transport he saw arrive, 80 to 90 per cent were selected to be murdered at once, stating:

> This process [of selection] proceeded in a relatively orderly fashion but when it was over it was just like a fairground. There was a load of rubbish, and next to this rubbish were ill people, unable to walk, perhaps a child that had lost its mother, or perhaps during searching the train somebody had hidden – and these people were simply killed with a shot through the head. And the kind of way in which these people were treated brought me doubt and outrage. A child was simply pulled on the leg and thrown on a lorry … then when it cried like a sick chicken, they chucked it against the edge of the lorry. I couldn't understand that an SS man would take a child and throw its head against the side of a lorry … or kill them by shooting them and then throw them on a lorry like a sack of wheat.

Gröning went to complain to his superior officer and said he wanted to leave, stating, 'It's impossible, I can't work here anymore. If it is necessary to exterminate the Jews, then at least it should be done within a certain framework.' The officer listened to his complaints calmly, reminded him of the oath of allegiance he had sworn and told him to forget about leaving the camp. Gröning, traumatised by what he had witnessed, subsequently put in for a transfer which was refused. However, what seemed to offend Gröning was not the policy of murdering the Jews but how it was carried out. 'How do you feel when you're in Russia, here's a machine gun in front of you, and there's a battalion of Russians coming running towards you and you have to pull the trigger and shoot as many as possible?' he asked. 'I'm saying it on purpose like this because there's always behind you the fact that the Jews are enemies who come from the inside of Germany. The propaganda had for us such an effect that you assumed that to exterminate them was basically something that happened in war. And to that extent a feeling of sympathy or empathy didn't come up.' The relentless Nazi propaganda about the Jews being the sworn enemy of the state he had heard growing up had made Gröning indifferent to their fate. When pressed on the issue of whether children, like the one he had seen thrown against the side of the lorry, were really the 'enemy within' he chillingly concluded, 'The children are not the enemy at the moment. The enemy is the blood in them. The enemy is their growing up to become a Jew who could be dangerous.'

Gröning like Niethammer came from a traditional conservative family who were intensely proud to be German. He was born in lower Saxony in 1921 where his father ran a textile business. When his father's business went bankrupt in 1929, he became a supporter of Adolf Hitler and told his son that the Nazis 'were the people who wanted the best for Germany and who did something about it'. Hitler had come to power when he was aged 11 and like all the other boys of his age he had joined the Hitler Youth. So, Gröning had grown up under the Nazis and been subjected to their propaganda from a very early age. This meant he believed that the Jews were degenerate *untermenschen* and by serving at Auschwitz he was helping rid Germany of the 'enemy within'. However, unlike many of the guards Gröning excelled at school and came top of his class, at the age of 17 training to be a bank clerk. Months later war was declared and wanting to join an elite unit, like his grandfather had done in the First World War, he volunteered for the Waffen-SS. Before being called up he worked as

Above: At the end of March 1941, Niethammer was entrusted with 'special duties' by Höß and given permission to carry out a bird survey of the camp which he began in May, shooting many of the birds for his collection. (Auschwitz Album via Wikimedia Creative Commons)

Right: As well as surveying birds Niethammer shot game to order for Höß, took his eldest son Klaus hunting and put up bird boxes around the camp and in Höß's walled garden, recording their breeding success. Höss's children in the garden, right Klaus and Brigette, left Hans-Jürgen and Heidetraud. (Institut für Zeitgeschichte München)

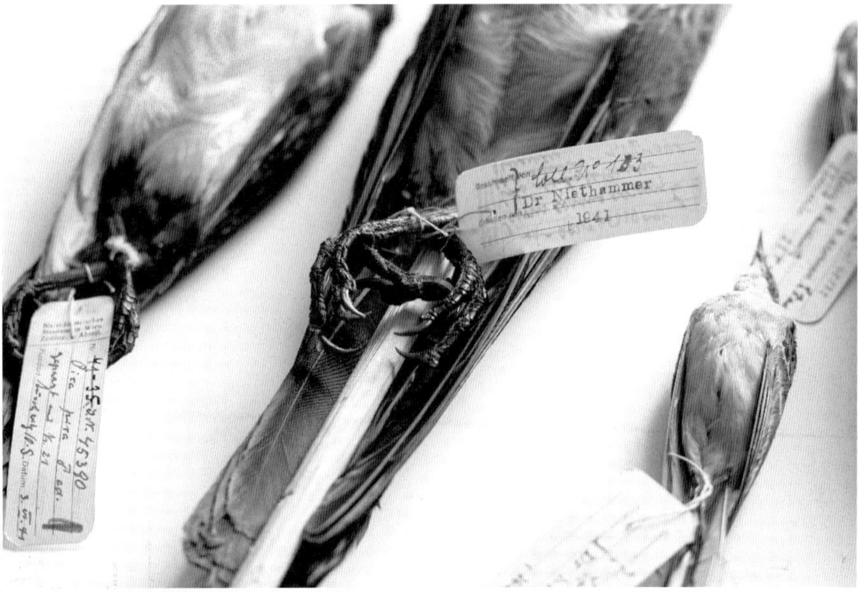

Working with Jan Grębocki, one of the Polish inmates, Niethammer created a macabre museum with the birds he shot. Like the inmates each was meticulously photographed and documented. (Natural History Museum, Vienna)

Niethammer recorded 124 species of breeding and wintering birds including snipe (*Capella gallinago,* now *Gallinago gallinago*) and brambling (*Fringilla montifringilla*), also sending skins back to the Natural History Museum in Vienna. (Natural History Museum, Vienna)

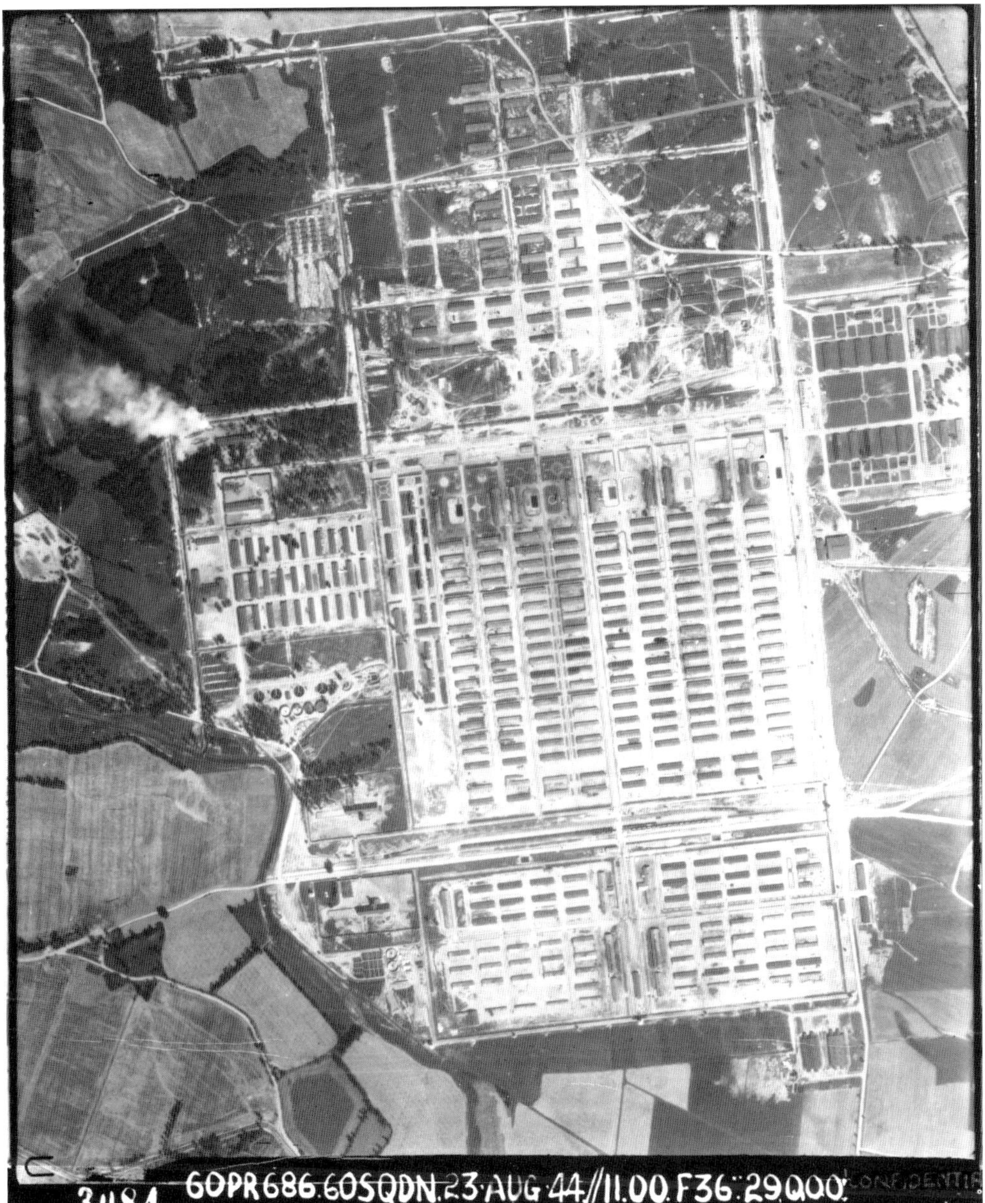

To record the birds at the camp, Niethammer systematically surveyed the grounds of Auschwitz and the fields, ponds and ditches which had been earmarked for the construction of Auschwitz II-Birkenau. An aerial view of the completed camp. (South African Air Force via Wikimedia Creative Commons)

Above: In the villages cleared to create Auchwitz II-Birkenau magpies took up residence after the Polish population had been expelled and worked together to kill the domesticated ducks left behind. Niethammer shot multiple specimens so he could study the feather changes associated with the magpie's moult. (Natural History Museum, Vienna)

Left: Niethammer found being a guard at Auschwitz a traumatic experience and after he had completed the survey successfully applied for a transfer, leaving in December 1941 to study birds on the occupied island of Crete. (Monument to the Fallschirmjäger, Professor Emeritus Hans Schneider via Wikimedia Creative Commons)

In May 1942 Niethammer's paper on the birdlife of Auschwitz was published in the prestigious *Annals of the Natural History Museum* in Vienna. The paper had four pictures including this shot of the Sola River taken in June 1941. As well as being a home for birds, it was also used to dump raw effluent, ground bones and human ashes from the crematoria at Auschwitz. (Author's collection)

In late August 1941 when the first Soviet prisoners were being gassed with Zyklon B, Niethammer recorded eight curlews flying over a pond within sight of the windowless room in the basement of Block 11. (Agatefilm via Wikimedia Creative Commons)

Left: In 1942 the third and final volume of the *Handbuch der Deutschen Vogelkunde* was published to great critical acclaim by German and Austrian ornithologists. The book included a colour plate of ducks' wings, Niethammer writing he was employed in the Waffen-SS. (Author's collection)

Below: In July 1942 Himmler (second left) visited Auschwitz and inspected the Judenrampe, watched as 400 Jews were gassed, toured the IG Farben factory and saw Niethammer's bird museum. (Institute of National Remembrance, Warsaw)

Right: During the war Stresemann began a correspondence with George Waterston, a British POW and ornithologist interned at Oflag VII-B, sending him a copy of Niethammer's *Handbuch der Deutschen Vogelkunde*. (Fair Isle Bird Observatory archives)

Below: In September 1942 Niethammer returned to Auschwitz by which time the Holocaust had begun in earnest, and the second camp Auschwitz II-Birkenau had been opened to 'process' the Jews. (Auschwitz Album via Wikimedia Creative Commons)

Left: Niethammer's return coincided with another guard arriving at the camp, Oskar Gröning, who was responsible for processing the inmates' money. (Auschwitz Album via Wikimedia Creative Commons)

Below: Like Niethammer he supervised one of the most traumatic parts of the process – the splitting up of families on the Judenrampe, the selection of who would live or die being overseen by SS 'doctors'. (Auschwitz Album via Wikimedia Creative Commons)

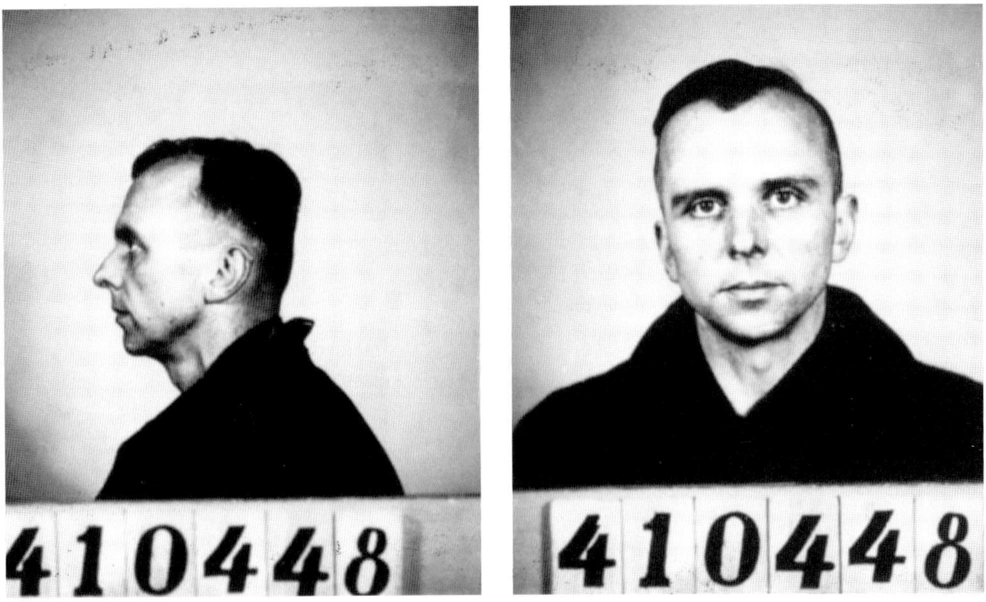

Above: After the war Niethammer was tried by a Polish court and sentenced to eight years in prison for his role in the Holocaust but this was reduced to three years following a concerted campaign by his fellow ornithologists and the British authorities. Photographed at the British Internment Camp, Recklinghausen, 1946. (Institute of National Remembrance, Warsaw)

Right: Höß during his trial in Warsaw, Poland. He wrote his autobiography *The Commandant of Auschwitz* while waiting to be executed but did not mention Niethammer to protect him. He was hanged on 18 April 1947. (Wikimedia Creative Commons)

BONNER ZOOLOGISCHE BEITRÄGE

Heft 1—3 Jahrgang 25 1974

Prof. Dr. Günther Niethammer

28. 9. 1908 — 14. 1. 1974

Above: Following his release Niethammer returned to the Museum Alexander Koenig in Bonn where his career flourished. He died in 1974 and received glowing obituaries including in his own journal, the *Bonner Zoologische Beiträge*, but his time at Auschwitz was erased. (*Bonner Zoologische Beiträge*)

Left: In 2015 Gröning, who became known as the 'Bookkeeper of Auschwitz', was found guilty of being an accessory to mass murder but died before he could begin his sentence. (Reuters)

a bookkeeper in an office, until the late summer of 1942 when the order came through that all fit and able-bodied members were to be transferred to active duty and desk jobs reserved for injured soldiers and veterans.

On arriving at the SS offices, Gröning was briefed by senior officers about unspecified top-secret work, reminded about his oath and was forced to sign a statement saying he would tell no one about his new role, including his friends and family. He was then put on a train to an unknown destination which turned out to be Auschwitz. On reporting to the central administrative building at the main camp, he was allocated a bunk in the barracks and was pleasantly surprised by the food in the canteen, which included tins of herring and sardines on top of the already generous SS rations of sausage, bread, vegetables, jam, coffee and sugar.

After being quizzed by SS officers about his background, he was allocated to a building where the prisoner's money was 'registered'. Here, talking to his fellow clerks, he began to realise what really happened at Auschwitz. 'The people there [working in the barracks] let us know that this money didn't all go back to the prisoners – Jews were taken to the camp who were treated differently. The money was taken off them without them getting it back,' Gröning recalled, asking them, 'Is this to do with the "transport" that arrived during the night? His colleagues replied, 'Well, don't you know? That's the way it is here. Jewish transports arrive, and as far as they're not able to work they're got rid of.' When Gröning pressed them on what 'got rid of' actually meant, one of the clerks replied to his astonishment and disbelief that they were gassed. Gröning recoiled:

> It was a shock, that you cannot take in at the first moment. But you mustn't forget that not only from 1933 [when Hitler came to power], but even from before that, the propaganda I got as a boy in the press, the media, the general society I lived in made us aware that the Jews were the cause of the First World War and had also 'stabbed Germany in the back' at the end. And that the Jews were actually the cause of the misery in which Germany found herself. We were convinced by our worldview that there was a great conspiracy of Jewishness against us, and that thought was expressed in Auschwitz. ... The enemies who are within

> Germany are being killed – exterminated if necessary. And between these two fights, openly at the front line and then on the home front, there's absolutely no difference – so we exterminated nothing but enemies.

Like Niethammer's guard duties, Gröning's bookkeeping work soon became routine. He still attended the transports that came into the camp day and night but took no part in the selection. Instead, he insured that the prisoners' belongings were taken to the Kanada sorting office and afterwards registered and counted their money. Similarly, Niethammer carried on with his guard duties, supervising the arrival of the transports and patrolling the grounds as well as doing his turn in the watchtower by the main gate, Post G. Both men carved out a role for themselves that didn't involve the killing of the Jews, instead in different ways they just focused on their work and what interested them – in Gröning's case money and in Niethammer's birds. Like other guards Gröning found the best way to forget about the horrors of Auschwitz was to bury himself in his work, his office soon becoming his refuge. Here he was insulated from the brutality and the sadism that was happening a few hundred metres away. If he had to leave the clerk's office and visit the Kanada sorting centre where they collected the death duties, he averted his eyes and said nothing. The only reminder that he was dealing in people's lives came in the form of the different currencies which came across his desk – German reichsmarks, American dollars, French francs, Czech korunas and Polish zlotys. Occasionally other personal items from the prisoners also came into his possession which helped him forget, like Russian vodka, French brandy, Greek ouzo or Italian samba.

> We didn't feel any empathy or sympathy towards one or other Jewish group from any particular country unless you were keen on getting a particular kind of vodka or schnapps – the Russians had a lovely type of vodka. … We drank a lot of vodka. We didn't get drunk every day – but it did happen. We'd go to bed drunk, and if someone was too lazy to turn off the light, they'd shoot at it – nobody said anything.

The life of a guard at Auschwitz had many other non-alcoholic compensations. As well as better pay and food, there were also shops and entertainment. The camp facilities were designed to make life seem as 'normal' as possible for the SS personnel working there. 'Auschwitz main camp was like a small town,' recalled Gröning. 'It had its gossip – it had a vegetable shop where you could buy bones to make broth [the reference to bones here would have been in relation to the camp animals]. There was a canteen, a cinema, a theatre with regular performances. There was a sports club of which I was a member. There were dances – all fun and entertainment.' The other quality that Auschwitz inspired was comradeship. 'I have to say that many who worked there weren't dull, they were intelligent,' said Gröning despite the reality that many only had a very crude education, guards like Niethammer being the exception. When he eventually left the camp in 1944, he went with some regrets: 'I'd left a circle of friends who I'd got familiar with, I'd got fond of, and that was very difficult. Apart from the fact that there are pigs who fulfil their personal drives – there are such people – the special situation at Auschwitz led to friendships which, I still say today, I think back on with joy.'

While Gröning was able to insulate himself from what was happening in the rest of the camp by burying himself in his accountancy books, Niethammer had no hiding place. He had to face the prisoners every day and must have seen the truth daily in their skeletal frames, hollow cheeks and dead eyes. His duties included patrolling up and down the electric fence, guarding the work parties and meeting the transports. On patrol he would have found prisoners who had thrown themselves on the electric fence to end it all. During his time in the watchtower by the front gate he would have witnessed the work parties leave each day at dawn and come back at dusk, exhausted and emaciated, many dying on their feet. And meeting the transports he would have seen the blind panic in the prisoners' faces as they were lined up and families forcefully separated. Despite this Niethammer may well have convinced himself that it was still a prison camp even if it was a brutal and at times a sadistic one. Yet the evidence was literally piling up all around him that Auschwitz was an extermination centre where prisoners were murdered in their droves while the remainder were worked to death.

Like Niethammer, Gröning was also in denial about the true purpose of the camp until one night his eyes were opened. Asleep in his bunk in the camp barracks, he awoke with a start when the alarm sounded. Another guard told him that some Jews on their way to the camp had escaped and run off into the forest. 'We were told to take our pistols and go through the forest,' said Gröning adding but 'we found no one'. Then he and the other guards fanned out and moved up towards the extermination area of the camp. 'We went in star formation up towards this farmhouse – it was lit from outside in diffused light, and out in the front were seven or eight bodies. These were the ones who had probably tried to escape and they'd been caught and shot. In front of the door of the farmhouse were some SS men who told us, "It's finished, you can go home."'

Despite being told to go home, curiosity got the better of Gröning and his comrades so they decided to hide in the shadows and watch what happened next at the farmhouse. They saw an SS man put on a gasmask and place Zyklon B pellets through a hatch in the side of the wall. Afterwards they heard a humming noise coming from inside the building which then 'turned to screaming' for a minute before being followed by a deathly silence. 'Then one man – I don't know whether he was an officer – stood and came to the door where there was a peephole, looked in and checked whether everything was okay and the people were dead.' Gröning then watched on in silence as the guards took out the lifeless bodies, extracted any gold teeth and shaved the head of the women before piling them into the railcar. He had stumbled upon Auschwitz's terrible secret, the mass extermination of the Jews and other prisoners. Trying to come to terms with the macabre sight, he felt the same sort of sick feeling 'as if you see two lorries crashing on the motorway. And you ask yourself, "Must it be that way? Is this necessary?" And of course it's influenced by the fact that you said before, "Yes, well, it's war," and we said, "They were our enemies."'

During the spring of 1942 when Niethammer was on Crete the number of Jews being killed was still in the low thousands. At this time the victims were being buried in mass graves but these became increasingly full. So, towards the end of the summer the camp guards started to burn them, first on wood pyres which could burn about 2,000 bodies at once and later in mass pits where they were burnt together with the bodies that had previously been buried. Firstly, oil was used to set fire to them, but later methanol was poured on to the corpses. 'Bodies were burnt in pits, day and night, continuously,' Höß reported. So, by the time Niethammer arrived back at the camp in September 1942 all the mass graves had started to be incinerated in the new crematoria.

The number of corpses in the mass graves amounted to 107,000,' wrote Höß with cold accuracy. 'This figure not only included the transports of Jews gassed up to the time when cremation was first employed, but also the bodies of those prisoners in Auschwitz who died during the winter of 1941/2 when the crematorium near the hospital building was out of action for a considerable time. It also included all the prisoners who died in Birkenau camp.'

Following Himmler's second visit Standartenführer Paul Blobel (1894–1951) from Eichmann's office had arrived at the camp with an order from the Reichsführer-SS that all the mass graves were to be exhumed and the bodies burnt (Blobel pioneered the use of the gas van and based on this experience developed the gas chambers for the extermination camps in occupied Poland). From late 1942 onwards, he led Sonderaktion 1005, who exhumed hundreds of thousands of bodies at the massacre sites and extermination camps across Eastern Europe to erase all evidence of the Holocaust. 'In addition, the ashes were to be disposed of in such a way that it would be impossible at some future time to calculate the number of corpses burnt,' recalled Höß.

Blobel had been experimenting with different methods of cremation at Kulmhof concentration camp north of Łódź in Poland and invited Höß and one of his officers, Obersturmführer Franz Hößler (1906–1945), to see what he had achieved. There they inspected a variety of makeshift ovens which were fired with wood and petrol. He had also tried to get rid of the bodies using explosives but had found that this was not an effective method of disposal, body parts being spread over too wide an area. So instead, the ashes had been ground down to a powder in a bone mill and then scattered over the surrounding countryside. Blobel's work was carried out by a special detachment of Jews who were given the code number '1005' and shot after each site had been completed, Auschwitz providing a lot of the Jews who carried out this ethnic cleansing. Among the areas at the camp where the ashes were deposited were the dykes and ditches which fed the ponds where Niethammer had carried out his bird survey (the human ashes and ground bones of those murdered were, however, mostly dumped into the Soła river). At Kulmhof, Blobel had also experimented with using the exhaust fumes from vehicles to kill people. 'On my visit to Kulmhof I was also shown the extermination apparatus constructed out of lorries, which was designed to kill by using the exhaust gases from the engines,' reported Höß. 'The officer in charge there, however, described this method as being extremely unreliable, for the density of the gas varied considerably and was often insufficient to be lethal.'

Niethammer's arrival back at Auschwitz in September 1942 also coincided with the round-up of a large transport of women arriving at the camp. The women's camp had been built in mid-May 1942 at Birkenau and after its construction had been designated as the principal place for 'processing both German and non-German women'. In July the Reich Security Main Office had informed police and security services that all arrested women were now to be sent to Auschwitz. As Niethammer had reported for duty Himmler had given the order that all the Jewish women interned in the Ravensbrück Concentration Camp were to be moved there so it could be made 'Jew-pure'. The largest camp designated solely for women, by the autumn of 1942 Ravensbrück held over 10,000 prisoners. Following Himmler's order all the Jewish women were separated from the other prisoners and transferred to Auschwitz which then became the largest camp holding women. Here the living conditions were incomparably worse than in the men's huts. 'Everything was much more difficult, harsher and more depressing for the women,' Höß wrote. 'They were far more tightly packed in, and the sanitary and hygienic conditions were notably inferior. Furthermore, the disastrous overcrowding and its consequences, which existed from the very beginning, prevented any proper order being established in the women's camp.'[2]

Niethammer would have heard about the conditions in the women's camp from other guards, Höß commenting that when those inside had 'reached the bottom, they would let themselves go completely. They would then stumble about like ghosts, without any will of their own, and had to be pushed everywhere by the others, until the day they quietly passed away. These stumbling corpses were a terrible sight.' Several non-Jewish inmates from Ravensbrück, principally alleged criminals and prostitutes, had accompanied the women and been designated to act as Kapos. According to Höß they far surpassed their male counterparts in terms of their toughness, squalor, vindictiveness, and depravity.

> Most were prostitutes with many convictions, and some were truly repulsive creatures. Needless to say, these dreadful women gave their full vent to their evil desires

> on the prisoners under them, which was unavoidable. The Reichsführer-SS regarded them as particularly well suited to act as Kapos over the Jewish women when he visited Auschwitz in 1942. Not many of these women died, except from disease. These were soulless and had no feelings whatsoever.

Along the Vistula river at the village of Budy, not far from where Niethammer had carried out his bird survey the previous year, a 'punishment company' of prisoners had been stationed to work on draining the land and constructing a sub-camp. Even by the standards of Auschwitz what went on there was particularly depraved. Completely cut off from the main camp, the Kapos of both sexes conducted a brutal reign of terror resulting in many of the prisoners being killed. 'I find it incredible that human beings could ever turn into such beasts,' wrote Höß without irony. 'The way the "greens" [green triangles signified criminal prisoners who were mostly German] knocked the French Jewesses about,' recalled Höß, 'tearing them to pieces, killing them with axes, and throttling them – it was simply gruesome.' While there were some compassionate guards left in Auschwitz, they often fell foul of the more brutal ones who thought they were not being hard enough on the prisoners. Niethammer was alarmed by how much the camp had changed in his absence, becoming a place of mass extermination and sadistic imprisonment. So, he decided that he needed to get out at all costs, this time permanently. After talking over his options with his ornithological contacts, Niethammer summoned up the courage to ask Höß if he could again be added to the list of guards eligible for a transfer, Höß surprisingly agreeing, perhaps wanting to save him from being associated with the worst excesses of the camp. However, in the meantime Niethammer had once again to join the camp roster and carry out the duties expected of a guard at Auschwitz.

Chapter 12

Birdie behind Barbed Wire

AT THE SAME time as Niethammer was starting on his next round of guard duties at Auschwitz in Poland, at another camp in Germany a British prisoner of war by the name of John Barrett was starting on his next prison term. John Henry Barrett had qualified as an RAF instructor four days before the outbreak of hostilities and by the time Neville Chamberlain declared war on Germany he was flying in Shropshire. Here he trained bomber crews although he had no operational experience, a baptism of fire only possible in wartime. In 1940 he had married, a baby daughter Jane soon following, so although a training role suited him, Barrett wanted to 'do his bit' and volunteered for operational duty with Bomber Command. Made Squadron Leader, Barrett was shot down on his first operational flight over Germany in 1941 by which time he had another child on the way, his family being told about his capture by the Red Cross. Before being interned with the three other ornithologist POWs, Edward Buxton, Peter Conder and George Waterston, at a camp near Warburg, Barrett had found himself on his own in Oflag XXI located near the small town of Schubin in northern Poland. On 5 September 1942 on his way to the camp he had nearly been killed when the transport train he was travelling in had been bombed during a raid after pulling over into a railway siding in Posen.

Despite being the only birdwatcher in the camp, Barrett soon started identifying the species he saw in the grounds and those passing overhead on migration. The other bemused prisoners soon christened him 'Birdie', a nickname which was to stick with him throughout the war (the other birdwatchers he was interned with in Warburg were also called similar names). A pair of storks had nested on the top of the camp hospital roof and Birdie became a regular visitor to the building, recording them laying eggs, feeding and fledging young. Inside the eaves of the mansion house where he was interned, he had found nesting house and tree sparrows. Often, he could be found squinting into the sun and looking up at the heavens, trying to identify the birds of prey soaring high up in the sky.

Barrett, like Niethammer in Auschwitz, found that the best time to see birds was to get up very early before the first roll call and walk the perimeter fence. Here in the stillness of the dawn he would be able to see and hear the birds in the nearby wood and on the marsh both, unlike Niethammer's study area, frustratingly out of reach.

Barrett's early morning walks soon became part of his daily routine, the RAF officer finding solace in the birds he saw both inside and outside the barbed wire. Just as importantly, walking the perimeter fence gave him some much needed time on his own to reflect and think, privacy being almost impossible to find in the crowded camp. However, his dawn sojourns had not gone unnoticed by the camp guards and an elderly security guard in his late fifties began to shadow him. His job was to check on whether Birdie was really recceing the fence as part of an escape attempt rather than watching the birds. The two men, despite being on opposite sides and different generations, soon began to develop a mutual respect.

On seeing the prisoner each day, the guard would greet him with a big grin on his face and say in broken English, 'Good morning, old sport. And what have we on offer today?' After the gentle mocking of a welcome, the two would then exchange a few brief words, anything more liable to arise suspicion, both among the other guards and prisoners (in most prison camps fraternisation with the enemy was strictly frowned upon, instead many prisoners taking part in 'goon baiting' or deliberately trying to provoke the camp guards). Over the weeks the two men slowly grew to know each other more, finding common ground walking the fence. During their snatched conversations Barrett learnt that the German guard had been a bookseller before the war who had also spent time in England, studying at Oxford. On his uniform the guard wore a First World War medal and on enquiring about it one day, Barrett learnt that he had fought at the Second Battle of Ypres, the same battle where Barrett's father had died. He also discovered that after the war the guard had gone back to England to study the book trade, before opening his own shop in Germany.

The discussion with the camp guard about books gave Barrett a vital opening – he was able to drop into the conversation that he had no bird books to help with identifying difficult species. He explained that in his previous camp the prisoners had access to a copy of Niethammer's *Handbook of German Ornithology* which, hoping to flatter the guard, he described as one of the great guides to the birds of Europe. Forlornly Barrett added that all his attempts to get hold of a copy in the present camp had failed. The guard listened and sympathised with his predicament but said that any requests for books had to be made directly to the commandant's office (a library was one of the luxuries enjoyed by POW camps holding officers but the books available were strictly limited). A few weeks later to his surprise Barrett received a brown paper package and on unwrapping it to his delight found all three volumes of the *Handbuch der Deutschen Vogelkunde*. That day, fearing difficult questions would be asked, he said nothing about the origin of books to either his fellow prisoners or to the guard. However, someone senior had noticed that the prisoner and the guard were becoming too friendly as the following day the guard was nowhere to be seen. Much to his disappointment Barrett never saw his benefactor again or learnt his real name (yet amazingly a couple of years later Barrett would go on to have a relationship of sorts with Niethammer himself).

By the autumn of 1942 Auschwitz was very short of guards due to the huge increase in the number of prisoners arriving at the camp and the number of sub-camps being created. 'Because of the mass of prisoners at Auschwitz, how to guard the outside working parties effectively was a constant problem,' Höß complained:

> There were never enough troops. Chains of sentry posts were useful, in that they could be used to enclose the larger working areas. But the constant moving of work parties from one site to another, and the mobility necessitated by the nature of the work itself, made proper supervision impossible in the case of agricultural work, digging ditches and so on. Owing to the small number of female supervisors available, it was necessary to employ as many dog handlers as possible.

In line with Himmler's orders the opportunity to become a dog handler was therefore offered to the guards. Many of the guards volunteered even if they weren't interested in being a dog handler including Niethammer, believing it would give him more freedom to birdwatch around the camp.

Auschwitz already had 150 dogs, mostly German shepherds, to intimidate, control and terrorise the prisoners. Intelligent, loyal and naturally aggressive, German Shepherds in the wrong hands also made for lethal weapons. One of the most trainable dog breeds, they worked throughout the German army as service, police and guard dogs. 'Even our one hundred and fifty-odd dogs were not enough,' complained Höß. Himmler had calculated that one dog should be able to replace two sentries, Höß agreed but only for the female prisoners, 'owing to the universal fear caused by the presence of the dog'. So, in the absence of enough guards, he brought in more dogs and decided to advertise not just in the camp but across the SS for people to train them. The new Auschwitz dog squad attracted 'the most astonishing military material. Astonishing in the negative sense,' reflected Höß. 'When volunteers were sought for training as dog handlers, half the SS regiment applied.'

For many guards the presence of a dog meant that they wouldn't have to do the work of manhandling the prisoners and bringing them into line. 'They imagined that such work would be easier and less monotonous,' said Höß. Instead of getting the dedicated dog handlers he had been hoping for, all the SS regiments encouraged their worst recruits to apply, hoping to get rid of them. 'Since it was impossible to take on all the volunteers, the companies hit upon a cunning solution, and gave up all their black sheep, so as to be rid of them,' he complained. 'Someone else could have the headaches now. Most of these men had been punished for some offence or other. If the commander of the guard unit had looked at these men's conduct sheets a little more closely, he would never on any account have allowed them to be sent away for training.'

All the successful volunteers, including the 'black sheep' but minus Niethammer who wasn't chosen, were sent to the Training and Experimental Establishment for Dog Handlers at Oranienburg. There young German shepherd dogs were taught to attack the prisoners on command. The first stage in the training was to establish a strong bond between the guard and the dog. Using rewards the dogs were taught to obey a range of simple, short commands. In particular the handlers were told to reward the dog for being aggressive toward strangers, barking and baring its teeth. To encourage them to attack prisoners the dogs were taught to recognise a prison uniform as a threat and then provoked by hitting them on the nose, the most sensitive part of their body, guards protecting themselves by using a thick leather glove. After training to attack on command, the dogs would then chase and maul the prisoners, locking onto their arm or leg and biting down hard, only releasing the limb when ordered by the handler.

After completing their training officers returned to Auschwitz where they were formed into a unit called the Hundestaffel or Dog Squad. Höß was not impressed with the new recruits, commenting sarcastically:

> it was not hard to see what a splendid new formation had here been created. And now it was time for them to be put to work. Either they played games with their dogs, or found an easy hideout and went to sleep, their dogs waking them up on the approach of an 'enemy,' or else passed the time in pleasant conversation with the female supervisors or the prisoners. A great many of them formed a regular liaison with the 'green' controllers. Since the dog handlers were always employed in the women's camp, it was not difficult for them to continue this liaison.

When the guards wanted to punish the prisoners, were bored or simply fancied some fun, they would set their dogs on them. Sometimes the guards would let loose several dogs, taking bets on which dog would maul the prisoner first. If they were reported for doing this, they would, according to Höß, 'maintain that the dog had done it of its own accord, owing to the peculiar behaviour of the prisoner, or that its lead had been lost, and so on. They always had an excuse. Every day, according to their regulations, they had to give their dog further training.'

Many of the guards formed a close working relationship with their dogs, treating them far better than the prisoners in their care. However, some of the more sadistic guards also mistreated their dogs, starving or beating them, and then letting them loose on the prisoners. Due to the amount of time and money it took to train new dog handlers, Höß could not relieve them of their roles unless they had been found guilty of some grave offence, usually one that involved punishment by SS court martial, or alternatively if they were caught badly ill-treating or neglecting their dogs. 'The kennelman, a former police sergeant, who had looked after dogs for more than twenty-five years, was often driven to despair by the behaviour of the dog handlers,' Höß reported. 'But they knew that nothing much could happen to them, and that they were unlikely actually to lose their jobs … I had much trouble with the Hundestaffel, and many clashes with the commander of the guard regiment over this [in reality guards were rarely if ever punished for mistreating the dogs].'

As the war in Russia began to turn against Nazi Germany, Himmler cut back further on the number of men employed as guards at the camp, Niethammer and the other guards living in constant fear of being sent to the Eastern Front. Instead of guards Himmler told Höß to use moveable barbed-wire fencing to enclose temporary work camps and more electrified fences for the permanent places of work. A double-layered electric fence, four metres or thirteen feet high, supported by concrete posts with barbed wire already surrounded both camps. The electrical fences were supplied with 400 volts and 0.1 amps continuously, a lethal charge which would quickly kill anyone coming into contact with it (a current of as little as 0.007 amps or 7mA across the heart for three seconds is enough to kill. 0.1 amps or 100mA passing through the body will almost always be fatal). The fences were so lethal that the prisoners could see them 'vibrating and howling', the buzzing sound coming from the very high voltage. The electric fences were guarded by Niethammer and his fellow guards, watchtowers being located in strategic places all around the camp to give the guards a bird's-eye view over the prisoners. The top of the fencing was deliberately designed to slope inward to make it more difficult to climb over. In addition to the two electrified fences there was a third 'deadline' fence just beyond. Any prisoner stepping over the low third fence was immediately shot dead without warning by the perimeter guards.

Despite the electric fence being deadly, Höß believed that it could be short-circuited. 'Even the double electrified fence can be neutralized in dry weather with a few simple tools, provided a man is sufficiently cold-blooded and gives the problem a little thought,' he wrote unconvincingly. 'This has frequently succeeded. Often too the sentries outside the wire have come too close to it and have had to pay for their lack of caution with their lives.' The electrical current for the fence, and for the entire Auschwitz camp, was supplied by a power plant at Siersza Wodna, about 20 kilometres north of the camp. The main electrical substation was situated at the sub-camp of Babice where two separate lines ran to the main camp and to Birkenau. At the main camp the voltage from the power plant was stepped down to 6,000 volts, and then finally to 400 volts, at which point it was connected directly to the camp fence. The Birkenau camp fence, being much longer than that of the original Auschwitz I main camp, used a significantly higher voltage of 760 volts. The total length of fencing in the camp including the internal fencing between the individual sectors, staggeringly stretched to over 17 kilometres.

Many prisoners were killed on the electric fences trying to escape while others tragically used them to commit suicide, the only way to end their suffering. Some were pushed on to the fence by other prisoners to rob them, settle scores or because they were working with the Nazis. One inmate who contemplated suicide was Alina Dabrowska, prisoner number 44165, who was transferred to Auschwitz in June 1943:

> I was an inmate at a prison in Nazi-occupied Poland – incarcerated for helping Allied forces – and one day in 1943, while walking the grounds, a new arrival warned me about it. She said, 'You're all going to Auschwitz! Do you know what kind of camp that is?' She told us that if someone is out of strength, they were immediately killed. She told us many horrible things. None of us believed her. When we got off the train, we were taken to a large hall, where we stripped down completely. Our hair was shaved and they tattooed numbers on our arms. I noticed an electric fence around the camp. Whenever we came back from working in the mornings, there was usually someone glued to it. If someone couldn't take it anymore, they jumped over the ditch and threw themselves onto the electric fence and their lives were over. A year later, I had had enough of the cold, the hunger and the death surrounding me. I too found myself in front of the fence. I was about to jump when a guard yelled at me. I instinctively turned around and never tried it again. I focused on doing whatever I could to survive. I had hope, but sometimes an officer with a cane selected some of us to go to the gas chamber. What left the deepest impression on me was watching those marches to the chambers where so many were murdered.[1]

The fences were backed up by the increasing use of minefields and by ever larger numbers of dogs. 'The Reichsführer-SS even imagined that dogs could be trained to circle around the prisoners, as though they were sheep, and thus prevent them from escaping,' Höß mocked.

> One sentry, aided by several dogs, was supposed to be able to guard up to one hundred prisoners with safety. The attempt came to nothing. Men are not sheep. However well

> trained the dogs were in recognizing the prisoners by their uniforms and their smell and so on, and however accurately they were taught to know how close prisoners might be allowed to approach, they were all only dogs, and could not think like human beings. If the prisoners purposely attracted them to one spot, the dogs would then leave a wide section unguarded through which they could escape. Nor were the dogs any use in preventing a mass breakout. They would of course savagely maul some of the escapers, but they would be immediately slaughtered along with their 'shepherds'.

Another of Höß's more bird-brained ideas was that dogs could stand in for the guards in the watchtowers, freeing them to patrol the camp. He also experimented with allowing the dogs to run loose between the double-wire fencing that encircled the original barracks and the new camp at Birkenau, allocating each dog to guard a certain section. The idea was that the dog would give warning of the approach of a prisoner by barking loudly, so preventing a breakthrough in the wire. However, according to Höß this was also unsuccessful as the dogs either found a spot in which to go to sleep or if the wind was blowing in the wrong direction wouldn't pick up on the prisoner's scent or its barking would not be heard by the sentry. For the prisoners the experiment was terrifying as they soon came to fear loose dogs because they randomly attacked them, especially when hungry or encouraged by the guards.

As dogs were of limited use, Höß ordered a lot more mines to be laid around the camp but commented that this was

> a two-edged weapon. They had to be accurately laid and their precise situation plotted on the plan of the minefield, since after three months at the most they became defective and had to be replaced. It was also necessary to walk through the minefield from time to time and this gave the prisoners a chance to observe the lanes where no mines had been laid.

Höß was aware that minefields had been tried at other extermination camps including one at Sobibor, where despite the area being guarded night and day, there had been a mass breakout. On 14 October 1943, Jewish prisoners there had bravely rebelled against their Nazi captors, killing 11 members of the camp's SS staff, including the camp's deputy commandant Johann Niemann. While close to 300 prisoners escaped, breaking through the barbed wire and traversing the lethal minefield surrounding the camp, only about fifty survived the war. Höß reflected, 'the Jews knew where the lanes through the minefield ran and were able by force to achieve a major breakout during which almost all the guard personnel were wiped out.' After carrying out lots of experiments with both dogs and mines to control the prisoners, Höß finally concluded, 'Neither mechanical devices nor animals can replace human intelligence.'

The autumn of 1942, when Niethammer arrived back at the camp, coincided with the Nazi 'eradication' of the Jewish ghetto at the city of Łódź, or Litzmannstadt in German. The second-largest ghetto in Poland and the conquered territories after the one in Warsaw, it contained 164,000 Jews and was situated 65 miles south-east of the capital. On 5 September1942, a mass deportation known as the Sperre began there – the round-up involved the removal of more than 13,000 children, elderly and ill Jews in a one-week period from the ghetto to Chełmno or Kulmhof camp (later deportations were sent to Auschwitz).

At 4 p.m. on 4 September, Chaim Rumkowski (1877–1944), the head of the Jewish Council of Elders, who governed the ghetto with an iron fist, told the workers in Łódź to give up their children and their parents, assuring them that if they did so the Germans had promised that the ghetto could be saved. The round-up profoundly shocked the community who up to that point had desperately clung to the illusion that people were being sent to labour camps. However, the brutal way the ghetto was cleared made it plain to many of those left that deportation meant death. Following Rumkowski's appeal the hospitals, schools and the rabbinate (the office of the rabbis) had all been cleared. In their place the remaining buildings were turned into a giant labour camp manufacturing war supplies for the German army (for his co-operation with the Germans, Rumkowski was killed in Auschwitz in 1944 by other Jews).

Niethammer also came back to a camp where individual acts of brutality were increasing every day. A typical example occurred on 11 September 1942 when SS-Oberscharführer (master sergeant) Josef Klehr (1904–1988), an SS medical orderly, killed a Dutch Jew called

Heiman Kohen, camp number 52425, with a poker in the corridor of Block 20 of the Auschwitz I camp. He ordered the body of the murdered prisoner to be moved to the morgue in the basement of Block 28 and issued a false death certificate stating that Kohen had died from natural causes. (The next year Klehr became head of the disinfection squad or Desinfektionskommando at the camp. In this role he administered the gas Zyklon B, using it to delouse living quarters and clothes and for the mass murder of prisoners, Klehr being responsible for inserting the gas into the rooms.) Niethammer may not have personally witnessed the act but he would have heard about it from other guards or seen the many other daily examples of cruelty. Most of the more sadistic guards often boasted about killing prisoners, seeing it as a sport. Others although not directly killing Jews, treated them with brutality and callous indifference, particularly those in charge of the work parties. It was an environment in which acts of violence, schadenfreude and savagery had become the norm and every day it increased Niethammer's desperation to get out.

At the camp during his spare time Niethammer wrote up his Crete bird survey and worked on a new ornithological project. One of the birds that he had become fascinated by was the collared dove. A species of Asian origin, during the 1930s and 1940s it was rapidly expanding its range throughout Central Europe. The reasons for the bird's expansion had been widely debated in ornithological circles, many German ornithologists avidly following its spread. As a result, a large-scale observation survey had been set up composed of both amateur and academic ornithologists throughout the Third Reich. Despite the war a steady stream of sightings had been sent into bird museums across Germany and Austria. From these records it soon became clear that the species was still extending its range, the reports generating much discussion and excitement. Fascinated by the exotic origins of the bird, Niethammer was determined to understand the reasons behind its rapid spread, a process known as biogeographic range expansion. The sightings sent into the museums therefore provided an outstanding opportunity to study the collared dove and track its growth. So, when not on guard duty Niethammer started to piece together the records from the different locations, working with Stresemann on the project.

While very different characters, what Niethammer and Höß had in common was a strong work ethic, Niethammer wanting to fulfil his scientific potential, Höß to fulfil Himmler's orders. 'My main task,' Höß wrote was 'namely, to push on, with all the means at my disposal, with the construction of all the installations belonging to the SS in the Auschwitz camp area.' Both men also shared an increasing desperation to make their mark as the war began to turn decisively against Germany. 'Sometimes, during a period of quiet, I used to think that I could see an end in sight to the construction work resulting from the numerous schemes and plans that the Reichsführer-SS had laid down for Auschwitz, but at that point new plans would arrive, involving further urgent action,' Höß protested. 'The perpetual rush in which I lived, brought about by the demands of the Reichsführer-SS, by wartime difficulties, by almost daily problems in the camps, and above all by the unending stream of prisoners flowing into the whole camp area, left me no time to think of anything except my work. I concentrated exclusively on this.'

As Höß struggled to cope with the workload and the huge demands placed on him, his officers and guards increasingly became the focus of his wrath:

> Harassed thus by circumstances, I passed on my harassment in double measure to all who came under my jurisdiction, whether SS, civilians, officials, business firms, or prisoners. I had only one end in view: to drive everything and everyone forward in my determination to improve the general conditions so that I could carry out the measures laid down. The Reichsführer-SS required every man to do his duty and if necessary to sacrifice himself entirely in so doing. Every German had to commit himself heart and soul so that we might win the war.

CHAPTER 13

The Greatest Human Extermination Centre of All Time

GERMANY WINNING THE war in the autumn of 1942 now looked increasingly less likely with every day that passed. In September on the Eastern Front the German army had found itself surrounded as the siege of Stalingrad continued, starting a new offensive but making little progress. America was now in the conflict and its huge military resources were beginning to turn the tide against Japan, Germany's Axis partner, in the Pacific war, defeating them in the Battle of Midway in June. In Africa the First Battle of El Alamein in July had resulted in a stalemate but with Rommel's position looking increasingly tenuous, three months later the Afrika Korps were routed at the Second Battle of El Alamein. In Poland following savage reprisals the resistance movement had been laid low but, in the autumn, Polish communists had been dropped into the country to set up the 'Worker's Party'. This included setting up a new resistance movement called the 'People's Guard'.

In Auschwitz Höß, Niethammer and all the SS personnel were now involved in both exterminating Jews and increasing the output from the armaments factories, the IG Farben rubber factory and the various sub-camps. 'In accordance with the will of the Reichsführer-SS the concentration camps were to become armaments plants. Everything else was to be subordinated to this. All other considerations must be set aside,' wrote Höß. Consequently, conditions in the camp deteriorated further as the prisoners were treated ever more brutally to get them to work harder. 'Armaments came first, and every obstacle to this must be overcome. I dared not allow myself to think otherwise,' reflected Höß:

> I had to become harder, colder, and even more merciless in my attitude toward the needs of the prisoners. I saw it all very clearly, often far too clearly, but I knew that I must

> not let it get me down. I dared not let my feelings get the better of me. Everything had to be sacrificed to one end, the winning of the war. I could not be at the front, so I must do everything at home to support those who were fighting.

Despite Germany looking as though it would lose the war, Höß still had implicit faith in final victory, and being a fanatical Nazi never stopped to question what he was being asked to do. Chillingly, he wrote, 'By the will of the Reichsführer-SS, Auschwitz became the greatest human extermination centre of all time.'

Reflecting on Himmler's command regarding the extermination of the Jews, Höß wrote:

> It was certainly an extraordinary and monstrous order. Nevertheless, the reasons behind the extermination programme seemed to me right. I did not reflect on it at the time: I had been given an order, and I had to carry it out. Whether this mass extermination of the Jews was necessary or not was something on which I could not allow myself to form an opinion, for I lacked the necessary breadth of view. If the Führer had himself given the order for the 'final solution of the Jewish question', then, for a veteran National Socialist and even more so for an SS officer there could be no question of considering its merits. 'The Führer commands, we follow' was never a mere phrase or slogan. It was meant in bitter earnest.

For Höß showing loyalty to Hitler, Himmler, National Socialism and the Waffen-SS was far more important than exhibiting any compassion towards the heartbreaking scenes he witnessed every day at Auschwitz. However, for some of his guards, like Niethammer, the gruesome scenes did deeply affect them and some of the braver ones even raised it with Höß personally when he did his daily rounds. 'This mass extermination, with all its attendant circumstances, did not, as I know, fail to affect those who took a part in it,' he wrote. 'With very few exceptions, nearly all of those detailed to do this monstrous "work", this "service", and who, like myself, have given sufficient thought to the matter, have been deeply marked by these events.'

When guards or other personnel at the camp raised issues with Höß, he would simply reply that it was Hitler's order and remind them of their oath to the Führer when they had joined the Waffen-SS. 'Again and again during these confidential conversations I was asked: is it necessary that we do all this? Is it necessary that hundreds of thousands of women and children be destroyed?' he recalled 'And I, who in my innermost being had on countless occasions asked myself exactly this question, could only fob them off and attempt to console them by repeating that it was done on Hitler's order. I had to tell them that this extermination of Jewry had to be, so that Germany and our posterity might be freed forever from their relentless adversaries.' Höß had over time become immune to the suffering of the Jews and other 'sub-humans' and was totally unable to put himself in their shoes. Despite this he claimed to be tormented by 'secret doubts': 'There was no doubt in the mind of any of us that Hitler's order had to be obeyed regardless, and that it was the duty of the SS to carry it out. Nevertheless, we were all tormented by secret doubts.' he stated. 'I myself dared not admit to such doubts. In order to make my subordinates carry on with their task, it was psychologically essential that I myself appear convinced of the necessity for this gruesomely harsh order.'

As he went about his daily rounds and spoke to his officers Höß became increasingly paranoid that his staff were monitoring and judging him. 'Everyone watched me,' he noted. 'They observed the impression produced upon me by the kind of scenes that I have described above and my reactions. Every word I said on the subject was discussed. I had to exercise intense self-control in order to prevent my innermost doubts and feelings of oppression from becoming apparent.' For Höß the most important part of being commandant was to show no emotion and to carry out orders unquestioningly. 'I had to appear cold and indifferent to events that must have wrung the heart of anyone possessed of human feelings. I might not even look away when afraid lest my natural emotions got the upper hand. I had to watch coldly, while the mothers with laughing or crying children went into the gas chambers.' But even Höß, who prided himself on being completely dispassionate in the execution of his duty, was on occasion moved by the heartbreaking scenes that played out in front of him.

> On one occasion two small children were so absorbed in some game that they quite refused to let their mother tear

> them away from it. Even the Jews of the Special Detachment were reluctant to pick the children up. The imploring look in the eyes of the mother, who certainly knew what was happening, is something I shall never forget. The people were already in the gas chamber and becoming restive and I had to act. Everyone was looking at me. I nodded to the junior noncommissioned officer on duty and he picked up the screaming, struggling children in his arms and carried them into the gas chamber, accompanied by their mother who was weeping in the most heart-rending fashion. My pity was so great that I longed to vanish from the scene, yet I might not show the slightest trace of emotion.

Höß's ability to coldly send the mother and her children to their deaths in the gas chamber was all the more inexplicable because he was a family man. The same was true of many of the guards who like Niethammer also had families. However, unlike Höß they were back in Germany or Austria, not living in a luxurious house with a beautiful garden on the edge of the camp. Yet on some level the killings did affect him because after certain incidents he found it hard to go back to his wife and children. 'I had to observe every happening with a cold indifference. Even those petty incidents that others might not notice I found hard to forget. In Auschwitz I truly had no reason to complain that I was bored,' he recalled with breathtaking irony. Like Niethammer, Höß's answer to the trauma of watching innocent people die was to find solace in animals, in his case horses. 'If I was deeply affected by some incident, I found it impossible to go back to my home and my family. I would mount my horse and ride until I had chased the terrible picture away. Often, at night, I would walk through the stables and seek relief among my beloved animals.'

Höß, however hard he tried, could never switch off from work, the many challenges and practical problems involved in running the camp being constantly on his mind. By his own admission this made him very difficult to live with as he drove himself ever harder to fulfil the targets set by Himmler, his family bearing the brunt of his mood swings. 'It would often happen, when at home, that my thoughts suddenly turned to incidents that had occurred during the extermination,' he wrote. 'I then had to go out. I could no longer bear to be in my homely family circle.

When I saw my children happily playing or observed my wife's delight over our youngest, the thought would often come to me: how long will our happiness last? My wife could never understand these gloomy moods of mine and ascribed them to some annoyance connected with my work.'

When thinking of his family, Höß claimed to be haunted by his work leading to many sleepless nights:

> When at night I stood out there beside the transports or by the gas chambers or the fires, I was often compelled to think of my wife and children, without, however, allowing myself to connect them closely with all that was happening. It was the same with the married men who worked in the crematoriums or at the fire pits. When they saw the women and children going into the gas chambers, their thoughts instinctively turned to their own families.

Yet Höß's answer to such a dark moral dilemma was not to reform the camp he had created but like Niethammer to find a way out. 'I was no longer happy in Auschwitz once the mass exterminations had begun,' he wrote. 'I had become dissatisfied with myself. To this must be added that I was worried because of anxiety about my principal task, the never-ending work, and the untrustworthiness of my colleagues.'

Höß convinced himself that the responsibility for the dreadful conditions at the camp lay not with him but his 'untrustworthy colleagues' and Himmler. 'Then the refusal to understand, or even to listen to me, on the part of my superiors,' he moaned. 'It was in truth not a happy or desirable state of affairs. Yet everyone in Auschwitz believed that the commandant lived a wonderful life.' However, in comparison to the prisoners Höß did live a wonderful life, his large house with pool, playrooms and well-kept garden being a world away from the cramped, disease-ridden dormitories in which the inmates existed. Here he played God as he had the power of life and death over others, which he exercised in a callous and calculating way. His family also benefitted from his rank and standing in the Waffen-SS, enjoying every luxury. 'My family, to be sure, were well provided for in Auschwitz,' he wrote. 'Every wish that my wife or children expressed was granted them. The children could live a free and untrammeled life. My wife's garden was a paradise of flowers. The prisoners never missed an opportunity for doing some little act of kindness to my wife or children and thus attracting their attention.'

By compartmentalising his work and home life, Höß was able to make extraordinary claims. 'No former prisoner can ever say that he was in any way or at any time badly treated in our house,' he wrote. 'My wife's greatest pleasure would have been to give a present to every prisoner who was in any way connected with our household. The children were perpetually begging me for cigarettes for the prisoners. They were particularly fond of the ones who worked in the garden.' Höß like Hitler found that animals were better companions than people and he sought solace in them: 'My whole family displayed an intense love of agriculture and particularly for animals of all sorts. Every Sunday I had to walk them all across the fields, and visit the stables, and we might never miss the kennels where the dogs were kept. Our two horses and the foal were especially beloved.'

The Höß menagerie soon extended to the rare and exotic, the commandant even on very rare occasions finding the time to play with his children in the garden or swim in the nearby river. 'The children always kept animals in the garden, creatures the prisoners were forever bringing them. Tortoises, martens, cats, lizards: there was always something new and interesting to be seen there,' he wrote. 'In summer they splashed in the wading pool in the garden, or in the Soła. But their greatest joy was when Daddy bathed with them.' He had, however, so little time for all these childish pleasures (writing after the war Höß added, 'Today I deeply regret that I did not devote more time to my family'). But it was not family that Höß put first but duty, his devotion being entirely focused on running Auschwitz. 'I always felt that I had to be on duty the whole time,' he wrote. 'This exaggerated sense of duty has always made life more difficult for me than it actually need have been. Again and again my wife reproached me and said: "You must think not only of the service always, but of your family too."' What Höß did do for his family was vehemently deny that they knew anything about what was happening at the camp, the only way he felt he could protect them. 'Yet what did my wife know about all that lay so heavily on my mind? he asked, before stating, 'She has never been told [despite his denials, it seems inconceivable his wife Hedwig and to some extent his older children did not know what was going on; the Höß family life being well portrayed in the 2023 film *The Zone of Interest*].'

The overwhelming emotion that Höß felt was not love for his family or even for his animals but pity – not for the victims but for himself. Seeing such unadulterated misery and death play out every day was hardest not on the Jews who innocently went to their deaths in droves but on him. From his vaulted position he had to oversee the whole process and it was he who everyone else looked up to, a position he relished though the commandant denied it. 'I had to see everything. I had to watch hour after hour, by day and by night, the removal and burning of the bodies, the extraction of the teeth, the cutting of the hair, the whole grisly, interminable business,' he complained:

> I had to stand for hours on end in the ghastly stench, while the mass graves were being opened and the bodies dragged out and burned. I had to look through the peephole of the gas chambers and watch the process of death itself, because the doctors wanted me to see it. I had to do all this because I was the one to whom everyone looked, because I had to show them all that I did not merely issue the orders and make the regulations but was also prepared myself to be present at whatever task I had assigned to my subordinates.

CHAPTER 14

Special Command 'K' in the Caucasus

AS A MEMBER of the Waffen-SS Niethammer's duties at Auschwitz in September 1942 involved doing what he was told and not questioning orders. It was an unenviable position which left him severely depressed. However, in early October 1942 his prayers were answered when Höß told him that his request for a transfer had been granted. On 12 October 1942, against all the odds in wartime, after just over a month, Niethammer found himself officially transferred again, this time to the Special Command 'K' in the Caucasus, a unit under SS-Sturmbannführer Dr Ernst Schäfer.[1] The Caucasus oilfields in southern Russia between the Black Sea and the Caspian Sea were deemed vital for the German war effort in the East. On 23 July 1942 Hitler had issued a directive to capture the oilfields, codenamed Operation *Edelweiß*. Two days later German troops captured Rostov-on-Don which had opened up the Caucasus region and with it the oilfields of Maikop, Grozny and ultimately Baku. In preparation several new oil firms such as 'German Oil on Caucasus' were established and awarded ninety-nine leases to extract the oil from the region. To transport the oil a large number of pipes were delivered and bombing of the oilfields not yet in German hands was forbidden. To defend the occupied ones from counterattack by the Soviets an SS guard and German Cossack regiment, composed of members of the Cossack National Movement of Liberation, were formed (when war broke out Cossacks found themselves on both sides of the conflict, but most fought for the Soviet Union). As part of the new command Schäfer was given special permission to carry out scientific studies of the region, combining the geology, ethnology and the natural history of the area.

Schäfer was a member of Himmler's personal staff and was one of the most important people in the Third Reich when it came to carrying out scientific studies of the newly conquered territories. He had followed Niethammer's career with interest, greatly admiring his work on the *Handbuch der Deutschen Vogelkunde* and his bird survey of the island of Crete. So, when an opportunity had come up to carry out an expedition to the newly conquered Caucasus region, he had requested from Himmler that Niethammer be on the team. Himmler had agreed so Schäfer had written personally to Höß requesting his guard be transferred to the new Special Command 'K' he was setting up to carry out a survey of the area. This time Höß, although he liked Niethammer, was probably less supportive given the chronic shortage of guards at the camp and the changing war situation but given the request had been sanctioned by the Reichsführer-SS he had little choice. For Niethammer the transfer could not have come at a better time, and he must have quietly thanked God many times for the opportunity to leave behind Auschwitz and the mass extermination of the Jews which by the autumn of 1942 was in full force.

Niethammer's new boss Schäfer was born in 1910 in Cologne, the son of a business executive and from early childhood he was fascinated by nature and in particular birds.[2] To pursue his hobby, he had volunteered as a field assistant at bird observatories in Denmark and on Heligoland. He also took up hunting, as a teenager shooting deer and other game in the forests near his home. From 1928 he studied the natural sciences at the University of Göttingen and the next year also attended the Veterinary School in Hannover where he majored in bird anatomy. Another pupil and protégé of Professor Erwin Stresemann, he studied at the British Natural History Museum in London in 1932/3 and then in 1933 joined the SS, graduating from the Kaiser Friedrich Wilhelm University in Berlin in 1936. A year later he obtained his doctorate and from 1939 he taught at the University of Munich where he was granted a *venia legendi* (teaching permit) and given the academic rank of Reader by the SS. In between studying and scientific research he travelled widely, taking part in no less than three expeditions to China and Tibet in 1931–1932, 1934–1936 and lastly in 1938–1939 just before the outbreak of the Second World War.

The first two expeditions to Tibet were sponsored by the American adventurer and naturalist Broke Dolan II (1908–1945, the II was to distinguish Broke from his father, also called Broke Dolan, who was a very wealthy American industrialist in Philadelphia). Tibet as well as being the base camp for Everest was also rich in wildlife, supporting over 5,000 species of plants and 800 species of animals, about 40 of which were endemic to the area. This included some of the most elusive creatures on earth like the snow leopard and the Tibetan antelope together with characteristic birds like the Tibetan snowcock, the black-necked crane and the bar-headed goose. Dolan organised two expeditions to the 'Roof of the World' to see if he could catalogue the indigenous wildlife and find any new species to science. A big motivation for Schäfer joining the expeditions was to pursue his passion for hunting, the survey team bringing back many specimens to America.

In 1936 Schäfer decided to organise his own trip to Tibet and travelled to the United States where he went about looking for wealthy philanthropists to finance it. However, Himmler had got wind of his visit and summoned him back to Germany, stating that he would personally finance the venture. Himmler's motivation for doing so was for Schäfer and the team to discover the origins of the Aryan race which he believed resided in the ancient tribes in Tibet. The subject obsessed the Reichsführer-SS and in Schäfer's expedition he saw the ideal way to bring back evidence and artefacts relating to a super-race who had given rise to the blonde haired, blue eyed Aryan ideal. As Himmler demanded that the trek be the sole preserve of the SS, he made all the participants officers and told the Reich Research Council to support the project with a grant of 30,000 reichsmarks.

As well as finding the origins of the master race, Himmler had other more practical reasons for supporting the expedition. He also wrote a top-secret document to Hitler and other top-ranking Nazis outlining his plans which stated:

> Mission Tibet.
> It is planned to dispatch to Tibet SS-Hauptsturmführer Dr Ernest Schäfer, who has already been to Tibet three times and returned from his latest research expedition in July of this year, with a small force of about 30 men and weapons for 1,000 to 2,000 men.

The large number of weapons were to bribe the Tibetan army and to encourage them to rise up against the British in the region. The Schäfer covert force was to undergo a special two-month training programme 'not only for medium and heavy mortars but also for heavy machine guns'. Consequently, Himmler's mission to Tibet had two related but contrary objectives – to carry out a scientific study of the area as a cradle of Aryan civilisation and to foster religious discontent to plunge the region into civil unrest (in the end the military objective was dropped following feuding among top Nazis about the political implications if the Germans were found to be arming the Tibetans to rebel against the British).

In 1935, Himmler had set up a unit within the SS called the Ahnenerbe or Bureau of Ancestral Heritage to find out where the Germanic people had come from and trace their origins. As part of their ancestry work, the Ahnenerbe had supported the trek, providing both 'scientific credibility' and materials. Commenting on the expedition to Schäfer, Himmler said, 'We, as men from the SS, could fearlessly go much further and do much more to promote the sadly inadequate understanding of the New Germany, than if, even with a pure conscience, we were to travel under the mask of an obscure though neutral scientific academy.' Privately Schäfer thought Himmler's views on finding the roots of the Aryan master race were hokum but he went along with the Reichsführer-SS so his expedition would get the funding.

As well as being a leading member of Himmler's staff, Schäfer as a very keen huntsman had been awarded many trophies for shooting game. However, the year before he had been involved in a tragic accident on a boat that he was sharing with his wife. Schäfer had slipped when taking aim at a duck and shot his wife in the head instead, killing her instantly. Despite the accident he continued to be an avid hunter and was keen to use the expedition to bring back specimens, particularly of the rare indigenous wildlife. Another member of the expedition was Bruno Beger (1911–2009), a young anthropologist who like Schäfer had joined the SS in 1935. He had attended the University of Jena studying anthropology where he had come under the influence of the infamous Hans Günther (1891–1968), a German writer and eugenicist who advocated scientific racism and had heavily influenced Hitler. It was Beger's job to take measurements of the local Tibetans so he could compare them with the German people to see if the two were related.

The five-man team started on the expedition in early in May 1938, their ship docking at Colombo in Ceylon (now Sri Lanka). From there, they took another boat to Madras (now Chennai) and a third one to

Calcutta (now Kolkata). The British authorities in India were at first reluctant to admit the team to Tibet, suspecting them of spying, but Schäfer used his considerable charm and by the end of the year they had entered the mountain kingdom complete with swastika flags attached to their mules and baggage. On arrival in Tibet, they were pleased to see that the swastika was flying everywhere, the ubiquitous lucky sign known locally as *yungdrung*. Schäfer and the team had also come across it during their time in India where, like in Tibet, it had long been a symbol of good fortune. The previous Dalai Lama had died in 1933 and as the new one was only 3 years old, the team were greeted by the Regent who made them feel very welcome (despite the Nazis believing that the Tibetan religion of Buddhism, like Hinduism in India, had 'diluted' the Aryans who had come to Tibet, sapping their 'spiritual strength'). There they made a film, collected ethnic artefacts, took measurements of the local people and above all hunted, killing large numbers of the local wildlife to bring back. They also got extremely drunk most evenings as a way of dealing with the cold, the 'tasteless' food and the boredom, the Tibetans sarcastically giving them the nickname 'dry cup'.

To enter Lhasa, the closed-off capital of Tibetan Buddhism, required the Dalai Lama's consent. After Schäfer again used his charm on the Regent the team became the first westerners to be permitted into the ancient kingdom, much to the jealousy of the British. Here Schäfer, who was called the 'master of a hundred sciences' by an impressed Regent, was allowed to roam at will if he left behind his scientific equipment and did not kill any of the wildlife. Schäfer completely ignored both instructions, taking geomagnetic measurements, conducting ethnological studies and shooting a large number of birds and other animals. Beger took lots of measurements to assess the local people, using a compass, skull tongs and a device to measure the lower jaw. He also smeared Negocoll, a plastic composition used for making model castings, onto the faces of test subjects to make skull impressions. The pseudo-scientific mission – a bizarre mix of ethnography, zoology and drunken revelry – ended three weeks before the start of the war. The team arrived home in Germany with more than 3,500 bird skins, 2,000 eggs, 400 skulls, hundreds of mammals, reptiles and amphibians, thousands of butterflies and other insects, 2,000 ethnological objects, dozens of new minerals, numerous topographic maps and 40,000 black-and-white photographs. There they were met at Munich airport in person on 4 August 1939 by a delighted Himmler. In recognition of the success of expedition, particularly their 'scientific achievements', Schäfer was presented with the highly prestigious SS Death's Head Ring and Honour Sword.

With the outbreak of the war, Schäfer had to put his scientific studies on hold but in 1942 founded the Sven Hedin Institute for Central Asian Research and Expeditions based in Munich and Salzburg with a staff of 30 scientists. The institute was named after the famous Swedish aristocrat and explorer Sven Hedin (1865–1952) who in his youth had studied in Berlin, after graduating regularly visiting Central Asia on expeditions. Hedin was also an ardent fan of Hitler and National Socialism and was a big supporter of the institute named after him. In recognition of his work for it, the University of Munich awarded him an honorary doctorate. The following year both men attended the opening of the Grand Tibet exhibition called 'Secret Tibet' in the 'House of Nature' in Salzburg, together with leading figures from the party and the army. Schäfer also produced a book and a film of the expedition. However, the film was not widely shown due to Himmler being unhappy with some of the content, in particular telling Schäfer he objected to it because of 'the mocking way in which indigenous people and states are … characterised' and that the 'reservations which I had about public showings of the film are thus justified.' Coming from Himmler this was a serious put-down and could be read as being extremely hypocritical given his views on race. However, it was a reflection of his warped view that the Aryan race was descended from people in the region who ironically therefore needed to be presented in a positive light.

The new expedition to the Caucasus being led by Schäfer relied heavily on Niethammer and the anthropologist Beger who had taken the measurements of the local people on the expedition to Tibet just before the war. While Niethammer was given the task of surveying the geology and natural history of the region, Beger's job was to measure the Jews in the area, particularly those from the mountains. Schäfer wanted to see if there were any anatomical differences with Jews who lived at lower altitudes in Central Europe, described in the Waffen-SS handbook of the expedition as a 'foreign body'. For this Schäfer requested heavily armed Waffen-SS troops and a wide range of surgical equipment including 'twenty scalpels of varying sizes, six strong scissors and five large mincing machines' (the mincing machines were for the removal of human flesh). Just as the expedition was getting ready to leave, the security situation in the Caucasus changed. The 1942 offensive in the region had slowed as the Wehrmacht met stiff resistance in the mountains, and following Soviet breakthroughs in the siege of Stalingrad, the Germans found themselves on the defensive. After studying a variety of intelligence reports from the front, Schäfer contacted Himmler who agreed that the expedition should be postponed until the military situation improved (the German army was forced to withdraw from the area that winter after a Soviet counterattack, codenamed Operation *Little Saturn*, threatened to cut them off and they never returned).

For Niethammer the postponement of the expedition was a severe blow, both to his career in the Waffen-SS and his quest to carry out a bird survey of the area to complement the ones he had done at Auschwitz and on Crete. More urgently it also meant that he, like the other members of the expedition, could now be transferred to another part of the Waffen-SS. For the German ornithologist that held out the daunting prospect of him making a very unwelcome return to Auschwitz concentration camp. So Niethammer appealed directly to Schäfer who, after hearing about his ordeal, sympathised with his predicament and appealed to Himmler. He agreed to Niethammer continuing as research biologist under his Special Command 'K' with a continued focus on the conquered territories.

The continuation of his employment came as a huge relief to Niethammer, a desk-based job while dull at least allowing him to finish writing up his paper on the birds of Crete. That year he was honoured when the Hungarian pioneering ornithologist András Keve (1909–1984) proposed naming a subspecies of the great rosefinch after him, with the latin name *Carpodacus rubicilla niethammeri.* The great rosefinch is a striking looking crimson-coloured bird with white flecks which nests in the alpine zone across the Greater Caucasus, like all finches the species possessing an imposing bill for cracking open seeds. The proposal was contained in a paper called 'Some new breeds of birds from Asia', Keve publishing it in the *Anzeiger der Akademie der Wissenschaften* in Wien (*Gazette of the Academy of Sciences* in Vienna). The year before Keve had become a docent (one grade below professor but with lecturing rights) at the University of Budapest so the proposal was probably his way of keeping in with the Third Reich's foremost ornithologist and having his pioneering work on the collared dove recognized (Keve was born Andreas Kleiner but changed his German name to the Hungarian

András Keve to keep in with his fellow countrymen and ironically so he would not be accused of being German).[3]

Instead of Niethammer being sent back to Auschwitz, Beger, the expedition anthropologist, was dispatched in his place and arrived there in June 1943. He had been told that 'particularly appropriate materials' had arrived at the camp in the form of Jews with interesting facial features and other anatomical points of note, including some like those in the Tibetan region. On his arrival Beger 'was lost in admiration for the avenues of blooming popular trees' and requested from Höß a range of 'interesting types for measurement'. He was not disappointed – 79 male and 30 female Jews, two Poles, two Uzbeks, a mixed race-prisoner with one Uzbek and one Tajik parent and one Chuvash from the region of Kazan were made available for his 'scientific studies'. 'The Uzbek, a great healthy son of the soil, might have been a Tibetan,' he wrote to Schäfer, clearly very impressed with the specimen, adding, 'His manner of speech, his movements and his way of presenting himself, were simply delightful, in a word : Central Asian … as for my Auschwitz impressions, I'll have to speak to you in detail, face to face.'

Once each prisoner had been carefully measured and catalogued by Beger, they were taken away in special hygienic overalls and transported by lorry under armed guard to another concentration camp at Natzweiler-Struthof in the Vosges Mountains. Here they were carefully gassed by Professor August Hirt (1898–1945), an *SS-Hauptsturmführer* (captain). Hirt was a Swiss-German anatomist who was the chairman of the Reich University in Strasbourg. He was insistent that the procedure couldn't be done at Auschwitz as each specimen needed to be gassed separately rather than en masse and their corpses specially preserved. The corpses were then sent to the Reichsuniversität Straßburg anatomical theatre for inclusion in his skeleton collection. Hirt had experimented with mustard gas on inmates at the concentration camp before starting to collect skeletons. He wanted to establish a collection of model specimens from across the world at the Institute of Anatomy in Strasbourg where they could be studied by Nazi anatomists. However, as the war turned decisively against Germany the project was put on hold and then cancelled so the gruesome collection was never completed.

Chapter 15

Natural Selection in Action

THE YEAR 1943 started with Niethammer working hard on both his paper on the collared dove and his bird survey of Crete. With Schäfer's agreement he was also now working with the Natural History Museum in Bonn where he had been based before the war as most of the staff had been called up. In April 1943 he published two papers in the *Journal für Ornithologie* – the first was a study of the birds of the Peloponnese peninsula region in southern Greece and was a prelude to his report on the birds of Crete (in the introduction Nietmammer thanked the Oberkommando der Wehrmacht, the High Command of the Army). The full title of the paper was *Beiträge zur Kenntnis der Brutvögel des Peloponnes. Ergebnisse einer biologischen Forschungsreise nach dem Peloponnes und nach Kreta 1942, ausgeführt im Aufträge des Oberkommandos der Wehrmacht ind des Reichsforschungsrates. Nr. I.* – Contributions to the knowledge of the breeding birds of the Peloponnese. Results of a biological research trip to the Peloponnese and to Crete in 1942, commissioned by the High Command of the Wehrmacht and the Reich Research Council. No. 1'.[1]

Niethammer's next paper was the write-up of his collared dove survey and was called the 'The brood of the Collared Pigeon in Vienna'. The collared dove is smaller than the ubiquitous wood pigeon but larger than the turtle dove, its most distinctive feature as its name suggests being its black half-collar which has a distinctive white edge. Originally from the temperate and subtropical parts of Asia, its distribution formerly ranged from southern China to Turkey. However, at the beginning of the twentieth century it had started expanding its range, firstly being recorded in the Balkans in the 1920s and then spreading west. By the time Niethammer wrote his paper the bird had spread to Bulgaria and Romania with sporadic records occurring throughout the

Protectorate of Bohemia and Moravia (the German name given to the former Czechoslovakia), Germany and Austria, where he monitored a nest in the capital Vienna near his home. What made the collared dove particularly attractive to him and other ornithologists was that it bred close to human habitation, making it an easy bird to monitor even in wartime. At eight pages long Niethammer's paper was therefore both a record of the spread of the species across Europe and his observations from the nest he had been monitoring in the Austrian capital.

The female collared dove lays two white eggs, both sexes taking it in turn to incubate them with the young typically fledging after fifteen to nineteen days. The paper made use of many of the records that ornithologists across the Third Reich had been sending into the natural history museums in Bonn, Berlin and Vienna since the beginning of the war. This showed that remarkably up to six broods could be raised in a year if food was available, although in practice with the cooler European summers three to four broods were more common. On publication Niethammer's paper was widely read as ornithologists sought to understand what was driving the dove's rapid expansion, Niethammer presenting their sightings as being an exciting new opportunity for study rather than a threat to existing bird communities. In its own way the collared dove was therefore a perfect avian metaphor for the expansion of the Third Reich, albeit in the opposite direction. What the collared dove study also provided to Niethammer and other German ornithologists was an interesting scientific distraction at a time when the war was going increasingly badly for Germany.

The beginning of the year had seen the German Sixth Army surrounded at Stalingrad before capitulating and the rump of Rommel's defeated forces evacuated from North Africa. In Russia the Germans had found themselves for the first time on the defensive although they had managed to retake the city of Kharkov at a great cost. In Poland just after Niethammer's paper had been published there had been an uprising in the Warsaw Ghetto. It was the largest act of Jewish resistance during the war and had come about after more than a quarter of a million Jews had been transported from the ghetto to concentration camps where they had been murdered. Against overwhelming odds, the remaining Jews, who suspected their fate, had risen up, building bunkers and then using guns and weapons smuggled into the ghetto to kill their oppressors. The insurgency was brutally put down by the Germans, over 13,000 Jews being killed in the process as well as 150 German guards and soldiers. Marek Edelman, a heart surgeon and Polish political prisoner who was a leader during the uprising, summed up the Jewish fighting spirit when he said they weren't willing 'to allow the Germans alone to pick the time and place of our deaths'.

When the news broke of the Polish insurgence, Niethammer would not have been surprised at the turn of events. As a former concentration camp guard at Auschwitz, he was only too aware that the Jewish people were being systematically exterminated on Hitler's orders and that at some point news of the Holocaust would leak out. However, Nazi propaganda sought to play down the scale of the Warsaw uprising, instead claiming that German forces had swiftly and successfully put down the revolt. In response Niethammer chose to ignore the news, just like he had done at Auschwitz, instead focusing on the very favourable response to his paper on the collared dove. While the paper was well received, annoyingly many records had come too late for inclusion, he complaining that 'it was only during the printing process that Dr. Kummerlöwe wrote that he also found the collared pigeon in 1943 in the central Bulgarian towns of Sliven, Nova Zagora and Kazanlük and observed it regularly in Rustschuk'. However, Niethammer was able to incorporate the records into a lecture he gave on the expansion of the collared dove at the 61st annual meeting of the Deutsche Ornithologische Gesellschaft which took place in Berlin on 3 July 1943. Here his work was widely praised by those present, including warm words of admiration from his great mentor Erwin Stresemann. Two days after the German ornithologists' club met, over a thousand kilometres away in Russia, the Battle of Kursk had begun. The largest tank battle in history, it would see the German offensive stopped and then repelled at the cost of an immense number of Soviet lives. The battle was the final attack that the Germans were able to launch on the Eastern Front, their defeat meaning that from then on, the Soviets were on the offensive. The net, although still over a thousand kilometres away, was slowly but surely beginning to tighten around Niethammer.

In October Niethammer published his long-awaited survey of the birds of Crete which he had carried out the previous year. He had spent months meticulously going through all his notes and the considerable haul of bird skins which had been brought back by the expedition team. It was Niethammer's most extensive report and, he hoped, his tour de force. The title was 'About the birdlife of Crete. Results of a biological research trip to the Peloponnese and Crete in 1942 on behalf of the Wehrmacht High Command and the Reich Research Council'. By including the German armed forces and the Third Reich's research council in the title, Niethammer made sure that both his protector and paymaster were prominently acknowledged. The report ran to a lengthy 54 pages and included 19 photos and a map of the island. Detailed and rigorous but rambling in parts, it was another example of how the war had created a scientific opportunity but one that had been compromised by the deteriorating security situation. Nevertheless, the report was still the most up to date and comprehensive survey of the breeding birds of Crete ever carried out. It was published in the well-respected *Annalen des Naturhistorischen Museums in Wien*, the *Annals of the Natural History Museum in Vienna*, where he worked. When it came out the report was again very well received by the ornithological community and like his paper on the collared dove, it also provided a much-needed diversion during wartime. However, the war was getting ever closer, in October 1943 B-17 Flying Fortresses of the United States Army Air Forces attacking Munich, the home of Nazism, and targets across Austria for the first time.

In the introduction Niethammer formerly acknowledged the major contribution made by Dr Wettstein, expedition leader and the director of the Kaiser Wilhelm Institute in Berlin, for his 'contribution to ecology'. Name-checking his boss, a staunch national socialist, no less than five times in the opening paragraph, Niethammer gushed he had 'significantly deepened our knowledge of the distribution of birds' and offered 'heartfelt thanks' for his support for the survey. It was another calculated move designed to keep the senior Nazi leadership onside. During the four months the team had surveyed the island, from late April to late July 1942, they had collected a grand total of 268 skins. Following the survey Dr Wettstein returned with 169 birds to the Natural History Museum in Vienna, the remaining ninety-nine skins being sent to the Natural History Museum in Berlin. After the acknowledgements Niethammer used his introduction to discuss the differences between birds occurring on Crete and those present on the Greek mainland and surrounding islands in the Aegean Sea. To explain the difference in bird distribution across the study area, Niethammer examined the impact of island biogeography and natural selection on the survey results (island biogeography theory states that smaller, more isolated islands have fewer numbers of plant and animal species, natural selection being the evolutionary process by which birds adapt and change).

Setting the context for the report, Niethammer wrote that ornithological research on Crete had lagged behind that of other similar islands and mainland Europe, citing the few studies that had been carried out, including that of the Austrian ornithologist Guido Schiebel who had published a paper in 1926 about the birds he had recorded and shot on the island, Niethammer regretting he did not have access to the collection which was housed in the Reichsmuseum in Berlin. Like his Auschwitz report the bulk of the paper was taken up by a systematic list of birds found on the island, both those recorded by the team and any other verified records. The survey focused on the breeding birds of the island, migrants and 'accidentals' being assigned to an appendix (they were covered in much more detail by Stresemann's paper on Crete, also published in the same year). Niethammer reported that the team had recorded seventy-five different species of breeding birds on Crete, a total he thought might increase in the future but not significantly. He wrote that 'measured against the size of the island and its strong vertical structure, the population of breeding birds must be considered quite low!' To illustrate this, he compared the island's total to the Peloponnese, the adjacent peninsula on the Greek mainland, which had 126 breeding birds and the adjacent country of Macedonia which had 215 breeding species. This paucity of species, Niethammer maintained, could not solely be explained by the island breaking away from mainland Greece way back in geological time.

Adamant that no birds had been missed by the survey team, he instead believed that they had always been absent from Crete. To prove his point Niethammer listed those species which were conspicuous by their absence. This included herons, Niethammer listing four species which did not occur on Crete, including the purple heron, due to 'ecological reasons', the island lacking any large areas of freshwater. However, he found it far more difficult to explain why the little owl was so rare on the island, 'whereas it is otherwise common throughout the Aegean islands'. Of fourteen characteristic Mediterranean species he found that eleven occurred across the Aegean Sea in Greece but none were found on Crete. Birds were also not well represented in the high mountains of the island, Niethammer stating that the red-billed chough, alpine chough, alpine accentor and the bearded vulture were the only regular breeding species present (he also recorded the griffon and black vulture, but they were mainly associated with lower-altitude habitats). As all four species were present in the Tarus high mountain region of Turkey, he concluded that they had colonised Crete when it was still joined to the country. However, birds of Asian origin were the exception, Niethammer stating that of the remaining forty-two species recorded as breeding on the island, the majority were of European origin.

The reasons for these differences fascinated Niethammer who believed the lack of birds on Crete could not just be explained by it being separated from the Greek mainland by the Aegean Sea. In addition, he thought that the island's limited habitats restricted its diversity, it lacking the vegetation to support certain species. He wrote, 'The absence of deciduous oaks on Crete accounts for the absence of middle spotted woodpecker and the Eurasian nuthatch, the absence of black pine the crossbill, and the absence of firs coal tit and mistle thrush.' But he could find no ecological explanation as to why the magpie did not breed on Crete when it was so common in the Peloponnese region of Greece. The same was true of the robin, the firecrest and the turtle dove, the latter having 'advanced from Attica to the Cyclades on Naxos and also nests on Rhodes'. To back up his arguments about the restricted number of species, Niethammer compared the birds on Crete with the Cyclades, the set of islands off the Greek coast.

Lying south-east of Greece, the Cyclades is an archipelago composed of 2,200 islands scattered across the Aegean Sea, thirty-three of which were inhabited. The largest inhabited island was Naxos, where Wettstein had spent time recording the breeding birds so they could be compared with Crete. However, the islands had not been easy to survey because of the security concerns in wartime. The first Italian occupation forces arrived there in May 1941 but by the time that Niethammer had published his paper in October 1943 the islands had been taken over by the Germans. This had followed the Italian surrender the previous month, the Germans also occupying the Italian part of Crete. Like the rest of the country during the Nazi occupation all the islanders had suffered from lack of food, many starving to death in what became known as the Great Famine. This had reached a peak the previous winter when thousands of people had died, any food coming into the islands being requisitioned for the German occupying forces. Soon, like on Crete, there were active resistance movements on all the major islands. Niethammer, however, was concerned purely with the birds of the archipelago, not the state of the people trying to eke out a living under the Nazi yoke.

Despite the limited number of bird species he found on Crete, Niethammer believed that the island had been isolated from the mainland long enough to evolve endemics (separate species occurring in a single geographical zone and nowhere else) and subspecies (members of the same species but with different physical characteristics, usually a geographically isolated race). In keeping with Nazi ideology, he gave considerable coverage in the report to these 'racial differences', commenting on the distribution and characteristics of different species. 'Some subspecies are more widespread in the Aegean islands, while others indicate Crete's relationships with mainland Greece or Asia Minor and Cyprus,' he wrote. However, he felt this was difficult to prove as some subspecies were only very slightly different from their mainland counterparts while for others any differences could only be detected in newly molted birds (abrasion soon erasing any colour variation). The birds Niethammer considered endemic to Crete were

Certhia brachydactyla spatzi (Cretan short-toed treecreeper)
Muscicapa striata eretica (Cretan spotted flycatcher)
Troglodytes troglodytes stresemanni (Cretan wren, notably named after his mentor Erwin Stresemann)
Fringilla coelebs schiebeli (Cretan chaffinch, named after a Spanish ornithologist)

In one of the most remarkable parts of the report Niethammer wrote that he had recorded evolution by natural selection in action on the island. It was a bold claim designed to back up his belief that endemic and separate subspecies had evolved on Crete. The claim was also very much in line with the teachings of one of his heroes, the naturalist and father of evolution Charles Darwin (1809–1882). By embracing Darwinism in his report, Niethammer again ensured that his racial theories supported those of the Nazi leadership. They had twisted the theory of human evolution defined by Darwin to back up their ideology. Central to this was Nazi teaching that the Aryan or Nordic race had evolved to a higher level than other races, their superior intellect being a product of natural selection. The Nazis also quoted Darwin to underpin other elements of their ideology including the racial struggle for survival and the evolutionary benefits of collectivism by which the individual was subordinate to the state.

To prove natural selection in action Niethammer had meticulously measured all the skins that had been collected during the survey, from both the islands and mainland, and concluded that variation could be detected in both beak and wing length.

> The most striking result of my systematic investigation of the available bird collection was the fact that the formation of [new] breeds on Crete started almost exclusively with the beak and wings and here caused the same effect in a considerable number of species. Within Europe, the island of Crete is almost a classic breeding ground for birds, which are distinguished from the other members of the same species by longer beaks or (and) shorter wings. The beak length of the Crete birds is in no case demonstrably shorter than in any other European breed of the same species, but in many cases significantly longer.

He listed the following subspecies as having a longer beak:

Coloeus monedula pontocaspicus (western jackdaw)
Oenanthe oenanthe virago (northern wheatear)
Fringilla coelebs schiebeli (Cretan chaffinch)
Saxícola torquata graecorum (European stonechat)
Lullula arborea wettsteini (woodlark named after Dr. Wettstein)
Troglodytes troglodytes stresemanni (Cretan wren)

And these subspecies as having longer beaks with shorter wings:

Chloris chloris mühlei (greenfinch)
Galerida cristata cypriaca (crested lark)
Lullula arborea wettsteini (woodlark)
Turdus merula insularum (Eurasian blackbird)
Montícola solitarius behnkei (blue rock thrush)
Saxícola torquata graecorum (European stonechat)

These changes in beak and wing length, Niethammer believed, perfectly illustrated Rensch's principle.[2] A German evolutionary biologist (1900–1990), Bernhard Rensch had studied how environmental factors had influenced the evolution of geographically isolated populations like the birds on Crete. In 1929 he had published a seminal book called *Das Prinzip geographischer Rassenkreise und das Problem der Artbildung* or *The principle of geographical racial groups and the problem of speciation*. This discussed the relationship between geography and speciation and stated that different racial groups will evolve over time in isolated populations where this gave them an evolutionary advantage. Originally based in the zoological museum in the University of Berlin where he was head of department, unlike Niethammer he had refused to join the Nazi Party. Following sustained harassment, in 1937 he was forced to leave the museum and took a much lower position at another zoological museum in Münster. In 1940 he was conscripted into the army but was discharged two years later for medical reasons (after the war Rensch published a rule that made his name: Rensch's rule states that in groups of related species, sexual size dimorphism or the difference between males and females is more pronounced in larger species).

The bulk of Niethammer's report was taken up with a systematic list of the seventy-five breeding birds he had found on the island together with the migrant and accidental birds, starting with the raven and finishing with the quail which in the autumn was 'shot, killed and caught by the hundreds'. Like his Auschwitz bird paper for each species, he gave a range of basic information but also included where he thought they differed from mainland species and some personal insights into their behaviour. In the case of Eleonora's falcon, a bird of prey found predominantly in the Mediterranean, he recorded twenty to fifty of them flying early one morning in the summer from the outer lying island of Theodoro to the sand dunes of Crete to forage on locusts. In contrast, during the heat of the day he found them sheltering in shaded rock crevices on the cliff faces of the island. When it came to breeding Niethammer noted that the falcon delayed egg-laying until August so the fledglings could be fed on migrating turtledoves, orioles, quails, hoopoes and other smaller birds. 'The late start of the breeding season is therefore closely related to the autumn migration of most small birds,' he wrote.

> In September, there are rich feeding grounds on the rocky islands and reefs, which are otherwise relatively scarce in birds, where the Eleonora's falcon breeds. ... The preferred food for the young hawks, as far as migratory birds are concerned, seems to be the hoopoe. In the late summer of 1942, Mr. Hans Bauer saw Eleonora's falcons on the island of Theodoro (in litt [*in litteris*, in correspondence] to Dr. v. Wettstein) and reported: 'I observed a falcon hitting a hoopoe. I also found remains and feathers of this bird on all resting places and nests.' The hoopoe, as a particularly conspicuous bird, seems to be easy prey for the Eleonora's falcons and to play a significant role in their food biology.

It was not just the hoopoe that was conspicuous, so were the 'fat young' of the falcon, starving boys risking their lives by climbing down the very steep cliff faces to take them for the pot.

The rarest bird on the island was the black vulture which Stresemann had already reported following Siewert filming them. Niethammer wrote, '*Aegypius monachus*. Black vulture. Frivaldszky reports that his collectors observed the black vulture in the vicinity of the "snowy mountains" on Crete [Aquila 1902, p. 208]. This old statement, which has remained unconfirmed for almost a hundred years [collectors saw the species near the snow-covered mountains in 1843–1845], regains significance through the finding of the black vulture by Siewert, who even filmed it on Crete in November 1942. The species is probably a breeding bird.' The report finished with a five-page description of the geography, geology and ecology of the island by Wettstein, another attempt by Niethammer to make sure that his boss's contribution to the expedition was properly recognised (after the war in 1970 von Jordans proposed a new Cretan subspecies of the great tit and named it after Niethammer, *Parus major niethammeri*. Today with advances in genetics we know that none of the species proposed by Niethammer are endemic although some ornithologists believe the Cretan short-toed treecreeper may be a candidate. However, many subspecies are recognised including the great tit).[3]

In October 1943 at the same time as Niethammer published his report on the birds of Crete, the Germany army was involved in murdering members of the local resistance on the island. Supplied and supported by British Special Operations Executive (SOE) agents, the resistance had increased considerably in both numbers and effectiveness in the year since Niethammer had left. Following a series of raids the previous month by the Wehrmacht, several resistance groups had been infiltrated or given up after captured members had been tortured by the Gestapo. One of those betrayed was a partisan group led by Manolis Bandouvas who fearing for his life had decided to flee and was hiding in the mountains. On 4 October 1943 his partisan group together with local resistance fighters came into contact with a German patrol and killed all its members. When the German commander on Crete, Bruno Bräuer (1893–1947), heard of the attack he ordered ruthless reprisals against the villages of Kali Sykia and Kallikratis. On 6 October, twelve women accused of helping the resistance were rounded up in the village of Kali Sykia, tied to stakes and burnt alive as a warning to the rest of the village. Two days later, on 8 October, the Germans surrounded the village of Kallikratis after having sealed off all the exit routes. The local people were then dragged from their homes at gunpoint and herded into the local church where they were told they were going to be shot unless they named the members belonging to local resistance groups and their location. Around thirty men who the Germans either suspected or refused to cooperate were marched from the church and executed outside their homes, many in front of their families. They were killed by members of the Jagdkommando Schubert headed up by Friedrich 'Fritz' Schubert (1897–1947), a ruthless paramilitary commander in charge of crushing resistance on the island.[4] During the executions women and children tried to escape but were turned back by heavy machine-gun fire directed just over their heads by soldiers on the outskirts of the village. Despite the Germans trying to cover the massacre up, many villagers and several men in the resistance movement who had been hiding witnessed it and lived to give testimony of the slaughter.

Chapter 16

The Hygiene Institute of the Waffen-SS

IN NIETHAMMER'S OTHER bird survey area of Auschwitz the number of people being killed was of a different magnitude. Transports were arriving there daily, and thousands of Jews were being murdered or 'processed'. Since he had left, the new camp of Auschwitz II-Birkenau been transformed beyond recognition, two sprawling new camps or segments having been completed. The sheer scale of the new site meant that it covered over 140 hectares and took over an hour to walk around. The first sector, known as BI, had been built in the village of Brzezinka or Birkenau during 1941/2, and was divided into two sub-sectors, BIa and BIb. This contained sixty-two residential barracks (thirty brick and thirty-two wooden), along with ten barracks containing washrooms and toilets, two kitchens, two bathhouses and two storage barracks. Work on the second sector, BII, had begun in 1942 and was finished by the time Niethammer published his report. This sector was divided into seven sub-sectors labelled from a to g and consisted of over 150 wooden barracks. Sector BIIa contained sixteen residential barracks, three barracks containing washrooms and toilets, and a kitchen barracks. Sub-sectors BII b, c, d, and e each contained thirty-two residential barracks, six barracks containing washrooms and toilets, and two kitchens. In sub-sector BIIf there were seventeen residential barracks and one bathhouse. Thirty barracks used mainly as warehouses were built in sector BIIg, along with one brick bathhouse used, ironically, as a sauna.

The four large gas chambers and the new crematoria had also been completed, coming into operation in the summer of 1942 and by the autumn were working at full capacity. Like the undressing rooms the new gas chambers at crematoria II and III were located underground while those at crematoria IV and V were above ground in the new camp. About 4,000 people a day were being processed in the crematoria, approximately equivalent to the number of words Niethammer was writing each month for his report on the birds of Crete. This meant that the crematoria at full capacity could in theory burn over 1.6 million corpses a year. However, prisoners who worked in the camp disposing of the bodies later stated that the daily capacity of the four crematoria in Birkenau was double the official total, at its peak about 8,000 corpses a day being burnt.

The Jews being sent to Auschwitz included 7,500 sent from Italy in October 1943 following the country capitulating to the Allies the month before. This marked the end of the twenty-one-year fascist regime of Benito Mussolini (1883–1945), after his arrest and imprisonment German forces moving quickly to free him and occupy the whole of the country – he was rescued in a daring raid from his prison at the Hotel Campo Imperatore high up in the Gran Sasso mountains on 12 September 1943 by a special Fallschirmjäger unit and Waffen-SS commandos led by Major Harald-Otto Mors, (1910–2001). One month after Italy had surrendered, on 13 October 1943, the Jewish ghetto in Rome was sealed off and then raided by German security forces, over 1,000 Jews being arrested and transported to Auschwitz. On the same day the new Italian government declared war on Nazi Germany, their one-time Axis partner, bringing the war ever closer to Niethammer.

After Niethammer sent out his Crete paper to the other German and Austrian ornithologists in his network, he was contacted by his mentor Stresemann. He commended his former pupil on the report, stating that it complemented his own study and that Crete had been transformed from being an island where there was virtually no recent ornithological information to one where there was now a comprehensive and up-to-date list of the breeding birds. Stresemann believed that combined the two reports formed a unique baseline assessment against which all future ornithological studies would be judged. The Wehrmacht and the Waffen-SS were also pleased with their reception, the paper increasing Niethammer's international standing (and propaganda value) and showing that, like his previous report on Auschwitz, serious scientific studies followed in the wake of great German military victories.

Stresemann, however, had an ulterior motive for praising the report. After commending the author, he suggested Niethammer consider sending his paper to one of the four British prisoners of war he had been in touch with – Peter Conder, George Waterston, John Barrett and Edward Buxton, all incarcerated in Oflag VII-B in Eichstätt, Bavaria, southern Germany. Stresemann had already taken a considerable risk in beginning a correspondence with the British ornithologists and had taken great pleasure in surreptitiously including the observations of Waterston in his own paper on Crete. To entice Niethammer, Stresemann mentioned that all four men had formed a birdwatching club behind barbed wire where they regularly consulted with his *Handbuch der Deutschen Vogelkunde.* Flattered, after assessing the risks, Niethammer asked which of the ornithologists he should address it to and Stresemann replied that he should send the report to Edward Buxton, the first of the four to get in touch with him.

Buxton, as well as being a birdwatcher, was also a budding poet, linguist, and archaeologist. Born in Cheshire, before the war he had lectured at Oslo University and had taken part in archeological digs in Palestine and Ireland. When war was declared he was reading for his Doctor of Philosophy at Oxford. Having first volunteered for the navy, he later responded to a special appeal from the War Office for men with language skills and had been taken prisoner during the Norway campaign in 1940. While a prisoner he had made full use of the libraries in the camps and had given lectures on birds. His literary career had started in 1936 when he had published his first book, *The Pilgrimage*, which was followed two years later by *Judas*, a play in four acts about the apostle Judas Iscariot. After he was captured Buxton wrote prolifically in prison, like birdwatching using it to while away his time behind bars. His first wartime collection of poems was called *Westward* and was published in 1942. The title saw him sitting on the cliffs of Skokholm surrounded by seabirds looking westward out to sea where there were no fences, barbed wire or guard towers, just an endless expanse of ocean. Extraordinarily *Westward* appeared in print while Buxton was still a prisoner, courtesy of his wife, many poems being included in his letters home to her. Another book of poems, appropriately enough called *Such Liberty*, was published two years later, a mixture of natural and military history. It included a poem called 'The Prisoner to the Singing Bird'.

> Sing on, sing on beyond the walls
> That I within may know
> Spring is in the woods again
> Where you may go

Sing on, sing on; then in my cage
I shall delight to hear
That you are glad and free out there –
So near, so near!

When he was not writing poems, Buxton was poring over the pages in Niethammer's bird book, so he was well suited to comment on his paper on Crete.

Sending a report through official channels to a British prisoner of war was a bold but highly risky move, especially as by the time Niethammer got round to dispatching the paper, it was early 1944 and Germany was facing ruin. Although the Allies hadn't yet opened a second front in Europe, most senior German generals believed it was only a matter of time. In the air American and British planes were now bombing German cities night and day, the Luftwaffe lacking the pilots, planes and above all the fuel to stop them. On the Eastern Front the Red Army had taken back much of the motherland occupied by the Germans who were now in full retreat. As the war turned decisively against Germany, in the occupied territories and on the home front the Gestapo had become increasingly active in search of traitors, collaborators and those seeking to reach out to the Allies to sue for peace.

Niethammer was not in any of these categories but knew that as a member of the Waffen-SS and an Auschwitz guard that when the time came, he would pay a high price. What particularly concerned him was that even sending an innocuous ornithological paper could easily be misinterpreted as an olive branch to the British. So, in February 1944 he dispatched a copy of his paper to Buxton as Stresemann had suggested but did not personalise it. Instead, his old boss at the Zoological Museum Koenig in Bonn, Adolf von Jordans, wrote an inscription on the flyleaf which read, '*Liet. John Buxton, mit besten Gruss*' and then added his scribbled signature underneath (writing after the war Niethammer proudly said, 'My work reached England too through Lieutenant Buxton and the Red Cross and was reproduced in an ornithological journal').

Von Jordans had been involved in setting up the museum in 1921 and was a world-renowned expert on the birds of the Mediterranean. In 1932 the Eurasian stone curlew was given the honorary scientific name of *Burhinus oedicnemus jordansi* after him. By the outbreak of the war, he had progressed from curator to the deputy director of the museum. The two had already previously published a paper together in 1940 on the birds of the Fukien region of China, after having been donated lots of bird skins by an entomologist who had been on a major expedition to the area. At 52 years of age von Jordans was too old to be in the military and as the most senior person left working at the museum, he and Niethammer agreed it would look far less suspicious coming from him. Buxton on receiving the report must have been delighted and bemused in equal measure. Given the long hours of boredom spent day after day in the camp any new reading material was avidly consumed but it is likely that the report was passed to Waterston who had been on Crete when the Germans had invaded and knew the island well.

In 1944 as the months went by the Germans military situation became more and more dire. On the Eastern Front the Russians in late March had moved on to Romanian soil for the first time and had launched a final all-out attack on the German forces in the Crimea. In Italy the Germans put up stiff resistance at Monte Cassino but following weeks of bitter fighting had withdrawn from the strategic monastery leaving the road open for the Allies to drive on to Rome. At Auschwitz every day brought the imminent threat of death to those who were still left alive like the Austrian-Jewish psychiatrist Viktor Emil Frankl (1905–1997). He was sent to Auschwitz in 1944 where his mother and brother were murdered. Separated from his beloved wife who had been sent to another camp, he fought a daily battle to stay alive which he did by finding solace in nature and talking to her:

> Another time we were at work in a trench. The dawn was grey around us; grey was the sky above; grey the snow in the pale light of dawn; grey the rags in which my fellow prisoners were clad, and grey their faces. I was again conversing silently with my wife, or perhaps I was struggling to find the reason for my sufferings, my slow dying. In a last violent protest against the hopelessness of imminent death, I sensed my spirit piercing through the enveloping gloom. I felt it transcend that hopeless, meaningless world, and from somewhere I heard a victorious 'Yes' in answer to my question of the existence of an ultimate purpose. At that moment a light was lit in a distant farmhouse, which

> stood on the horizon as if painted there, in the midst of the miserable grey of a dawning morning in Bavaria. '*Et lux in tenebris lucent*' – and the light shineth in the darkness. For hours I stood hacking at the icy ground. The guard passed by, insulting me, and once again I communed with my beloved. More and more I felt that she was present; that she was with me; I had the feeling that I was able to touch her, able to stretch out my hand and grasp hers. The feeling was very strong: she was there. Then, at that very moment, a bird flew down silently and perched just in front of me, on the heap of soil which I had dug up from the ditch and looked steadily at me. [Frankl's wife died of typhus in Bergen-Belsen, the bird, probably a robin, being the messenger. After the war Frankl became one of the leading psychiatrists of his era, devising a branch of psychiatry called logotherapy based on the premise that the primary motivational force of an individual is to find meaning in their life. He also wrote many books including the bestselling *Man's Search for Meaning* which drew on his time in four concentration camps.][1]

For his part Niethammer also feared being sent back to Auschwitz concentration camp. In mid-May 1944 the Waffen-SS Special Command 'K' unit which he had been working for was disbanded as the Caucasus and much of the other conquered territory in Russia was now in Soviet hands. However, this time rather than being sent back to Auschwitz, both Schäfer and von Jordans intervened on his behalf, making representations to Himmler's office. At the end of May, Niethammer was instead transferred to the Waffen-SS's 'Hygiene Institute' on the Knesebeckstrasse in Berlin where he was classified as a zoologist.[2] The institute was involved in a wide range of work including testing vaccines, biological warfare and notoriously human experimentation, both on live prisoners and corpses. The scope of these experiments touched on nearly every branch of medicine from surgery to serology, anatomy to oncology, pathology to bacteriology, infectious diseases to immunology and gynecology to genetics. However, what characterised all of them was that medical ethics were replaced by Nazi racial ideology.

The head of the institute was the chief SS physician Professor Joachim Mrugowsky (1905–1948), a German bacteriologist and staunch Nazi who had joined the SS in 1933. Its scientific supervisor was Professor Heinrich Zeiss (1888–1949) of the University of Berlin, another German doctor who was an epidemiologist. Like his boss he had joined the party early in 1931 and the Nazi Medical Association the next year. He had been a member of the expert advisory board for population and racial policy at the Reich Ministry of the Interior before in 1937 joining the institute. The institute's scope included every SS division which had a field hygiene unit responsible for the soldiers' health at the front. In addition, the SS had two laboratories 'for special purposes', one at Raisko attached to Auschwitz-Birkenau, and another located at Buchenwald. The head of the Buchenwald laboratory was the SS physician Erwin Ding-Schuler (1912–1945), who conducted extensive experiments on over a thousand inmates working on vaccines for a variety of diseases including spotted fever, yellow fever, smallpox, typhus and cholera.

On joining the institute Niethammer's Waffen-SS record as a camp guard was soon put to good use when he was appointed as a liaison officer to the *Hygienisch-Bakteriologische Untersuchungsstelle der Waffen-SS Auschwitz* or the Hygiene and Bacteriology Lab of the Waffen-SS in Auschwitz (also known as the *Hygiene Institut der Waffen-SS und Polizei Süd-Ost* or The Hygiene Institute of the Waffen-SS and Police for the South-East). It was located near Auschwitz and operated as a branch of The Hygiene Institute and had been established following a typhus epidemic which had erupted and quickly spread among the inmates in 1942. Not only did hundreds of emaciated prisoners die but so did SS staff and their families including the wife of Obersturmführer Caesar, a high-ranking SS officer who was head of the farms attached to the concentration camp. Typhus therefore threatened not only to kill the prisoners but also their captors, so to prevent it happening again Dr Eduard Wirths (1909–1945), the *SS-Standortarzt* or SS physician of the garrison, turned to Mrugowsky for help.

On 8 April 1943 he set up the laboratory at the camp and appointed the SS physician Obersturmführer Dr Bruno Weber (1915–1956) as its head, with SS-Untersturmführer Dr Hans Münch (1911–2001) as his deputy (another of his appointments was the infamous 'Angel of Death' Doctor Josef Mengele, 1911–1979, to the position of chief physician of the *Zigeunerfamilienlager* or the Romani family camp at Birkenau).[3] Initially the institute's labs were situated in Blocks 10 and 20 in Auschwitz I, but on 5 May they were moved to a two-storey building in the village of Raisko near the town of

Auschwitz. This included offices accommodating the head, his deputy and clerks, laboratories specialising in bacteriology, biology, histology and chemistry, units for animal, agricultural and botanical experiments together with sterilisation and 'washing-up' rooms and garages. The laboratory even had its own meteorological station, as it was important to know which way the wind was blowing when disinfecting the gas chambers and operating the crematoria. Following several accidents in which SS guards had been accidentally gassed, Höß ordered that they were forbidden to enter the rooms until five hours after they had been aerated.

The remit of the laboratory meant that it required prisoners with specialist skills, particularly in the fields of bacteriology and immunology. So, Weber asked the Gestapo to find him the best specialists from universities and camps across the occupied territories. These included Polish inmates from the camp, professors of biology, pathology and mathematics from across Poland and from 1943 a group of scientists associated with the Rudolf Weigl Institute for typhus and virus research plus their families (Rudolf Weigl, 1883–1957, was a Polish biologist who created the first effective vaccine against typhus). Weber also brought in bacteriologists, histologists and chemists from Czechoslovakia, France and Germany. Together with inmates who did the administrative and cleaning work, around 150 prisoners worked in the Raisko laboratory. The bacteriology section had a separate *Nährbodenküche* or culture media facility where a cooked meat broth was prepared for microbiology. This used an established recipe containing beef or veal and if they weren't available, horse meat. Professor Stefan Ślopek (1914–1995), a Polish doctor and microbiologist who worked at the Rudolf Weigl Institute, made a simple type of broth using the following recipe:

> Mince 1kg [2.2lb] of beef or veal without the fat, put it in water and let it stand overnight at a temperature of 4–6°C [39–43°F]. Remove the fat from the surface, heat to 45°C [113°F] and keep it at 45–50°C [113–122°F] for an hour, then heat for half an hour (do not stir). Next filter through glass wool or linen, topping up with distilled water to the original volume. Sterilize and store.[4]

The day-to-day operations at the institute were run by Unterscharführer (squad leader) Hans Fugger who served as its administrative officer and Scharführer (section leader) Zabel who was one of its disinfection officers. They supplied the meat for the broth and gave it to the prisoners who prepared it for them. However, being on meagre camp rations the inmates were always hungry so when the guards were not looking, they often ate the meat after cooking and seasoning it with salt. They kept this a strict secret from the other prisoners, the guards and Weber fearing they would be reported and put to death in the gas chambers. One prisoner Mieczysław Kieta, No. 59590, who worked as a warehouse attendant in the institute reported that at its peak production about 30–40kg (66–88lb) of meat was delivered to the institute several times a month. The meat was delivered in a motorcycle sidecar or if this was not available, Weber's car.

At first the prisoners would consume large quantities of the boiled meat believing Fugger and Zabel obtained it from the butcher or abattoir in the town of Auschwitz but over time they started to have their doubts. As a result, they began to discreetly monitor the SS men and their meat deliveries. What they discovered was that before going to collect the meat Fugger and Zabel would borrow a range of instruments and then return them to the washing room. After making enquiries with the prisoners who worked there, they found out that the SS men would take out saws, knives, scalpels, and tweezers involved in post-mortem work and then return them covered in blood so they could be cleaned. Together with the instruments they would bring back three buckets of meat which was then used to make the broth. Horrified, the prisoners recognised the buckets – they were from Block 11 where inmates were executed. The meat was not beef, veal or horsemeat but human flesh from prisoners who had been shot or gassed in the chambers. This macabre discovery was confirmed by one of the Kapos working at the camp, Dr. Mikołaj Korn, No. 32387, who one day took a sample with a piece of pale-coloured skin attached to the chemistry lab. When it was analysed by the fellow prisoners, they confirmed it was human flesh. Unbeknown to them, the prisoners had been consuming human broth and were eating their fellow inmates.

The shocking and sickening truth was that the prisoners in the laboratory's at Auschwitz had unwittingly been practising necrophagia. A French prisoner, Dr Léon Landau, No. 64063, confirmed that he had come to the same conclusion after recognising human thigh buttocks and the flesh off human chest bones in the buckets. Another prisoner,

Dr. Jakub Lewin, No. 28476, wrote, 'Apparently prisoner Genci, who worked in the culture media facility, was the first to make the discovery of those "red muscles". One lump of it had a piece of pale skin covered with fair hair. It looked like a woman's skin.' Dr Lewin also confirmed that Mrugowsky on visiting the institute for an official inspection, was overheard in a discussion with Weber talking about the *Menschenbouillon* or human broth. Both Weber and Mrugowsky reacted to this gruesome disclosure by laughing out loud. After the war Dr Hans Münch, who served as deputy head of the Raisko Hygiene Institute, in an interview with the former prisoner Stanisław Kłodzinski, No. 20019, said the following about the human broth:

> The Institute of Hygiene received its horse meat from an SS farm about 50 kilometres away from the city of Oświęcim. Meat was in short supply, primarily because it was pilfered on the way. Zabel often had his fingers in that pie. At first, he made up for the shortfall in Birkenau. Initially the prisoners working in the culture medium room didn't know and continued to bake that meat as well. One day during a booze-up in the institute Zabel spilled the beans. So, Weber had a systematic set of tests conducted to check out the potential of using human flesh from the gas chambers. There were no differences, except that crucially it was more difficult to extract the fat. So, Weber put a ban on the use of human flesh. However, Zabel, who was in charge of the 'broth kitchen', ordered the resolution of the *Fettproblem* [problem with fat] as soon as possible. Whenever he went to Birkenau to collect blood samples, he always brought back flesh from the crematoria. As of the summer of 1944 he no longer needed to do that. At night we used to steal the Wehrmacht's draught horses put out to graze in the meadows in the environs of the institute and killed them.

After word got round that the meat broth was made from human flesh, no prisoner ever ate it again and instead it was buried in the prison garden.

Niethammer, as a former guard with the camp, was not involved in the day-to-day running of the institute but as a liaison officer provided technical and administrative support to Weber and Münch. Like at

Auschwitz Niethammer soon looked for a way out of the gruesome work so while working there he put forward an ambitious proposal to explore Mount Olympus in Greece, believing that like on Crete, species there had 'developed their own, as yet unknown breed'. He was particularly keen to see if large mammals like deer and bears had evolved but, like the expedition to the Caucasus, partisan activity prevented the expedition. While the Greek study was shelved, amazingly despite the rapidly deteriorating security situation, he was still able to participate in two more expeditions – to Bulgaria and Trieste in northern Italy, both still under German control. Like his previous bird studies of Auschwitz and Crete, the expeditions owed more to Nazi realpolitik than they did ornithology. However, this time rather than having to use his influence with either Schäfer or von Jordans to secure the trip, Niethammer instead was sent to Bulgaria on behalf of the Oberkommando der Wehrmacht to personally support Adolf Hitler's efforts to bring the country into the war on the side of Nazi Germany.

At the outbreak of the war Bulgaria remained neutral until 1 March 1941 when it entered an alliance with Nazi Germany out of self-interest and fear. Although it did not take part in the attack on the Soviet Union in June 1941, the pro-fascist Bulgarian government did symbolically declare war on both Britain and the United States by the end of the year to keep Hitler happy. Bulgaria's king was Tsar Boris III who, as well as being ruler, was an expert ornithologist.[5] His pride and joy was a huge collection of bird skins housed in the National Museum of Natural History in Sofia (NMNHS). The museum had been founded in 1889 by his father, Ferdinand I, also a keen ornithologist who had personally taken three years to identify and arrange the collection. Catalogued in 1907, it amounted to 8,229 bird specimens of at least 1,538 species and subspecies and contained 2,210 bird eggs, forty-five bird nests and several dozen fluid-preserved specimens, most of them morphological abnormalities or juveniles. After Ferdinand's abdication in 1918 in favour of his son, Boris III took over the collection, frequently working in the museum. This included in 1927 founding the Bulgarian Ringing Centre at the NMNHS to monitor bird movements. On learning of his passion for birds the German Foreign Office soon sought to exploit it and turn Boris's interest to their advantage. With the war situation rapidly turning against Nazi Germany it had put out a special request that an ornithologist was needed to help with the bird collection in

Sofia, building on the king's legacy. Given his years of ornithological experience including creating the bird museum at Auschwitz there was only one man for the job.

In 1944 Niethammer was dispatched from Berlin to Sofia to study the bird collection and work on a range of other exciting projects including extracting snake venom and looking at the feasibility of capturing Pyrenean horses. There he worked with Dr. Pavel Patev (1889–1950), the Director of Sofia Zoo and the first Bulgarian ornithologist to become the curator of the museum in 1928. Since his appointment, Patev had added an extra 9,000 specimens to the collection, considerably increasing its size. Some of these skins were collected during joint field trips with the British ornithologist Dr. James Harrison (1892–1971) to Greece and other countries in the region. Patev had also organised expeditions throughout Bulgaria including to the swamps along the Danube River such as Srebarna lake (now a United Nations Biosphere Nature Reserve). Working with Alexi Popov, another eminent Bulgarian naturalist and collector, Patev had added another 166 bird skins, most of them water birds including herons, spoonbills, waders, cormorants and ducks. This meant that by the outbreak of the war the museum housed one of the best natural history collections in Europe.

During the early years of the war Patev had continued collecting but by 1943 the first air raids had taken place on Bulgaria by Allied planes and the war situation prevented further expeditions. By this time the king was under huge political pressure from Hitler both to deport all the Jews in the country and to declare war on the Soviet Union. Hitler had personally harangued him on several occasions, and this intensified as the war turned against Germany. On 9 August 1943 the Führer summoned Boris to a stormy meeting at his Wolf's Lair at Rastenburg, East Prussia. Here despite being threatened the king refused to agree to either demand, becoming an unlikely hero.

At the start of the war under pressure the king had passed antisemitic laws but unlike many other countries in occupied Europe, the Bulgarian public did not accept them. Led by the Church and prominent politicians from across the political spectrum, huge numbers of protest letters were sent to him. They included a mocking letter from a former government minister which read, 'Poor Bulgaria! We are seven million people, yet we so fear the treachery of 45,000 Jews who hold no positions of responsibility at the national level that we need to pass exceptional laws to protect ourselves from them!' Despite the scale of the protest under huge pressure the king agreed to the date of 10 March 1943 for the deportations to begin but on learning of the order the Bulgarian people rose up as one to prevent it. Threatening to block the trains and free the prisoners, Boris, sensing the public mood, cancelled the deportation order.

When the Führer learnt that the king had interceded, he was furious. In his meeting with him, Hitler demanded the deportation of all Bulgarian Jews. 'Hitler went into a rage when I refused his demands,' the king recalled. 'Screaming like a madman, he attacked me, and Bulgaria, in a torrent of accusations and threats. It was horrible. But I did not surrender one inch!' Instead, the king told Hitler that the Jews were needed for labour projects in the country and although thousands of men were moved into camps the deportation never went ahead. However, despite the heroic stand of the Bulgarian people, over 11,000 Jews living in the Bulgarian occupied territories of Thrace and Macedonia were deported to death camps including Auschwitz. The king also paid a heavy price for his defiance, suddenly dying of a heart attack in suspicious circumstances on 28 August 1943. Many Bulgarian people believed he had been killed for refusing Hitler's demands, although there was no proof of this and he was succeeded by his 6-year-old son Simeon II. Due to his age a regency council was then appointed headed up by the prime minister.

Just before Niethammer's visit on 30 March 1944 the capital Sofia suffered a heavy air raid by Allied bombers which caused many of its inhabitants to flee. The city was widely damaged, including the museum which was hit by five bombs. These destroyed the taxidermist laboratory where the bird skins were prepared, many other laboratories and several offices while part of the library was also badly damaged. A large fire burnt down parts of the bird and other zoological collections, the archive of the Bulgarian Ringing Centre and many of the books in the library on the ornithology and zoology of the Balkans. Following the raid Niethammer arrived and helped Patev to rescue the remains of the collection. However, with the destruction of the museum and its collection, Niethammer reported back to the institute that his presence was no longer welcome. As a member of the Waffen-SS he was resented by the staff who blamed Germany as much as the Allies for the raid. No longer politically useful, after a few weeks he was recalled to Berlin.

Chapter 17

Liberation of Auschwitz

NIETHAMMER'S NEXT AND last expedition of the war was equally political in nature. He was sent to Trieste in northern Italy on the border with Yugoslavia, again on the surface to carry out scientific studies of the birds and support the natural history museum there. Like the visit to Sofia the institute had an ulterior motive for the trip which was to fortify the city in the face of the Italian surrender. So, after receiving his orders Niethammer got in touch with the Civic Museum of Natural History in the city offering his services. Among the oldest natural history museums in the world, the *Museo Civico di Storia Naturale di Trieste* had been set up in 1846 and was widely respected for its research and collection. It housed a huge number of biological specimens, prize exhibits being a human jaw over 6,400 years old with a dental filling made of bees wax and the largest preserved white shark in the world. Called Carlotta, it measured 5.4 metres in length and had been captured at the beginning of the century in the Kvarner Gulf (today the collection also includes the most complete dinosaur ever found in Italy called Antonio, *Tethyshadros insularis*, a genus of the hadrosauroid or duck-billed dinosaur superfamily).

In all the museum hosted over two million exhibits gathered over a century and a half, including hundreds of bird skins, much to Niethammer's pleasure. Trieste also had a long history of its own, operating as a free city and independent port and shipbuilding centre for hundreds of years. After the Napoleonic Wars it became part of the Austrian Empire where it continued to prosper as the 'Imperial Free City of Trieste' or *Reichsunmittelbare Stadt Triest*. By the beginning of the twentieth century it had become a truly cosmopolitan centre, visited by artists like James Joyce (1882–1941) and a busy hub for international shipping. While German was the language of the Austrian bureaucracy which ran the city and Slovenian the language of the surrounding area, reflecting its international heritage the city had its own Italian dialect called Triestine which was widely spoken by the population.

In 1920 Trieste was transferred to Italy after the disintegration of the Austro-Hungarian Empire but the city had preserved its cultural identity from the rest of the country. From 1943 it was governed by the fascist regime of Benito Mussolini but after it fell and the Italian government capitulated to the Allies, the Germans annexed the city. They declared it part of the *Zone of the Adriatic Littoral* together with the provinces of Udine, Gorizia, Pula and Fiume. The government of the Adriatic Littoral Zone was entrusted by Hitler to the Gauleiter of Carinthia, Friedrich Rainer (1903–1950), an Austrian Nazi who hated Italy. In line with all conquered territories, he ordered the army to round up Slovenes and Jews from across the zone for deportation. However, the prisoners weren't destined for Auschwitz or any other camp on Polish soil but instead were deported much closer to home, to the Risiera de San Sabba. This was the only concentration camp built on Italian soil during the war and was situated in the suburbs of Trieste.

Before the conflict there were around 5,000 Jews in Trieste but after the passing of antisemitic laws in 1938 and the establishment in the city of one of the notorious 'Centres for the study of the Jewish problem' (there were four throughout Italy), many decided to emigrate abroad. Of those that were left the Nazis managed to deport more than 700 Jews from Trieste to Risiera de San Sabba and other extermination camps (only about twenty survived the war). The job of deporting the Jews was given to Odilo Lotario Globocnik (1904–1945), an associate of Adolf Eichmann, who had been born in Trieste, was linked to Himmler and already had played a key role in Operation *Reinhard*, the codename for the German plan to murder the two million Jews living in German-occupied Poland (in addition to Auschwitz three killing centres at Belzec, Sobibor and Treblinka were established during Operation *Reinhard* between 1942 and 1943 to murder the Jews).

In Globocnik's wake followed the Einsatzgruppen or Einsatzkommandos, specialist units who were responsible for fighting partisans and carrying out Nazi ideology towards *untermenschen* or 'sub-humans' in the occupied territories. In all nearly 100 'specialists' arrived from the autumn of 1943 in Trieste, including Niethammer whose experience carrying out scientific studies of bird collections was put to good use at the museum. A few miles away as the crow flies from the exhibition, Globocnik was busy organising his large 'extermination staff' at the new camp. The presence of so many personnel, exceptional given the size of the Jewish population in the city, was because the Adriatic Littoral Zone was of key strategic significance to the Third Reich. The last European conquest by the Nazis, the zone was vital economically and politically for German control of the Mediterranean. Militarily it was the fulcrum between the Balkan sector, devastated by a long partisan war and threatened by the Soviet advance, the Italian front and southern Germany. Here Hitler held out the vain hope of using the region as a springboard for the German recolonisation of Southern Europe.

On Globocnik's orders a former six-storey rice mill at San Sabba was turned into a concentration camp, though at first it was used as temporary prison camp for captured Italian soldiers after they had changed sides the previous year. However, it was then converted into a *Polizeihaftlager* or police detention camp, where hostages, partisans, political prisoners and Jews were locked up. The mill had its own workshops where the inmates were employed making clothes and shoes, dormitories where they slept and cells where they were incarcerated, including 'death cells' where prisoners were executed or gassed imminently and 'torture cells' where they were interrogated. The camp also had its own crematorium to burn bodies, the oven originally being used to dry the rice. Hidden underground, the oven was accessed by descending a staircase, a pipe connecting it to an outside chimney. Prisoners were usually 'dispatched' first with a blow to the back of the head or were shot by firing squad. They were also gassed using vehicle exhaust fumes which were piped into a sealed room near the garages. However, this method of killing was notoriously ineffective, so often Jews were still alive when they were cremated (3,000–5,000 passed through the camp, but many more were rounded up and went from Risiera di San Sabba to concentration camps throughout the Third Reich including Auschwitz).

While he was helping out at the natural history museum in Trieste, Niethammer's contribution to the SS and specifically to scientific studies of birds in the conquered territories was formally recognised when he was promoted to *Obersturmführer* or senior stormtrooper in May 1944, the equivalent rank of lieutenant, it theoretically putting him in command of fifty to a hundred men. After he had left Auschwitz, Niethammer had been given the special rank of SS second lieutenant, a commissioned officer, although he had no troops directly reporting to him. However, although he had been actively encouraged to apply twice for a promotion by Höß and Schäfer in the Waffen-SS, the combat wing of the organisation, he had declined their offers. Instead, he had decided to remain only a *Untersturmführer* or stormtrooper in it because one of the stipulations was that he had to leave the church (as well as Niethammer's religious convictions it is likely that he turned down promotion twice as he did not want to pursue a career in the Waffen-SS. He also probably thought that being 'just a guard' at Auschwitz was the best way of distancing himself from the horrendous crimes that happened there and made it more likely that he would qualify for a transfer as he was not essential to the running of the camp).

Back in Auschwitz in the summer of 1944 a determined attempt to break out of Birkenau was made by the Jewish Special Detachment who worked taking away the corpses. By this time the number of inmates numbered over 105,000, mainly Jewish prisoners, accommodated at the original Auschwitz site, Auschwitz II-Birkenau and the largest sub-camp, Monowitz (also known as Auschwitz III) together with over 40 other sub-camps. With the help of other prisoners from the women's camp, including the Kanada stores, they killed four SS officers, took their weapons and tried to escape. However, their brave attempt to break out was brutally put down by Niethammer's fellow guards, 455 prisoners being killed, many being mowed down in cold blood by the machine guns fired from the watchtowers.

By late 1944 the Germany army was in full scale retreat on all fronts, in Italy the Allies advancing towards the Po River in the north and bringing them ever closer to the city of Trieste. In late October on the Eastern Front the German forces created a defensive line at Syrmia and east Slavonia to safeguard their troops withdrawing from the Balkans. However, after a series of hard-fought battles the Soviets and the Yugoslav armies broke through and headed towards the city. Inside Trieste the Italian resistance stepped up its campaign against the occupying forces while to the south the Allies were pushing ever deeper into northern Italy. This created the 'Race for Trieste' between the Yugoslav army and the Western Allies to see who would be the first to liberate the city. With the threat of encirclement all personnel not vital to the running of the city or the camp were ordered back to Berlin to defend the capital. So, in early 1945 Niethammer once again found himself heading back on a train to the institute where he was shocked to see so much of Berlin in ruins and its people preparing to make a desperate last stand to defend the city. This time, however, on arriving back at his offices he was told that due to the increasingly perilous war situation no soldiers could be spared for special duties and there would be no more transfers or expeditions. Instead, as the net threatened to engulf him, Niethammer was told he was going to have to do something he had never done before – fight.

On 27 January 1945 as Niethammer was leaving Trieste, Auschwitz concentration camp was being liberated by Red Army soldiers who had advanced under heavy fire to the Vistula and Oder rivers. In anticipation of their arrival ten days earlier, the SS had killed thousands of prisoners and dismantled the camp before beginning the evacuation of Auschwitz and its sub-camps. By 21 January many of the guards had left the camp, leaving behind a small number of SS patrols. The evacuation involved marching 65,000 prisoners, mostly Jews, at gunpoint towards southern Poland in sub-zero temperatures. Most were marched north-west 55 kilometers (30 miles) to Gliwice (Gleiwitz) or west 63 kilometers (35 miles) to Wodzislaw (Loslau) in the western part of Upper Silesia where they were joined by prisoners from other camps. Anyone who fell behind was shot, many also dying from the cold weather of hypothermia or starvation, 15,000 perishing en route.

Although most of the prisoners were forced to take part in these death marches and the Nazis tried hard to cover up their crimes, about 5,000, mainly sick and physically debilitated prisoners, were left behind in the main camps with another 500 in sub-camps (it is likely that the SS were told to kill them but in their haste to leave had not been able to complete the task). They were left with no food or power to the camp so after the remaining SS guards had left, the inmates had to fend for themselves. To survive they raided the warehouses from which they took food, clothing and blankets, some tragically dying as a result of eating too much in one go, their shrunken stomachs unable to digest the food. The Soviet troops on finding them were deeply shocked at what they saw – the emaciated bodies of the prisoners, the horrific conditions at the camp and in particular the piles of half-burnt or buried corpses.

Some of the fitter prisoners left the camp of their own accord and headed to Kraków. However, most were in such a bad state that they could not walk and were in desperate need of medical care. More deaths followed when the Soviet troops gave their rations to the survivors, the food causing acute diarrhoea from which they died. A survivor, Zofia Jankowska-Palińska, recalled:

> They all [the Soviet soldiers] looked at us in a funny way. They couldn't believe we were human and alive. We were more like embalmed mummies. The soldiers saw how emaciated we were, so they started giving away their rations, especially their hardtack and tinned meat. They shared everything they had with us. On orders from their commanding officer, they slaughtered a horse and started cooking the meat. Hungry survivors wanted to eat their fill as soon as possible and snatched pieces of meat that were still red and hard, partly raw, and devoured them as fast as they could. We were starving and all that we had had to drink over the past few days was water from melted snow. We behaved like savages, not decent people. Despite the best of intentions, Soviet troops brought about the death of many survivors by providing us with too much food. There were no doctors to warn us not to eat too much food that was hard to digest. After such a long spell of starvation we had to get used to eating. I was saved by the fact that before I got some meat I had quite a lot of hardtack which made me almost full up, so I couldn't take very much meat. On the same day in the evening or next morning a Soviet army doctor arrived and ordered all the food the soldiers had given us confiscated.

Soviet doctors arriving shortly afterwards ordered that only easily digestible food like boiled potatoes and cooked cereals be given to the inmates which reduced the number of deaths from diarrhea; they then set up a makeshift military hospital. The first people the troops allowed into the camp after its liberation were doctors and nurses from the Polish Red Cross who entered Auschwitz on 5 February 1945. They included Józef Bellert (1887–1970), a surgeon and Polish army officer with the rank of captain who had fought in the First World War and took part in the 1944 Warsaw Uprising. He was in charge of a hospital during the uprising and was the chief physician with the Polish Red Cross team. On arrival at the camp, he was put in charge of the survivors' hospital at Auschwitz-Birkenau and took detailed notes of what he found, writing:

> After reporting our arrival to the camp commander (I cannot recall his name), we were allocated a typhus barrack and

> spent our first night in the camp there. Mr Kodż [Henryk, the administrative head] and I were fluent in Russian, which made communication with the Soviet authorities in the camp much easier. Our help was warmly welcomed since the situation in the camp was really desperate and severely ill survivors had been left with no medical aid. The Germans had incompletely evacuated the camp in a piecemeal fashion and the last big group of prisoners were led out of the camp on 21 January 1945. The survivors still in the camp were severely ill and incapable of walking too far – there were approximately 4,800 of them. After surveying the situation, we made a record of the following data:
>
> Birkenau: about 2,200 persons
> Auschwitz: about 1,800 persons
> Monowitz: about 800 persons [the largest sub camp of Auschwitz – all these figures were later revised upwards]

The team asked the prisoners still left in the camp which country they were from and recorded many different nationalities, mostly Poles, Hungarians, Czechs, Russians, French, Dutch and Yugoslavs from the conquered territories but also Austrians, Germans, Italians, Belgians, Greeks and Romanians. They also included two Norwegians, one Lithuanian and one American prisoner. The situation the team found at Birkenau particularly shocked Bellert who found the experience 'very hard', their work not helped by the fact that the camp stretched over 8 kilometres and they had no transport which meant walking between the different locations.

When they arrived at the barracks, Bellert noted that the camp had been designed to hold approximately 200,000 prisoners in wooden bunks on two levels but instead of each bunk having one person in it, up to six had to share. He also inspected the heaters which were broken but when working gave out barely enough warmth to prevent the prisoners from freezing to death overnight. In his notebook he wrote:

> The bunks were occupied by severely ill prisoners, next to the dead and the moribund, lying in their excrement which was trickling down to the lower bunks. There was no light or

> running water, and in front of the barracks there were about 300 frozen corpses. The surroundings were contaminated with waste and human excrement. Barrack Nos. 20–35 accommodated 20 mental patients, six of them in a state of raving agitation. The situation was desperate.

All the survivors were severely malnourished, Bellert noting they were 'just ashen skin and bone'. The adults weighed 25 to 35kg (55 to 77lb, under half their normal weight) and their swollen bodies were covered with festering wounds, weeping pus and bed sores. Many had frostbite on their hands and feet with gangrene and bones showing through the wounds.

A group consisting of 13 Polish Red Cross workers then began to clean the barracks, taking out the dead, bringing food for those still living and repairing the heaters. The food they found allocated to the prisoners consisted of dried potato flakes for soup, 'peas pudding', soup with groats and sometimes a little meat and ersatz 'coffee' made of cereal grains and bread. Many of the survivors were deeply impressed by the dedication and commitment of the hospital's staff. Terezie Freundova-Jírová from Czechoslovakia recalled:

> Everything around us was so depressing that we did not want to wait for help any longer. When the Red Cross nurses saw us, they were amazed how miserable we were. They got down busily to their task, which called for a lot of self-sacrifice. That was because some of the sick women had been lying completely debilitated for whole days with no care at all, in their excrement and in an unimaginable condition. The nurses put them in new beds, washed them, and got food and medications for them.

Among the most desperate groups inside the barracks were new mothers, the team counting twenty-four with babies aged from nine days to six weeks old. All the mothers were found to be incapable of producing breast milk due to being so malnourished, so meals were brought into the camp from the local community to supplement their meagre rations. A maternity hospital was also specifically set up for them but even so two of the children died.

One of the most chilling places the team came across were the laboratories associated with the 'Hygiene Institute', Niethammer's former employer. Bellert recorded:

> 2 kilometres from the sub-camp in Rajsko [Raisko] the Germans had set up their laboratory with various strains of contagious diseases, apparently including bubonic plague and cholera, which they had wanted for experiments on prisoners. The lab had been looted and we were notified of the danger of disease and epidemics spreading.

The team found both tuberculosis and typhus among the prisoners, sixty-three being diagnosed with the latter. As well as the adult survivors, eighty children were also found in the camp aged from two to 14 years old. The Polish Red Cross took the children away, most being fitter than the adults, to the nearby city of Katowice where they were all given special rooms in 'pretty barracks'. The children received a really warm welcome from the Polish Red Cross nurses based there and were given toys, many of them never having owned any. The team found it difficult to identify all the children due to many not being able to spell their names and the large number of different nationalities present.

Among the adult survivors were a dozen doctors whom they invited to join with them in helping the other survivors. Many were not fit enough to work but they were helpful in identifying prisoners, record-keeping being very difficult as the team could not gather everyone together at once and they spoke so many different languages. While the Soviet military strictly controlled who could enter the camp, the Polish Red Cross were able to work with their field hospital unit which also provided meals for the former prisoners. Medicines from Kraków also arrived but the number of doctors and nurses was completely insufficient, those working in the team barely able to help the most urgent cases. Bellert recalled:

> We could barely administer the most urgent medical aid, clean up the blocks a bit, bury over 300 people who had died before our arrival and dispose of the corpses the Germans had not managed to burn, as well as the arms and legs lying around near the ditches in which the Germans had been burning the bodies of those they had killed and those who

> had died. By that time the crematoria had been demolished. All that was left were piles of ashes which the Germans had failed to dispose of in the Soła River.

Each prisoner was given a Red Cross postcard so they could contact their relatives, those wishing to leave also being given an identity card. After the Soviets relaxed the entry restrictions, many distraught people began to arrive at the camp looking for relatives. Bellert put out a request for more medical staff and then a second Soviet field hospital arrived after which conditions began slowly to improve. The Polish Red Cross team decided to move everyone from Birkenau and Monowitz to the original main camp where they were put up in the brick barracks which were better insulated and given a medical record card. Despite getting round-the-clock care around a hundred people still died, the team carrying out several autopsies. In all the Polish Red Cross staff consisted of sixty-three people, the hospital being called Szpital Obozowy Polski Czerwony Krzyż (PCK) w Oświęcimiu – the Polish Red Cross Camp Hospital at Oświęcim. The most serious cases were transferred to the local hospital in Kraków, some of the first patients to be sent being the mentally ill who were transferred to a psychiatric unit.

One of the most harrowing discoveries were the warehouses and Kanada stores where thousands of personal belongings were found from the murdered prisoners – shoes, glasses, toothbrushes, combs, artificial limbs and a huge mountain of human hair together with thousands of personal items (these possessions now form the centrepiece of the Auschwitz Museum). Billert continued to head up the hospital at the site until the 1 August 1945 when he was appointed director of St. Lazarus Hospital in Kraków. Despite all his medical care during that time over 300 more people died because of their time in Auschwitz, new cemeteries having to be dug to accommodate them.

In the last chaotic weeks of the war as the former prisoners at Auschwitz were being marched across Poland, Niethammer was assigned to the 269th Infantry Division. Here despite his rank, he served as an infantry soldier under General Hans Wagner (1896–1967) taking part in the last desperate battles to defend Saxony from the rampaging Soviets. Created just before the war in August 1939, the 269th Division had first seen combat in the Battle of France in 1940, afterwards being posted to Denmark as part of the occupying forces.

Mobilised for Operation *Barbarossa*, the attack on the Soviet Union, in the summer of 1941, the 269th Division was part of Army Group North which advanced on Leningrad. Here it was involved in bitter fighting as the Germans fought street by street to take the city, followed by the subsequent 900-day siege as they tried to starve the city into submission. Spending the winter and the next summer on the defensive along the Volkov river front, the division fought off repeated Soviet attempts to restore communications to the besieged city. Escaping the subsequent encirclement and humiliating defeat, in December 1942 the rump of the division was transferred to Norway where it remained for the next two years. The 269th Division returned to action in November 1944, firstly in the west where it fought against American forces following D-Day and finally in 1945 in the east where a much-depleted *Kampfgruppe* or battlegroup found itself facing the maurading Red Army.

Chapter 18

An Accomplice to the Crimes Committed at Auschwitz

ON 22 APRIL 1945 Niethammer took up arms for the first time as Red Army troops fought pitched battles with the remnants of his division. Numerically superior with far greater firepower, the Soviet troops easily overcame the German resistance. Three days later Soviet and American troops met at the Elbe River, near Torgau in Saxony, marking a historic step towards victory over the Nazis. With the Soviets advancing from the east and the Americans from the west, Germany was now effectively cut in two. Niethammer fought on with his division until 7 May 1945. After months of fierce fighting, the Germans agreed to Allied demands for unconditional surrender, finally ending nearly six years of war that had left millions dead and much of Europe in ruins. After two weeks of intense fighting Niethammer's brief war was also at an end. However, his overall war record was unprecedented in the annals of the history of the German Army. Thanks to his ornithological contacts, membership of the Nazi Party and his involvement with the Waffen-SS he had carried out bird surveys and research in Poland, Greece, Crete, Bulgaria and Italy while playing a part in the Holocaust, one of the most evil events in human history.

The following day, Tuesday, 8 May 1945, Victory in Europe was declared, marking the formal end of the war in Europe (Niethammer's army record states he fought on with the division until 8 May 1945). The Allies were now faced with occupying a conquered and destroyed nation with millions of displaced persons and former soldiers like Niethammer. To administer Germany and Austria it had already been agreed among the victorious nations that they would be divided into four occupation zones: Soviet, American, French and British. The German capital of Berlin, despite being deep inside the Soviet occupation area, had also been split into four separate zones. As soon as the zones had been worked out the hunt for Nazi war criminals began. Thousands of men and women suspected of involvement in the concentration camp system and other crimes across Europe were named on a most wanted list. The round-up included apprehending many lower-ranking Nazis, the hunt for war criminals soon becoming the major preoccupation of the occupying forces.

During the final months of the war Niethammer's great mentor Erwin Stresemann had also found himself in combat at the advanced age of 56. His initial enthusiasm for Nazism had waned as the early victories had evaporated and been replaced by occupying German forces known for their cruelty and barbarity. Then the war came home to Germany as the Allied air forces reduced Berlin to rubble, forcing him to confront the full horrors of the regime. Despite bombs falling all around him, he had stoically carried on working in the zoological museum in the city. However, on the nights of 22 and 23 November 1943 part of the museum was destroyed following a very heavy raid. After the attack one of Stresemann's colleagues, Professor Walter Arndt, had been arrested by the Gestapo for 'defeatist statements' (in response to the destruction, he had been overheard saying 'it was now the end of the Third Reich and all that remained was to punish the guilty persons'). Stresemann had then begun to worry about his own fate after one of his students, a member of the party, had reported him for allowing a Jewish ornithologist by the name of Salomonsen to become a member of the German Ornithological Society. This concern became a reoccurring nightmare when he learnt that the People's Court had sentenced Professor Arndt to death and he was beheaded on 26 June 1944, his family as well as collecting his decapitated corpse having to foot the bill for the judgement made against him.

On 29 January 1945, as Niethammer was fleeing Trieste, Stresemann was drafted into the Volkssturm or People's Storm, a militia of old men and boys charged with the large-ditch defence of Berlin against the Soviets. While his wife and daughter fled the besieged capital, Stresemann was being taught to use the Panzerfaust or 'tank fist', a crude bazooka which was meant to stop the Soviet tanks in their tracks (often unreliable, it only stood a chance of doing so if directed at the tracks at close range). On 3 February more bombs hit the museum, this time destroying the whole right wing of the building. In March Stresemann wrote to his friend Richard Heyder in Saxony, 'Soon we shall be surrounded unless there is a miracle – one of the many for which we have waited in vain so far.' But there was no miracle and Stresemann and other members of the Volkssturm could do little to stop the Soviets taking the city. During a brief period of leave from the front Stresemann drove to a village on the Oder under a hail of Soviet shells where his library was stored for safety and brought it back with him to Berlin. He saw out the final days of the war hiding in his basement, his house miraculously escaping damage from the Soviet artillery pounding the capital night and day.

Unlike many of his fellow troops Niethammer did not become a prisoner of war when Germany finally capitulated. Instead, he found himself in the town of Oederan when the formal surrender was announced. Lying in the district of Mittelsachsen in Saxony, Oederan was the location for a sub-camp of Flossenbürg concentration camp, situated in the remote Fichtel Mountains of Bavaria, near the border with Czechoslovakia. At the camp just outside the town in the final days of the war the SS had massacred many of its Jewish inmates before evacuating the site. Liberated by the Red Army in April 1945, Soviet soldiers found hundreds of corpses and began the hunt for those responsible. Like many other SS troops on the run Niethammer decided that his best option was to get to the west as quickly as possible rather than face the wrath of the Soviet troops. In reprisals for the German invasion, they were seeking bloody revenge for the suffering their people had experienced at the hands of the Nazis. Fearing for his life, Niethammer approached Stresemann's ornithologist friend Richard Heyder who lived locally and asked him for help. Heyder gave him a set of civilian clothes to replace his SS uniform and told him to head to Marburg in the American zone, a distance of over 360 kilometres. To make his escape Heyder gave him a bicycle and several days' food. So, after disposing of his uniform he spent the next week cycling, mostly under cover of darkness to avoid the Soviet patrols, before he finally arrived in the town.

As a member of the Waffen-SS who had been a concentration camp guard at Auschwitz, Niethammer had every reason to fear for his life. Of all the different branches of the German armed forces, he knew the SS was the most feared and the most loathed. Groups of Soviet soldiers roamed Oederan after the city had formally surrendered looking for former German troops, in particular members of the SS – on finding them they were often dealt with by summary execution instead of being handed over as prisoners of war. To escape a similar fate many former higher-ranking soldiers assumed false identities and were issued with fake documents to aid their escape. However, Niethammer knew that if he was taken prisoner, he could not hide his identity because of his SS tattoo, the Soviets always checking soldiers to see if they had one. So Niethammer fled but on arriving at Marburg he found that he was not safe there either as in all the three Allied occupation zones of Germany the authorities were searching for SS, in particular former concentration camp guards. Following the end of the war the Allies had made the German people confront their collective guilt for the Holocaust and had published truly shocking pictures of piles of bodies as the concentration camps were liberated. In particular, the emaciated, haunted faces of Auschwitz prisoners stared back from newspaper pages and cinema screens. So, Niethammer decided his only option was to go underground, writing to Heyder on 29 January 1946:

> I happened to meet Joachim Steinbacher by coincidence on the streets in March and shortly thereafter von Boxberger [both ornithologists], who was a district administrator at that time. From June I took up a job as a night watchman in an orphanage under construction, which was located magnificently in the countryside in Neuhöfe (near Marburg) and provided me with the opportunity to begin a beautiful collection of small mammals (130 skins of 19 species).

Niethammer also worked on a farm where he was given the responsibility of feeding and milking the cows before reverting to working on vaccines, drawing on his experience working for the SS 'Hygiene Institute'. He wrote that he was:

> a kind of 'dairyman', whereby I ascertained that this was not so difficult, for I was considered in general to be an old, experienced milker although I had never before pulled at an udder, which I prudently concealed. I changed my profession in the autumn and went to the Boehringer works [in Marburg], a position of trust for an acknowledged feeder of 'juicy lice' [manufacture of typhus vaccine]. I would have been able to survive here for any length of time even if Jordans had not started pulling strings in the meantime. I visited Jordans in December and we planned a return to the field of zoology. I also discussed this with the English authorities. Now I will return the day after tomorrow to Bonn.

With his approval Niethammer's former boss at the Museum Koenig in Bonn, von Jordans, had approached the British occupation authorities about his case, stating that he was an eminent ornithologist who had been a member of the Waffen-SS but was 'just a guard'. In return the security officer had given him a vague promise that if his record checked out, he would be released after verification. Writing to Heyder about this, von Jordans stated:

> With Nieth's permission I opened your letter of 16.11 to him, which was received yesterday. He spent 10 days with us a good three weeks ago, before he – definitely I hope – was unreachable by anyone for no longer than 6–8 weeks altogether. I advised him to do this and prepared him for this final arrangement and hope and believe that this is the best solution for him.

For the next couple of months while von Jordans negotiated with the British over his surrender, Niethammer lay low and continued with his work manufacturing typhus vaccines. Within a few weeks of the war ending, the initial rush to arrest Nazi war criminals had waned as the Allies focused on the new threat from the Soviets so Niethammer decided to give himself up. At the beginning of February 1946, he reported to the British 320th Field Security Section in Bonn where he gave his name to the security officer J. E. Shaw and declared that he had been a member of the Waffen-SS and a guard at Auschwitz. On 11 February he was sent to Recklinghausen and the 4th Inter Civilian Internment Camp (ICIC) with the number 410448, later being sent to Neuengamme, the 6th ICIC. To encourage Niethammer to give himself up, the authorities had promised von Jordans that he would be tried by a British court. However, on 22 November despite the promise he was deported by ship to Poland via Lübeck after the British and Polish governments had signed a treaty stating that all war criminals who had been based in Poland would be handed over to the Poles for trial.

On arrival, Niethammer was taken to the Montelupich Prison in Kraków and put in a cell as a prisoner awaiting trial. After almost a year, on 11 November 1947, he was finally put on trial after an indictment was agreed against a group of Auschwitz SS guards. Niethammer was accused of the following crimes: membership of the Waffen-SS (his tattoo proved this), serving as a guard with a loaded rifle in Auschwitz concentration camp and being an accomplice to the crimes committed there – the charge sheet stating that when he arrived in Auschwitz, he was well aware of what went on there. On 4 March 1948, after a hearing before the District Court in Kraków, Niethammer was sentenced to eight years in prison (the minimum punishment in the case being five years and the maximum ten years). He also lost his public and civil rights, again for a period of eight years, and had all his property seized.

The severity of the sentence devastated Niethammer who believed that as 'just a guard' he would not be charged with being an accomplice to the crimes committed at Auschwitz. As soon as the sentence was passed all his ornithological contacts including von Jordans and Stresemann contacted the authorities saying the judgement was unjust and asking for a reduction in his sentence or a pardon. Niethammer's wife Ruth, now alone with four children back in their house in Bonn, wrote asking that Dr. Andrzej Dunajewski (1908–1944), in charge of the ornithological collection in the Museum of Warsaw, be questioned as a character witness for the defence, not realising he had died in the Warsaw Uprising in 1944 (Dunajewski had worked in the national zoological museum in Poland from 1933 to 1939, receiving a doctorate from the University of Warsaw; he also studied in Berlin with Stresemann. After the Germans removed him from the museum, he joined the resistance during the war and died either in the bombardment or while trying to escape in a sewage tunnel under the city during the Warsaw Uprising in 1944. Even had he lived it is highly unlikely he would have made representation on Niethammer's behalf, believing he might have been responsible for plundering the bird skin collection at the museum early in the war). She even wrote to the Polish president, asking for a pardon but received no reply.

A concerted campaign was now being waged on Niethammer's behalf to reduce his sentence. The legal representations and character references from his friends, colleagues and family all stressed Niethammer's great contribution to science, his many ornithological papers and that he was 'just a guard' who took no role in the Holocaust. Niethammer himself wrote to the Public Prosecutor's Office and asked that they search for a Polish prisoner by the name of Grębocki who had helped him prepare the bird skins for his ornithological museum at Auschwitz and would certainly vouch for him. However, the court did not grant the request and even if they had, unbeknown to Niethammer, Grębocki was already dead, having drowned when the prison ships *Cap Arcona* and *Thielbeck* were bombed by the Allies on 3 May 1945. Despite the campaign waged on his behalf, the Polish authorities remained unmoved. In desperation Niethammer hired a lawyer in Kraków who put together a defence case appealing to the Supreme Court of the Republic of Poland and challenging the judgement.

The lawyer consulted widely while putting together Niethammer's defence, gathering testimony from across the extensive network of German and Austrian ornithologists that he had built up over his career. Principal among these was Stresemann but many others also provided character references, including von Jordans, Kummerlöwe (who at the end of the war changed his name to Kumerloeve to prevent himself being traced) and even disgraced ones like Schäfer. The elite ornithological community was closing ranks to protect one of its own. The appeal against Niethammer's sentence was heard by the Supreme Court in the autumn 1948, and shortly afterwards it revoked the judgement at a sitting in Kraków and ordered a new hearing. His ornithological community and 'old boys' bird network', many of whom had lived and prospered under Nazism, had won him a reprieve. The reason given by the court judge for revoking the sentence was that the District Court in Kraków had not fully considered 'mitigating circumstances' and had failed to apply them to his case. Those mitigating circumstances were that Niethammer did not know what went on at Auschwitz when he had been sent to the camp and after he had started there and had 'personally experienced the full truth, he had applied immediately and emphatically for a transfer, which had been granted to him'.

During the appeal ruling no mention was made of the fact that in 1940 Niethammer had served at the camp for six months before applying for a transfer, that he had carried out a bird survey of the camp while thousands were sent to their deaths within his 'patch', that he had been very close to the commandant Höß and dedicated the scientific paper on the bird survey to him or that he had returned to the camp in September 1942 when the Holocaust was happening and thousands of Jews were being exterminated daily. On 7 December 1948, after carefully weighing up the new evidence presented to it, the District Court in Kraków announced its second judgement: Niethammer's sentence was to be reduced from eight to three years' imprisonment, taking into account time already spent in prison while awaiting trial from 29 September 1946. He would also lose his public and civil rights for three years not eight, and the property found on him when he was arrested would be confiscated (his file in the Polish archives still contains his cards and wallet with some reichmarks in it).

To serve the remainder of his time in jail Niethammer was transferred to the Mokotow Prison in Warsaw where he served 11 months, finishing his sentence on 10 November 1949. Two days later he was deported from Poland by train, arriving in Hannover on 14 November 1949. Here on the platform, he was reunited with his wife and four children in a highly emotional reunion. During his time in prison Frau Niethammer had found life very difficult, not only having to bring up four children on her own but suffering a lot of abuse after word had got out that her husband was on trial for being a guard at Auschwitz. Forced to vacate the affluent villa in Vienna, the family had moved into much more modest accommodation in Bonn. She had been very grateful to all the ornithologists who had campaigned on his behalf but was bitter at the British authorities who she believed had broken their promise and abandoned her husband to his fate at the hands of the Polish legal system. The first people in touch following his release were Stresemann and von Jordans who were delighted that the author of the *Handbook of German Ornithology* and so many other scientific studies was once again free to pursue his career in ornithology. After a short break at the beginning of 1950 Niethammer returned to the Zoological Museum Koenig in Bonn to resume his career.

Despite Frau Niethammer's belief that Niethammer had been abandoned, his reduced sentence was thanks to a series of remarkable interventions by the British and the United Nations on his behalf. Contradicting her view that the British had not supported her husband, his court file in fact showed that the authorities had been sympathetic to his case. It also showed that all the character references from German and Austrian ornithologists sent to his lawyer had been dismissed because they were considered biased. Despite this the British authorities had supported the appeal, feeling that the original judgement had not fully taken into account Niethammer's efforts to leave the camp. They did not appeal to the Polish court on his behalf and never issued any character references, agreeing that a Polish judge should hear crimes that had taken place in their country when it was occupied. However, the British authorities did instruct the Judge Advocate General of the British Army to make representation on Niethammer's behalf and he then approached the United Nations War Crimes Commission in London, consisting of representatives from the Allied nations.

The British delegate to the Commission asked his Polish counterpart, Colonel Dr. Marion Muszkat, to provide information on all the individual accusations against Niethammer so that they could be considered in light of the 'new mitigating circumstances'. Even the British authorities in Germany got involved in the case, they informing the head of the Polish Military Mission, Captain Romuald Spasowski, based in Bad Salzuflen, of their intention to distance themselves from the decision to deport Niethammer to Poland if they did not provide satisfactory answers. (The high-level intervention by the British authorities on behalf of a guard at Auschwitz is now difficult to comprehend but at the time it was probably designed to send a signal to the wider population that those who had simply been following orders or were very low down in the Nazi hierarchy would not be unfairly prosecuted. The political situation with the Soviet Union also probably played an important part, the British wishing to show that in contrast to the Soviets they would treat people fairly according to the law rather than seeking retribution from the German population, many of whom had little control over the conduct of the war.) The Polish Military Mission responded that the court would pursue a second judgement, which it did after some delay, considerably reducing Niethammer's sentence, the British authorities being satisfied that after some pressure the right decision had been reached.

While the German and Austrian ornithologists' testimonies had been ruled inadmissible, one person the court did take notice of was the Polish Doctor Włodzimierz Marcinkowski of Kraków who played an important role in getting Niethammer's sentence reduced. Marcinkowski was the doctor and psychologist at Mokotow Prison who had interviewed a range of German prisoners about their experiences and treatment. He had published these testimonies in a Kraków newspaper and became something of a local expert. Of all the prisoners he interviewed, he found Niethammer's story the most moving and over time became a friend, telling colleagues he wanted to take care of the 'German ornithologist' as he was a good man who had found himself in a very dark place. To do this he appointed Niethammer as the prison pharmacist while he was serving his sentence which helped him survive the harsh prison conditions, any prisoner with access to drugs being popular inside (in contrast, in his previous prison he had to work in the colliery, a hard physical role, though even that was desirable in comparison to any job at Auschwitz). During the court hearing Marcinkowski was a witness for the defence; his statement read:

> From the conversations that I had with him, I was convinced that he was a good man and a conscientious scientist, who felt guilty for all the German atrocities as a German but not as a human being in a personal sense. He told me that during his time in Auschwitz as a guard, instead of torturing the Poles he spent the time making numerous birdwatching excursions to nearby wetlands and had prepared bird skins. I would like to emphasise that the behaviour of the accused in the prison towards the other German [and] Polish prisoners was extremely good and correct. When I asked the accused if he knew what Auschwitz was, he replies – contrary to other German prisoners – that it sufficed to stay there for a moment to comprehend this great criminal act.[1]

It was Marcinkowski's testimony that made the difference to the court, in particular his assertion that Niethammer had treated all the prisoners in a 'good and correct' way. However, the most crucial part from the court's perspective was Niethammer's personal admission that he knew Auschwitz was a camp where 'a great criminal act' had been committed, a plea that made him stand out from other guards brought to trial who all denied knowledge of the atrocities. This mea culpa was an astute move, given that he had worked there for over six months before applying for a transfer. It was a strategy also deployed by a very high-ranking Nazi who made a similar admission which probably saved his life.

Before Niethammer's case came to trial in 1947, the German city of Nürnberg had played host to the greatest war trial in history. Here from 1945–1946 all the captured leading Nazis had been charged with war crimes and their cases tried before the world. Uniquely among them Albert Speer, Hitler's architect and later armaments minister, had expressed remorse for the crimes committed against the Jews but he had denied firsthand knowledge of the plan to exterminate them. Based on his testimony, he was convicted of war crimes and crimes against humanity but was only sentenced to twenty years in jail in comparison to many of his co-conspirators who were sentenced to death. (Speer served out his sentence in full at Spandau Prison in West Berlin. Until his death, he continued to publicly claim that he had been unaware of the 'final solution'. However, in a letter made public in 2007 but written in 1971, he admitted to having been present at a 1943 conference when Himmler announced that all the Jews would be exterminated.) The trials of the leading Nazis generated huge publicity and it is likely that Niethammer's lawyer had noted how a plea of remorse without admitting to knowledge of the 'final solution' had seen Speer's sentence reduced. So, he had advised Niethammer as a lowly guard to enter a similar plea – to admit knowing about the purpose of the camp without pleading guilty to being involved in the Jews extermination.

Despite the disposition, the court did not hear evidence from one key witness. Niethammer's admission that he knew what happened at Auschwitz and Marcinkowski's view of him treating the prisoners in a 'good and correct' way was contradicted by a medical graduate named Andrzej Zaorski. He had been among the first people from the Polish Red Cross to enter the concentration camp after its liberation on 27 January 1945 by Soviet troops. All together the Red Cross team was composed of eight doctors, thirteen nurses and seventeen paramedics who had been sent urgently to Auschwitz to treat the remaining survivors in the 'camp hospital'. Most of the team were themselves thin, underfed and poorly clothed after years of war and had participated in the Warsaw Uprising so had suffered terribly under the Nazis. In spite of this they had all volunteered for what they knew would be a very traumatic experience. However, nothing that they had read or heard about the camp could have prepared them for what they were going to find on entering Auschwitz.

Monday, 5 February 1945 was the date agreed with the Soviet authorities for the Polish Red Cross medical team to enter the camp, Zaorski being among the first to turn up at the meeting point in front of the Hotel Francuski in Kraków. There they had boarded an old truck and had set off for the camp with Dr. Grabczyński, a survivor, as their guide. Despite the freezing February temperatures some of the party had to stand in the back of the lorry for the bitterly cold trip. The road to the concentration camp led through Chrzanów and then through fields and a forest. The ditches were full of disk or teller mines removed from the roads and they had to get out and walk behind the lorry every time it went over ground which had not been cleared of mines. It was a long and uncomfortable journey to the camp as Zaorski and his party had to navigate blown-up bridges and the long, winding columns of Soviet troops heading west.

When he eventually arrived, Zaorski was shocked at the horrific conditions he saw all around him as he visited the different parts of the camp. He was, however, stupefied when he saw the residential area for camp staff. For here among the comfortable barracks, sports facilities and the cinema were bird nesting-boxes. Made by Niethammer and some of the Polish prisoners, the sight of them stopped him in his tracks. How could the officers and camp guards encourage birds to nest when at the same exterminating so many people? After seeing the same nesting boxes in the Höß family garden, Zaorski's gruesome tour finished at the commandant's office where in the open safe he found a copy of Niethammer's paper on the birds of Auschwitz. Picking it up he saw the title *Beobachtungen über die Vogelwelt von Auschwitz* (*Observations on the birdlife of Auschwitz*) and then at the top read with incredulity the personal dedication from the author to Rudolf Höß. In Zaorski's eyes Niethammer was not 'just a guard' who had no control over the operations of the camp but the guard who had civilised an extermination centre and disguised from the world the true purpose of Auschwitz under the guise of a scientific study.

The man whom Niethammer had dedicated his paper to, the Commandant of Auschwitz Rudolf Höß, like him had gone on the run at the end of the war. In November 1944 he had been moved to Ravensbrück, the women's concentration camp, 90 kilometres north of Berlin with his family (the move, nominally at his request, was also due to an alleged affair). After the completion of the gas chamber there, Höß had coordinated the murder of more than 2,000 female prisoners. In early January 1945 as the Russians advanced ever further westward, Höß had left the camp and travelled to Auschwitz to ensure that Himmler's last order, that the camp be destroyed, was carried out (Höß would have been particularly keen to ensure there was no trace left as he knew that it would implicate him). It was to be the last time as a free man that Höß would travel to the camp which, on and off, had been his home for the last four years and in which he had built his career. On the journey he came across columns of dishevelled prisoners struggling through deep snow, many on death marches. However, he was only able to get as far as the Oder river near Ratibor in southern Poland, about 85 kilometres west of the camp, due to the speed of the Red Army advance and the difficulty in travelling as the Third Reich collapsed. To avoid capture Höß had instead headed north towards Gross-Rosen, where the Nazis had another concentration camp near the German town of Striegau in Lower Silesia (now Strzegom, Poland). On arrival he found the situation just as chaotic, the camp and railway station crammed to overflowing with refugees.

So, Höß had returned to Ravensbrück and after organising its evacuation, Himmler had told him to disguise himself as a Kreigsmarine sailor and go on the run. Taking his family with him, he headed first to Darss, a peninsula in the Baltic and then on to Schleswig-Holstein, 300 kilometres to the north 'in accordance with the orders of the Reichsführer-SS. What we were supposed to do for him, or what duties we were still intended to do, we could not imagine,' he wrote. 'For days on end we scurried from one clump of trees to the next,' he recalled, 'for the enemy's low-flying planes were continually machine-gunning this principal escape route.' A couple of days later while sheltering in a farmhouse he heard that Hitler was dead. 'When we heard this, my wife and I were simultaneously struck by the same thought: now we too, must go! With the Führer gone our world had gone. Was there any point in going on living? We would be pursued and persecuted wherever we went. We wanted to take poison.' Höß had been given some cyanide capsules for himself, his wife and children in case they were captured by the Soviets but he couldn't bring himself to take one or give them to his family. 'I have always regretted it since,' he lamented. 'We would all have been spared a great deal, especially my wife and the children. How much more suffering will they have to endure? We were bound and fettered to that other world, and we should have disappeared with it.'

Höß reported for the last time to Himmler at Flensburg, where the Reichsführer-SS had withdrawn with other Nazis on the run. 'I shall never forget my last meeting with the Reichsführer-SS,' Höß recalled. 'He was beaming and in the best of spirits; yet the world, our world, had crumbled beneath our feet. He said: "Well, gentlemen, this is the end. You know what you now have to do."' Despite preaching to the SS for years about death before dishonour, Himmler instead instructed Höß to escape by disguising himself as an ordinary sailor and take his chances along with thousands of other troops fleeing the Russians. 'Such was our farewell message from the man to whom I had looked up so respectfully, in whom I had had such implicit trust, whose orders and utterances had been gospel to me,' Höß wrote ruefully.[2]

What Höß didn't know was that Himmler had first tried to negotiate a surrender with the Allies and only when this failed had he fled and headed towards Flensburg in the north of Schleswig-Holstein disguised as Sergeant Heinrich Hizinger. While crossing the River Oste on 21 May, Himmler had to pass through a British checkpoint, where his poor disguise and nervous behaviour attracted the attention of the guards and he was detained. He was then moved between several camps before on May 23 being brought to the British Civilian Interrogation Camp in Barnstedt near Lüneburg. There, under routine interrogation from the duty officer, Captain Thomas Selvester (1910–1998), he admitted to being Heinrich Himmler. The prisoner was then quickly transferred to the British Second Army headquarters in Lüneburg, where a Dr. Wells began a medical examination. Wells tried to inspect Himmler's mouth but he pulled his head away and bit through a cyanide capsule hidden in a molar tooth. He then collapsed on the floor and despite efforts to save him died fifteen minutes later. Höß's mentor and the man who had inspired him to create the most notorious extermination camp in history was dead. The body of the Reichsführer-SS, once one of the most powerful men in Nazi Germany and the architect of the Holocaust, was then unceremoniously dumped in an unnamed grave on Lüneburg Heath (the exact location has never been disclosed). Himmler's death attracted media headlines around the world and left Höß in little doubt as to the fate that awaited him if he was captured.

To evade the authorities Höß had also been issued with false identity papers in the name of a boatswain called Fritz Lang who before the war had been a farmer. After travelling for days under the cover of darkness he had heard one day on the radio of Himmler's arrest and death. Like his former boss Höß had contemplated taking his own cyanide pill but had instead decided to wait on events. After passing through several British checkpoints without difficulty, he had reported to the local labour office where like Niethammer he was found work on a farm in Gottrupel, a quiet hamlet in Schleswig-Holstein (many farmers were pro-Nazi and when the war was over happily accepted men of fighting age without asking any questions about their past). There Höß kept a low profile for nearly a year, working as a labourer and gardener. However, on 11 March 1946, his luck ran out when he was captured by British troops after his identity was exposed. According to Höß his cyanide capsule had broken two days previously so he could not commit suicide, even if he had summoned the courage to do so. The person who gave him away was none other than his wife Hedwig who had settled close by and was being monitored by the British following a tip-off. Refusing to reveal her husband's whereabouts, in response the British had arrested their eldest son Klaus, aged 16. Telling Hedwig he would be shipped off to the Soviet Union where he would be tortured and imprisoned, she had finally given away Höß's location in exchange for a guarantee of Klaus's safety.

Höß was well aware that the Allies were looking for him and that he was one of the most sought-after criminals in the former Third Reich. Despite this he was taken by surprise by his arrest while asleep at the farm. Hearing the arrival of several vehicles one night, he ignored the commotion, thinking that the farm was being robbed, a common occurrence in rural areas where food was in very short supply. However, the men arriving at the farm were not thieves but soldiers of the Field Security Section 92, including German Jews from the Pioneer Corps who had fought against the Nazis and had lost family members at Auschwitz. Höß was arrested by a Berlin-born Jew named Hanns Alexander, who was serving as a captain with the British army.[3] Fearing the former commandant would fight or try to take his own life, Alexander had requested additional back-up and had arranged for a doctor to be present. Travelling in a small convoy of trucks and jeeps Alexander and twenty-five armed men had rolled into the farmyard in Gottrupel at 11 o'clock at night on 11 March 1946. On opening the door Höß was confronted by the doctor and Alexander brandishing a pistol which without warning he thrust into Höß's mouth. After the doctor confirmed that he did not have a cyanide pill hidden in the back of his mouth, Alexander introduced himself in perfect German as a captain with the British War Crimes Investigation Team and demanded to see his papers. Höß handed over his false identity documents with the name of Franz Lang and a temporary work card with the number B22595. Alexander barely glanced at the card and instead thrust forward a photograph of Höß in uniform and asked him directly if he was the former commandant of Auschwitz. Flatly denying it, Höß reiterated he was a farm labourer called Franz Lang, but Alexander dismissed his claim out of hand.

At gunpoint he ordered the man to roll up his shirtsleeves to see if there was a blood group tattooed on his arm, but could not find one.

As Höß continued to deny his identity Alexander became frustrated until he noticed his wedding ring. Demanding to see it, Höß refused so Alexander threatened to cut off his finger. Realizing he would lose the ring either way, a furious Höß reluctantly handed it over. Looking inside the band, Alexander saw the engraved names of 'Rudolf' and 'Hedwig'. Alexander had identified the infamous commandant of Auschwitz. However, before formally arresting Höß, Alexander turned to his men and said, 'In ten minutes I want to have Höss in my car – undamaged,' and walked off. The men moved forward en masse and beat Höß with their rifle butts until the doctor called them off. At around midnight a bruised and bloody Höß was bundled into the back of the one of the waiting trucks.

Once in the prison in the town of Heide, Höß was interrogated by Alexander and another member of the team. Alcohol was forced down his throat and after handcuffing Höß, they beat him with his own whip, taken from the barn where he had been arrested. With the temperature in the cell well below freezing, Höß's bare feet soon developed frostbite. His harsh treatment, while illegal under military law, was but a small taste of what so many prisoners in Auschwitz had endured. Three days later, on 15 March 1946, Alexander delivered Höß to a British-run prison near the town of Minden in North Rhine-Westphalia. There, the War Crimes Investigations Team's lawyer, Colonel Gerald Draper, intensively questioned Höß again. A few hours later, Höß admitted to who he really was and his role in the Holocaust, his statement being typed up into an eight-page confession. It was the first time that a concentration camp commandant had spoken on the record about the final solution, Höß confessing to killing over one million people.

Chapter 19

The Verdict

THE NEW YORK TIMES reported Höß's arrest on 17 March 1946, stating that after a nine-month search, British soldiers had captured the person who was 'probably the greatest individual killer in the history of the world'. At the end of March, Höß was moved to Nuremberg, where the Americans questioned him at the International Military Tribunal in relation to the trials of Ernst Kaltenbrunner (1903–1946, the highest-ranking member of the SS to stand trial and the Director of the Reich Security Main Office from 1943–1945) and IG Farben (against the directors of the company who had profited so much from the camp and manufactured the Zyklon B gas used in the genocide). He was also analysed by a psychiatrist to see if he was sane and understood the consequences of his actions. Asked if he knew that one day he could be held to account for killing so many people, Höß replied, 'At the time there were no consequences to consider. It didn't occur to me that I would be held responsible. You see, in Germany it was understood that if something went wrong, then the man who gave the orders was responsible [this was Höß's attempt to blame Himmler, deploying the well-used excuse of war criminals that he was just following orders].' When the psychiatrist asked how being in charge of Auschwitz had affected his mental health, Höß said, 'That just didn't enter into it. I suppose you want to know in this way if my thought and habits are normal … I am entirely normal. Even while I was doing the extermination work, I led a normal family life.'

At the trials Höß was also asked why he had carried out orders that resulted in the deaths of so many people and replied:

> I am constantly reproached for not having refused to carry out the Extermination Order, this gruesome murder of women and children. I have given my answer …. what would have happened to a group captain who refused to lead an air attack on a town which he knew for certain

> contained no arms factory, no industrial plant of value to the war effort, and no military installations? An attack in which he knew for sure that his bombs must kill principally women and children? He would surely have been court martialled. People say that this is no comparison. But in my opinion the two situations are comparable. I was a soldier and an officer, just as was that group captain. Some say that the Waffen-SS was not a military organization, but a kind of party militia. However, we were just as much soldiers as were the members of the other three armed services.

During his time in prison Höß was encouraged by the prison authorities to write his autobiography in which he tried to justify his actions (first published in Polish in 1951, five years later it came out in German, afterwards various English language editions appearing). In the book he wrote about his early life, setting up Auschwitz and the mass extermination of the Jews and other prisoners in the Holocaust. The book also mentioned by name those senior Nazis with whom he had come into contact during his life, in particular Himmler and other high-ranking ones including Eichmann and Eicke. Many of his officers and guards also got mentions but one name notable by its absence was that of Günther Niethammer (it is unlikely that Höß had forgotten him or not thought him worthy of inclusion; instead, by deliberately not mentioning Niethammer, the commandant was trying to protect him).

Höß's own trial by the Polish Supreme National Tribunal for mass murder began on 11 March 1947 in the auditorium of the teachers' union in Warsaw. Following the uprising it was the only venue not in ruins large enough to hold the number of people who wanted to attend. Specially adapted for the trial, extra security points were installed together with equipment for simultaneous translation into several languages and a press gallery. Able to accommodate 500 people, the auditorium was packed throughout the three weeks of the trial, many of those present being former Auschwitz prisoners. When Höß had appeared on the witness stand the previous year at the International Military Tribunal in Nuremberg, he had not denied his crimes but had maintained throughout that he had only been following orders. In his own trial the 47-year-old when questioned about his role in the Holocaust by the prosecution used the same defence: blaming Himmler. He said, 'The concentration camps became what they were during the war entirely and solely because such was the intention of the Reichsführer-SS. It was he who issued the directives to the Reich Security Main Office, and he alone could do so.' Calm and controlled throughout, Höß harboured no illusions about the fate that awaited him. To the end he contended that 'only a million and a half people' had died at Auschwitz, not the five or six million claimed by the prosecution. Just before the verdict was read out Höß had asked that his wedding ring, which had given him away but was his most precious personal possession, be sent to his wife. On 2 April 1947 the court announced its verdict, sentencing Höß to death by hanging.

The day after the verdict some former prisoners present at the trial formally requested that the execution take place on the grounds of the camp, the tribunal judge agreeing to their request. On 10 April Höß received the sacrament after having returned to the Catholic church of his youth. The next day he wrote a final letter to his wife Hedwig in which he stated:

> Based on my present knowledge I can see today clearly, severely and bitterly for me, that the entire ideology about the world in which I believed so firmly and unswervingly was based on completely wrong premises and had to absolutely collapse one day. And so my actions in the service of this ideology were completely wrong, even though I faithfully believed the idea was correct. Now it was very logical that strong doubts grew within me, and whether my turning away from my belief in God was based on completely wrong premises. It was a hard struggle. But I have again found my faith in my God.

Reflecting on his relationship with Himmler and the extermination of the Jews, he wrote:

> Himmler was the crudest representative of the leadership principle. Every German had to subordinate himself unquestioningly and uncritically to the leaders of the state, who alone were in a position to understand the real needs of the people and to direct them along the right path. Anyone who did not submit to this principle must be eliminated

> from public life. With this purpose in mind Himmler trained and formed his SS, and created the concentration camps, the German police, and the Reich Security Main Office. But the extermination of those population elements which remained hostile was in any case a mistake. If the peoples of the occupied territories had been treated with decency and common sense their resistance movements could have been reduced to insignificance. There would then have been few serious opponents left.
>
> I also see now that the extermination of the Jews was fundamentally wrong. Precisely because of these mass exterminations, Germany has drawn upon herself the hatred of the entire world. It in no way served the cause of antisemitism, but on the contrary brought the Jews far closer to their ultimate objective. The Reich Security Main Office was only the executive, the long arm, of Himmler the police chief. The Reich Security Main Office and the concentration camps were only the tools that were used to carry out the wishes of Himmler, or the intentions of Adolf Hitler, as the case might be.

But tellingly, to the end Höß maintained that he 'never maltreated a prisoner' and was just following orders:

> I for my part never sanctioned them. I myself never maltreated a prisoner, far less killed one. Nor have I ever tolerated maltreatment by my subordinates. In my disgust at the errors and abuses that I discovered, I may have spoken many hard words that I should have kept to myself. But I was never cruel, and I have never maltreated anyone, even in a fit of temper. A great deal happened in Auschwitz that was done ostensibly in my name, under my authority and on my orders, which I neither knew about nor sanctioned. But all these things happened in Auschwitz and so I am responsible. For the camp regulations say: the camp commandant is fully responsible for everything that happens in his sphere.
>
> My life is now nearly at its end … Let the public continue to regard me as the bloodthirsty beast, the cruel sadist and

> the mass murderer; for the masses could never imagine the commandant of Auschwitz in any other light. They could never understand that he too, had a heart and that he was not evil.

Höß's biography, which ran to 114 pages, was finished in February just weeks before his execution. His main reason for writing it, apart from telling his side of the most notorious crime in modern history, was to try to protect his family by making it clear that they knew nothing of what went on in the camp (it seems inconceivable that his wife Hedwig and eldest son Klaus did not know what was going on in Auschwitz but they were not implicated in his crimes. Instead, they were allowed to live their lives although they never escaped his past). The date for his execution was set for 14 April 1947 but it was postponed until two days later because of fears that the residents of Oświęcim would lynch Höß while he was being transferred to the camp.

On 16 April Höß was collected very early from his cell and driven under heavy guard one last time to Auschwitz. A short-drop gallows with a trapdoor had been erected at the former Gestapo building by German prisoners of war. Due to security fears, armed guards were posted throughout the grounds, and no one was admitted without a special pass. Höß arrived at 8 a.m. and was taken to the building that had once housed his office and from where he had overseen the operation of the camp. After requesting a cup of coffee, which he drank, Höß was led to a cell in the 'bunker', the camp jail in Block No. 11, also known as the 'Death Block', where so many prisoners had been summarily executed and the first ones gassed. Punctually at 10 a.m. he was led out to his own execution, an observer describing him as being 'calm and walking to his death with energetic steps, almost strutting'.

On reaching the gallows Höß was helped on to the stool above the trapdoor as his hands were handcuffed behind his back. A Catholic priest, Father Tadeusz Zaremba, whose presence had been requested by Höß, approached the gallows as the prosecutor read out the sentence. The noose was placed around Höß's neck and he adjusted it with a circular movement of his head. At 10:08 a.m. the hangman pulled the stool out from underneath Höß's feet and the trapdoor opened leaving Höß hanging by the rope, subjecting the prisoner to death by slow strangulation. Father Zaremba recited a prayer for the dying and at

10.21 a.m. a physician pronounced Höß dead. No official announcement was made about the fate of Höß's corpse but it was probably cremated.

Despite the high profile of the case and the unprecedented scale of the crimes Höß had committed, the press coverage of his execution was limited as newspapers were forbidden by the tribunal judge from printing eyewitness accounts. Early in 1947 the authorities had all but banned executions of Nazi war criminals in public following the death the previous year of Arthur Greiser (1897–1946, Gauleiter or Reich Governor of the German territory of 'Wartheland', he had organised the Holocaust in occupied Poland). A picnic atmosphere prevailed among the large number of people who had gathered to witness his hanging on the slopes of the Citadel in the Polish city of Poznań. Afterwards church officials and some politicians had protested to the authorities about the inappropriate spectacle, pointing out that children and ice-cream sellers had been present. Following this the Polish ministry of justice decided that the number of people attending Höß's execution should be strictly limited. As a result, just over a hundred people including former prisoners, senior officials from the Polish ministry of justice, the state prosecutor's office and the security bureau witnessed Höß's hanging. It was to be the last and the most important execution for war crimes in Poland.

Niethammer would have read about the execution of his former commandant while awaiting his own trial in Montelupich Prison in Kraków. The escalating Cold War and the limited publicity given to Höß's hanging helped him as extensive coverage would have raised more difficult questions about Niethammer's own role at the camp. After his release in 1949 Niethammer continued with his career at the Zoological Museum Koenig in Bonn where he was appointed curator of the bird collection but could never entirely escape his past at Auschwitz. Back in his old role Niethammer tried to foster international links and assuage his conscience by reaching out to the British ornithologists with whom he had been in contact during the war but to his disappointment none of them answered his letters (it is likely that writing to them was also part of an attempt by Niethammer to get support from fellow ornithologists on the other side in case he was ever brought to trial again). Though he didn't know it, George Waterston, the Royal Artillery Officer who had been captured on Crete and had been in regular contact with Stresemann during the war, felt sorry for him. Like his fellow POWs who had been incarcerated in Oflag VII-B, he did not reply to Niethammer's letters, feeling it would not be appropriate to correspond with a former Auschwitz guard. However, writing to his fellow ex-prisoner Edward Buxton after Niethammer's release in 1950, he commented, 'Niethammer seems to have had a tough time of it and it is good to hear that there are people like Shaw who are doing their best to alleviate the beastly suffering of some of these unfortunates.'

Shaw was the British intelligence officer who had formally taken Niethammer's statement after he had surrendered and believed that his biggest crime was to be incredibly naive about what went on at Auschwitz. Shortly after Niethammer's release Shaw wrote to Waterston, 'Again, he takes pleasure in ordinary things. His wife. His work. Green fields. Birds singing.'[1] Despite being rebuked by the former POWs, Niethammer became a member of the British Ornithologists' Union in 1957. Like him they would go on to have spectacular careers of their own. George Waterston founded the Fair Isle Bird Observatory, Edward Buxton helped found the Skomer Bird Observatory, John Barrett became the first warden at Dale Fort Field Centre in Pembrokeshire and Peter Conder went on to become the director of the Royal Society for the Protection of Birds.

It was not just former British POWs who did not want to talk about Auschwitz. In a flourishing 1950s West Germany there was a strong collective desire on the part of German society to move on from the horrors of the war and in particular the word 'Auschwitz' became 'socially unacceptable', no one wanting to discuss or read about it. The prevailing attitude of the time benefitted Niethammer who was only too keen to leave the past behind him and concentrate on rebuilding his career. This he did spectacularly over the next twenty years, in particular travelling all over the world and helping to rapidly expand the museum's bird skin collection, adding many African and Palaearctic species. He also oversaw the return of one of oldest and scientifically most important bird collections in the world, the Christian Ludwig Brehm collection. Brehm (1787–1864) was a German pastor and ornithologist who had collected over 9,000 skins which resided in the British Natural History Museum after having been bought by the banker and zoologist Lord Rothschild (1868–1937) in 1932. Its return to the German museum in Bonn, its rightful home, was widely credited as Niethammer's greatest achievement.

In recognition of his work Niethammer had many subspecies of birds named after him including in 1952 the red-fronted tinkerbird *Pogoniulus pusillus niethammeri* and the linnet *Carduelis cannabina guentheri*, in 1963 the Asian short-toed lark *Calandrella rufescens niethammeri*, in 1967 the Eurasian jay *Garrulus glandarius hansguentheri*, (proposed by Keve who during the war had named a subspecies of the great rosefinch after him, the latin name being shared with his former boss Hans Kummerlöwe), in 1968 the Andean tinamou *Nothoprocta pentlandii niethammeri* and the Angolan lark *Mirafra angolensis niethammeri*, in 1969 the zebra waxbill *Amandava subflava niethammeri* and in 1970 the Cretan great tit *Parus major niethammeri* by his former boss von Jordans.[2] A subspecies of the European hare *Lepus europaeus niethammeri*, a lizard *Algyroides marchi niethammeri* and even a genus of pyralid moths known as *Niethammeriodes* were also named after him.

Despite the many subspecies named after him and negotiating the return of the prestigious Brehm collection, Niethammer's goal to become the director of the Zoological Museum Alexander Koenig in Bonn was never to be realised. It was an aspiration that was more than justified given his academic achievements but was blocked by the board who believed that having a former Auschwitz guard as the head of their institution would bring the museum into disrepute. However, the taint of Auschwitz did not prevent him from becoming president of the prestigious German Ornithological Society in 1967, having acted as its vice-president for the previous twelve years. He took over in the role from his great mentor Erwin Stresemann, the so-called Pope of Ornithology, and between 1962 and 1970 was also editor of the *Journal fur Ornithologie*, again succeeding Stresemann. It followed on from him in 1950 founding and editing the *Bonner Zoologische Beiträge* or *Bonn Zoological Articles,* the in-house publication for the museum, a major part of which was devoted to ornithological papers (it remained in print until 2010 when it was succeeded by the *Bonn Zoological Bulletin).*

Although Niethammer was reluctant to talk about his past, as he grew older there was increasing media interest in Auschwitz as a new generation of Germans began to grapple with their history. Former Jewish Holocaust survivors like Simon Wiesenthal (1908–2005) and Mossad, the Israeli national intelligence agency, had successfully tracked down many leading Nazis like Eichmann and attention was increasingly turning to those who had played supporting roles in the genocide. Towards the end of his life as his career came to an end the religious Niethammer decided to open up more about his past, wanting to make peace both with those who had suffered and God.

In 1972 he agreed to speak to the Austrian Auschwitz survivor and historian Hermann Langbein (1912–1995) who interviewed him for his book *Menschen in Auschwitz* or People in Auschwitz.[3] In it he stressed that he had always tried to be kind to the inmates, giving them extra food and tobacco but when it came to their fate 'it was impossible to do anything about it'. Published in 1972, much to Niethammer's relief, when the book came out, he only warranted a small mention. However, the stress had clearly taken its toll as shortly after the interview Niethammer had a heart attack, but survived. Now increasingly frail, he was devastated when his mentor and lifelong ornithological partner Erwin Stresemann died the same year, also from a heart attack. In failing health at the end of the next year, he resigned from his role as president of the German Ornithological Society after six years.

Two weeks after resigning from the role he loved so much during a hunting trip to Morenhoven Forest near his home in Bonn, Niethammer died of a second heart attack on 14 January 1974 at the age of just 65.

In many of the obituaries which followed Niethammer's death his time at Auschwitz was erased or glossed over. Those that did mention his military service just stated he had been in the army or had ended up a prisoner of war in Poland. Typical was this obituary in *Ibis*, the journal of the British Ornithologists' Union, published in 1975 which didn't mention his wartime record at all, instead stating, 'In 1932 he joined E. Stresemann at the bird department of the Zoological Museum in Berlin. Five years later he moved to the Museum Alexander Koenig in Bonn where he worked – with an interruption caused by the Second World War – ever since, and where he became curator of the bird department in 1949.'[4] The same obituary gave a glowing account of his character which read:

> The scientific work of Günther Niethammer was characterized by an amazing breadth in the subjects and geographical areas treated … Perhaps his greatest achievement in ornithology, however, was the compilation of the three volumes of the

> *Handbuch der Deutschen Vogelkunde* which for a long time was, and for many species still is, one of the most important handbooks on European birds. Its successor, the *Handbuch der Vogel Mitteleuropas*, was again initiated and its first two volumes edited by Niethammer. In addition to his ornithological research, Günther Niethammer was very interested in mammals and published many papers on various aspects of mammalian morphology, ecology and zoogeography. Everybody who knew Niethammer admired his charming personality, his constant cheerfulness despite many serious setbacks, his great hospitality and last, not least, his enormous energy and personal engagement. He will be remembered affectionately by the many ornithologists all over the world who profited by his advice and help in various matters which he gave only too readily.

The Zoological Museum Koenig mourned his death with two articles published in 1974 in the *Bonner Zoologische Beiträge,* the magazine Niethammer had edited for so long. One was written by his colleague H. E. Wolters and the other by his former boss and friend Hans Kummerlöwe. Both were moving tributes to a man who had been one of the driving forces in ornithology during the twentieth century and were notable for being highly personal tributes rather than the normal dry academic papers which characterised the magazine. The centre piece of the tributes was a very impressive list of twelve books, book translations and contributions to other people's books and 238 scientific articles produced by Niethammer during his lifetime compiled by his eldest son Jochen (who like his father went on to become a highly respected zoologist, specialising in mammals). Noticeably absent in the two testimonies was any reference to Niethammer's wartime record. Perhaps understandably the tributes reflected the zeitgeist of the time when Germany was trying to forget the war. But unforgivably for a scientific publication, they contained a deliberate deception – instead of including in the year 1942 the publication *Beobachtungen über die Vogelwelt von Auschwitz (Ost-Oberschlesien)*, in its place in the year 1940 was listed *Beobachtungen über die Vogelwelt von Ost-Oberschlesien* (*Observations on the birdlife of Eastern Upper Silesia*). The name of Auschwitz and its concentration camp had been deliberately erased from the tributes (see bibliography).[5]

If Niethammer had lived longer it is likely that his past would have been increasingly investigated by researchers, historians and the West German government. After the fall of Communism many more files on the camp became public, the Auschwitz-Birkenau Memorial and State Museum, which had been created by a Polish Act of Parliament in 1947, received international recognition and German state law changed in relation to former Nazi war criminals, anyone associated with the concentration camp system being liable for prosecution.

In 2015 at the age of 94, Oskar Gröning, the camp clerk who had arrived at Auschwitz in September 1942 along with Niethammer, was put on trial and charged with being an 'accessory' to the murder of hundreds of thousands of prisoners while serving with the Waffen-SS.[6] Gröning had believed that he would never be prosecuted as he was a lowly clerk and had just been following orders. But while Niethammer had counted birds, Gröning had counted the money of the Jews and other prisoners who had been gassed at the camp and he had not successfully applied for a transfer. However, like Niethammer, he had admitted to 'moral guilt' but denied that he had ever committed a crime, stating he didn't personally kill anyone. This defence was dismissed and on 15 July 2015 he was found guilty of knowingly facilitating mass murder and was sentenced to four years in prison. Due to his advanced age and increasingly fragile health Gröning's lawyers appealed the judgement and when this failed, stated that their client was too ill to go to jail. Gröning died in hospital in 2018 just before he was due to start his sentence, but had he been fit enough, he would have gone to prison.

In contrast to Gröning, Niethammer's 'legacy' continues to divide historians and ornithologists, some maintaining he was simply naïve, and seduced by the Nazis. Others believe he was far more calculating and saw in them a unique opportunity to progress his career. What stands out are his considerable scientific achievements in the fields of zoology and ornithology, particularly during wartime. Set against this, like Gröning, is the fact that he was also guilty of being an accessory to genocide and one of the worst crimes in human history.

Endnotes

Chapter 1

1. www.holocaust.cz/en/history/concentration-camps-and-ghettos/sachsenhausen-3/
2. Riedel Dirk 2010 'A "Political Soldier" and "Practitioner of Violence": The Concentration Camp Commandant Hans Loritz *Journal of Contemporary History* Vol. 45 No. 3 pp. 555–75
3. https://en.wikipedia.org/wiki/Rudolf_Höss
4. Hoess Rudolf (1959) 2000 *Commandant of Auschwitz* Weidenfeld & Nicolson p. 105
5. Hoess Rudolf (1959) 2000 *Commandant of Auschwitz* Weidenfeld & Nicolson p. 106
6. Hoess Rudolf (1959) 2000 *Commandant of Auschwitz* Weidenfeld & Nicolson p. 110
7. https://en.wikipedia.org/wiki/Günther_Niethammer

Chapter 2

1. Nowak Eugeniusz 2018 *Biologists in the Age of Totalitarianism* Cambridge Scholars Publishing p. 69
2. www.profil.at/oesterreich/vogelfaenger-auschwitz-10058605
3. https://en.wikipedia.org/wiki/Crop_(anatomy)
4. Nowak Eugeniusz 2018 *Biologists in the Age of Totalitarianism* Cambridge Scholars Publishing p. 1
5. Jolowicz Dr. Leo. 1938 *Nature* 142 p. 244. https://doi.org/10.1038/142244b0
6. *British Birds* April 1938 'Reviews' Vol. 31, issue 11 p. 359
7. Nowak Eugeniusz 2018 *Biologists in the Age of Totalitarianism* Cambridge Scholars Publishing p.69
8. *Polar Record* Volume 48 Issue 2 April 2012 Cambridge University Press pp. 113–22

9. www.profil.at/oesterreich/vogelfaenger-auschwitz-10058605
10. Nowak Eugeniusz 2018 *Biologists in the Age of Totalitarianism* Cambridge Scholars Publishing p. 70
11. https://en.wikipedia.org/wiki/Lorenz_Diefenbach
12. Hoess Rudolf (1959) 2000 *Commandant of Auschwitz* Weidenfeld & Nicolson p. 77
13. https://en.wikipedia.org/wiki/Karl_Fritzsch

Chapter 3

1. Hoess Rudolf (1959) 2000 *Commandant of Auschwitz* Weidenfeld & Nicolson p. 129
2. Nowak Eugeniusz 2018 *Biologists in the Age of Totalitarianism* Cambridge Scholars Publishing p. 78
3. Hoess Rudolf (1959) 2000 *Commandant of Auschwitz* Weidenfeld & Nicolson p. 111
4. Hoess Rudolf (1959) 2000 *Commandant of Auschwitz* Weidenfeld & Nicolson p. 205

Chapter 4

1. Nowak Eugeniusz 2018 *Biologists in the Age of Totalitarianism* Cambridge Scholars Publishing p. 70
2. Nowak Eugeniusz 2018 *Biologists in the Age of Totalitarianism* Cambridge Scholars Publishing p. 78
3. Nowak Eugeniusz 2018 *Biologists in the Age of Totalitarianism* Cambridge Scholars Publishing p. 73
4. Nowak Eugeniusz 2018 *Biologists in the Age of Totalitarianism* Cambridge Scholars Publishing p. 88
5. 'Architecture of Murder: The Auschwitz-Birkenau Blueprints Through the Lens of History' Mini Exhibits from the Yad Vashem Collections www.yadvashem.org/yv/en/exhibitions/through-the-lens/auschwitz-blueprints.asp

Chapter 5

1. Hoess Rudolf (1959) 2000 *Commandant of Auschwitz* Weidenfeld & Nicolson p. 146
2. www.auschwitz.org/en/history/resistance/escapes-and-reports/
3. *Nature* 1945 Obituary: Prof. F. von Wettstein 156 p. 328

Chapter 6

1. https://en.wikipedia.org/wiki/Kurt_Student
2. Nowak Eugeniusz 2018 *Biologists in the Age of Totalitarianism* Cambridge Scholars Publishing p. 71
3. https://en.wikipedia.org/wiki/Volkswagen_Kübelwagen
4. Hoess Rudolf (1959) 2000 *Commandant of Auschwitz* Weidenfeld & Nicolson p. 150

Chapter 7

1. Niethammer Günther 1942 *Beobachtungen über die Vogelwelt von Auschwitz (Ost-Oberschlesien)* (z. Z. bei der Waffen-SS) Mit 4 Figuren auf Tafel XI und XII. www.zobodat.at/pdf/ANNA_52_0164-0199.pdf
2. Kommandantursonderbefehl Auschwitz, 9. Juni 1941 www.tenhumbergreinhard.de/taeter-und-mitlaeufer/kommandanturbefehl/kommandantursonderbefehl-23.html
3. Ibid
4. Schulze-Hagen Karl 1997 *Otto Natorp und seine Vogelsammlung: Schicksal und Hintergründe Mauritiana* (Altenburg) 16 2, S. pp. 351–79
5. Rundell Katherine 2021 'Consider the Stork' *London Review of Books* Vol. 43 No. 7

Chapter 8

1. Kosmidis Pierre 'Operation Albumen: The daring SBS raids in Crete' 1942 National Archives www.ww2wrecks.com/portfolio/operation-albumen-the-daring-sbs-raids-in-crete-1942/
2. Nowak Eugeniusz 2018 *Biologists in the Age of Totalitarianism* Cambridge Scholars Publishing p. 17
3. Nowak Eugeniusz 2018 *Biologists in the Age of Totalitarianism* Cambridge Scholars Publishing p. 19
4. Nowak Eugeniusz 2018 *Biologists in the Age of Totalitarianism* Cambridge Scholars Publishing p. 22
5. Stresemann Erwin 1943 Ueberblick über die Vögel Kretas und den Vogelzug in der Aegaeis *Journal für Ornithologie,* Vol. 91 Issue 4 pp. 448–514

Chapter 9

1. Niemann Derek 2012 *Birds in a Cage* Short Books p. 114

Chapter 10

1. United States Holocaust Memorial Museum, Washington, D.C. 'Wannsee Conference and the "Final Solution"' https://encyclopedia.ushmm.org/content/en/article/wannsee-conference-and-the-final-solution
2. Hoess Rudolf (1959) 2000 *Commandant of Auschwitz* Weidenfeld & Nicolson p. 215
3. Hoess Rudolf (1959) 2000 *Commandant of Auschwitz* Weidenfeld & Nicolson p. 212

Chapter 11

1. Lees Laurence 2015 'The Life of an Auschwitz Guard' *Politico* www.politico.com/magazine/story/2015/07/oskar-Gröning-auschwitz-guard-120036/
2. Hoess Rudolf (1959) 2000 *Commandant of Auschwitz* Weidenfeld & Nicolson p. 134

Chapter 12

1. www.npr.org/2020/01/27/798480937/75-years-after-auschwitz-liberation-survivors-urge-world-to-remember

Chapter 14

1. Nowak Eugeniusz 2018 *Biologists in the Age of Totalitarianism* Cambridge Scholars Publishing p. 71
2. Nowak Eugeniusz 2018 *Biologists in the Age of Totalitarianism* Cambridge Scholars Publishing p. 324
3. Udvardy Miklos 1986 'In Memoriam: Andrew Keve' *The Auk* 103 p. 207

Chapter 15

1. Niethammer Günther Beiträge zur Kenntnis der Brutvögel des Peloponnes *Journal fur Ornithologie Heft* 2/3 April/Juli 1943 pp. 167–238
2. https://en.wikipedia.org/wiki/Bernhard_Rensch

3. Michaella Moysi et al 2023 Genomic data reveal contrasting patterns of divergence among island and mainland birds of the Eastern Mediterranean *Ibis* 165 (3) pp. 829-843
4. https://en.wikipedia.org/wiki/Friedrich_Schubert

Chapter 16

1. Frankl Victor 2003 Man's *Search for Meaning* p. 44
2. Nowak Eugeniusz 2018 *Biologists in the Age of Totalitarianism* Cambridge Scholars Publishing p. 72
3. www.auschwitz.org/en/history/medical-experiments/other-doctor-perpetrators/
4. https://pl.wikipedia.org/wiki/Stefan_Ślopek
5. Boev Zlatozar 2002 'The Ornithological Collections of the National Museum of Natural History' *Bonner zoologische Beiträge Band* 51 Heft 2/3 pp. 157–63

Chapter 18

1. Nowak Eugeniusz 2018 *Biologists in the Age of Totalitarianism* Cambridge Scholars Publishing pp. 75–76
2. Hoess Rudolf (1959) 2000 *Commandant of Auschwitz* Weidenfeld & Nicolson p. 172
3. Burchell Helen 2003 'The Northampton shoemaker who caught the Auschwitz commander' BBC News www.bbc.co.uk/news/uk-england-northamptonshire-66875251

Chapter 19

1. Niemann Derek 2012 *Birds in a Cage* Short Books p. 119
2. https://en.wikipedia.org/wiki/ Günther_Niethammer
3. Nowak Eugeniusz 2018 *Biologists in the Age of Totalitarianism* Cambridge Scholars Publishing p. 79
4. *Ibis* 1975 Vol. 117 Obituaries Günther Niethammer p.3 89 https://onlinelibrary.wiley.com/doi/pdf/10.1111/j.1474-919X.1975.tb04230.x
5. *Bonner Zoologische Beiträge* Heit 1–3 Jahrgang 25 1974 Prof. Dr. Günther Niethammer
6. Rees Laurence 2015 'The Life of an Auschwitz Guard' *Politico* www.politico.com/magazine/story/2015/07/oskar-Gröning-auschwitz-guard-120036/

Sources

A LIST OF papers published in 1974 in the Bonner Zoologische Beiträge attributed to Professor Doctor Günther Niethammer during the war. Compiled by his son Jochen, part of 238 papers listed for his lifetime.

Any reference to Auschwitz concentration camp was excluded, instead a paper, 'Observations on the bird life of Eastern Upper Silesia', was wrongly included for the year 1940.

1939

'On a healed forearm fracture of a dwarf sager'. *Rhine. Natur-freund* 3: 38–39.

'Migratory bird sightings in South West Africa (October to January)'. *Vogelzug [Bird Migration]* 10: 127–30.

1940

'Bird watching at Lake Neusiedl'. *Deusche Vogelwelt* [*German Birds*], 97–100.

'On the breeding occurrence of the little tern in the Ostmark'. *Orn. Monatsber* [Monthly]. 48: 109–12.

'Observations on courtship and studies on the oesophagus of South African bustards'. *Orn. Monatsber*. 48: 29–33.

von Jordans, A. & G. N.: 'A bird yield from Fukien'. *Verh. Orn. Ges. Bayern*. 22: 98–136.

'On the breeding occurrence of the tawny owl in the Rhineland'. *Orn. Monatsber*. 48: 80–82.

'The saker falcon (*Falco cherrug*) in the Ostmark'. *Orn. Monatsber*. 48: 141—144.

'Pomeranian cormorant, *Phalacrocorax carbo sinensis* in Saxony'. (Shaw & Nodder), *Mitt. Verein sachs. Ornithologen* 6: 121–22.
'On the breeding occurrence of the red-throated pipit in the Ostmark'. *Orn. Monatsber*. 48: 89–90.
'*Oceanodroma castro* [band-rumped storm petrel] in Germany'. *Orn.* Monthly. 48: 124–25.
'*Motacilla flava feldegg* [yellow wagtail] in der Ostmark', *Orn. Monatsber*. 48: 163.
'Back to the "Wood pigeon as a cabbage eater"'. *Orn. Monatsber*. 48: 193.
'Observations on the bird life of Eastern Upper Silesia'. *Ann. Naturhist. Mus. Wien*. 52: 164–99.

1942

'About the klipspringer [antelope] in German-South West Africa'. *Zool. Garten* (NF). 14: 139–49.
Addendum to the ornithological observations in Eastern Upper Silesia. *Ann. Naturhist. Mus. Wien*. 53: 337–39.
'Large decrease in the coot'. *Beitr. Fortpfl. Vögel*. 18: 112.
'Nestling duration of the stonechat'. *Beitr. Fortpfl. Vögel*. 18: 113.
'Duck sightings in Eastern Upper Silesia'. *Ber. Ver. Schles. Ornithologen*. 27: 1–4.

1943

'The brood of the collared dove in Vienna'. *J. Orn*. 91: 296–304.
'Contributions to the knowledge of the breeding birds of the Peloponnese'. *J. Orn*. 91: 167–238.
'Three new breeds of birds from Crete'. *Anz. Acad. Wiss. Wien, Math.-Nat. Klasse*, Nr. 3: 7–10.
'About the bird life of Crete'. *Ann. Naturhist. Mus. Wien*. 53: 5–59. (1942; issued in 1943).
'The collared dove in Vienna'. *Orn. Monatsber*. 51: 96–97.
'*Haematopus ostralegus longipes* [Eurasian oystercatcher] in Hungary'. *Orn. Monatsber*. 50: 300.
G. N. & Merzinger On the participation in the breeding success of the magpie by age and sex'. *Beitr. Fortpfl. Vögel*. 19: 21–2.

1944

Haematopus ostralegus longipes [Eurasian oystercatcher] on migration in south-eastern Europe. *Orn. Monatsber.* 52: 161–64.

Books and websites

Auschwitz-Birkenau State Museum website www.auschwitz.at/gunther-niethammer-en

Hoess Rudolf (1959) 2000 *Commandant of Auschwitz*, Weidenfeld & Nicolson

Museum Koenig Bonn website https://bonn.leibniz-lib.de/en

Natural History Museum Vienna Naturhistorisches Museum Wien website www.nhm-wien.ac.at/

Niemann Derek 2012 *Birds in a Cage*, Short Books

Niethammer Günther 1942 *Beobachtungen über die Vogelwelt von Auschwitz (Ost-Oberschlesien)*, Annals of the Natural History Museum in Vienna, 52: 164-199

Niethammer Günther 1974 *Bonner Zoologische Beiträge Heit 1–3*, Jahrgang 25, 1974 Prof. Dr. Günther Niethammer

Nowak Eugeniusz 2018 *Biologists in the Age of Totalitarianism*, Cambridge Scholars Publishing

Rees Lawrence 2005 *Auschwitz: The Nazis and the Final Solution*, BBC Books

UK Holocaust Memorial Foundation website www.gov.uk/government/organisations/uk-holocaust-memorial-foundation

Index